Mapping *Smallville*

Mapping *Smallville*

Critical Essays on the Series and Its Characters

Edited by
CORY BARKER,
CHRIS RYAN *and*
MYC WIATROWSKI

McFarland & Company, Inc., Publishers
Jefferson, North Carolina

LIBRARY OF CONGRESS CATALOGUING-IN-PUBLICATION DATA

Mapping Smallville : critical essays on the series and its characters / edited by Cory Barker, Chris Ryan and Myc Wiatrowski.
    p.   cm.
Includes bibliographical references and index.

    ISBN 978-0-7864-9464-4 (softcover : acid free paper)
    ISBN 978-1-4766-1751-0 (ebook)

    1. Smallville (Television program).   I. Barker, Cory, 1988– editor. II. Ryan, Chris, 1983– editor.   III. Wiatrowski, Myc, editor.
PN1992.77.S626M37 2014
791.45'72—dc23   2014018968

BRITISH LIBRARY CATALOGUING DATA ARE AVAILABLE

© 2014 Cory Barker, Chris Ryan and Myc Wiatrowski. All rights reserved

No part of this book may be reproduced or transmitted in any form or by any means, electronic or mechanical, including photocopying or recording, or by any information storage and retrieval system, without permission in writing from the publisher.

On the cover: Tom Welling in *Smallville*, Season 10 (2010-2011) © The CW Network (Photofest)

Printed in the United States of America

McFarland & Company, Inc., Publishers
   Box 611, Jefferson, North Carolina 28640
      www.mcfarlandpub.com

Acknowledgments

The editors would like to thank the collection's contributors for their tireless work, flexibility, and patience throughout the process from proposal to final publication.

Cory would like to thank his co-editors for everything they have done over the last few years. This project began in May 2011 in his small apartment in Bowling Green, Ohio, on the night of *Smallville*'s series finale and it faced many stumbling blocks (some self-inflicted). Seeing everything finally come together is very rewarding. He would also like to thank his partner Emily Davis for her love and support, and his parents John and Sherry Barker for letting him watch so much TV as a child. Finally, Cory would like to thank all the people who spoke with him about *Smallville* and this project, and the places and things that helped him carry it through to completion: Craig Byrne, Andy Daglas, Noel Kirkpatrick, Barbara Klinger, *Kryptonsite*, Adam Lukach, and the *Smallville* Wikia.

Chris would like to thank his co-editors for their diligence in keeping this project on track (even when it threatened to jump the rails a few times, leaving no survivors). They helped turn a conversation into a compilation. Cory got the project running and Myc put it in front of people who cared. Without them it never would have started, and it definitely would not have finished. Chris would also like to thank his wife, Mackenzie. Cory and Myc may have kept the lamplight burning for the book itself, but Mackenzie kept the fire lit under Chris to do his part to see the project through.

Myc would like to thank his co-editors and ever-supportive friends for their work, Cory in particular. This project would not have been possible without the superheroic passion and drive that Cory brought to the team. Myc would also like to thank his family—Laura and Lucas—for their abiding encouragement and patience, his mother Ruth who never had the opportunity to see this project reach fruition, and his colleagues at Bowling Green State University and Indiana University for their support and feedback.

Table of Contents

Acknowledgments — v
Introduction—Cory Barker, Chris Ryan and Myc Wiatrowski — 1

Part One:
Smallville's Decade-Long Mythical Journey

Mythicizing Clark Kent: Archetypes and Mythic Structures of *Smallville*—Daniel P. Compora — 13

The *Smallville* Destiny: The Superhero's Shaping by His Archetypal Fathers—James F. Iaccino — 25

"Always hold on to Smallville": Domesticity and the Male Hero—Bridget Kies — 45

Part Two:
Powerful Women

Sidekicks or Heroines? The Feminist Successes and Failures of *Smallville*'s Leading Ladies—Valerie Estelle Frankel — 59

Another Way: Tess Mercer as Ethical Hero—Peter Melville — 83

Girl Friday Power: Chloe Sullivan and the Hacker Sidekicks of Twenty-First Century Teen Television—Tara K. Parmiter — 100

Part Three:
Bodies, Identities and Politics

Rummaging Through the Closet: (Un)Masking the Signified Other in *Smallville*'s First Four Seasons—Jonathan A. Austad — 115

Kryptonian Encounters: Model Immigration and Superman's Impossible Dream—Roger Almendarez — 132

Bodies as Unreliable Signifiers: The Inconsistency of
   Smallville's Character Construction—DANIEL KULLE   145

PART FOUR:
RECEPTION

Finding Clark Kent: Sites of Nostalgia and Affect—
   GREGORY BRAY and JOHN PATRICK BRAY   161

"Chlark" Versus "Clois": Shippers, Anti-Fans and Anti-Fan
   Fans—CORY BARKER   174

Selected Bibliography   193
About the Contributors   207
Index   209

Introduction

Cory Barker, Chris Ryan and Myc Wiatrowski

Who cares about *Smallville*? The WB/CW series ran for ten seasons from 2001 to 2011, however its ratings peaked early in the second season and eventually bottomed out at one quarter of its initial viewership by the end of season ten. Critics were never particularly high on the series, and the only Primetime Emmy awards it took home were for Sound Editing. In terms of cultural cachet, *Smallville* is certainly not *The Wire* (2002–2008) or *Breaking Bad* (2008–2013). *Smallville* is not even *Buffy the Vampire Slayer* (1997–2003). So why does this book exist?

Why *Smallville*?

Smallville itself was never supposed to exist. As the story goes, producers Mike Tollin and Brian Robbins wanted to make a television series about a young Bruce Wayne, but the project never got off the ground because Warner Bros. wanted to resurrect the Caped Crusader on the big screen (and it eventually would with Christopher Nolan's *Batman Begins* in 2005). Undeterred, Tollin and Robbins worked with Warner Bros. to develop a series around a young Clark Kent instead, later bringing in Alfred Gough and Miles Millar to shepherd the project that would ultimately become *Smallville*.[1]

In the beginning, *Smallville* was a legitimate hit. When the series debuted on the WB's schedule in 2001, it broke the network's ratings records in total viewership (8.4 million) and in the all-important 18–34 age demographic.[2] From there, *Smallville* quickly followed the familiar trajectory of a buzzworthy new series. *Smallville* and its stars, Tom Welling, Kristin Kreuk, and Michael

Rosenbaum, were the subject of a *Rolling Stone* cover story in March 2002.[3] In September 2002, *Smallville* picked up its first Emmy win for Outstanding Sound Editing. In 2002–2003's season two, ratings soared higher, critical appreciation improved, and another Superman, actor Christopher Reeve, turned in an important guest performance in one of the series' highest-rated episodes.[4] With *Dawson's Creek* (1997–2003) off the air and *Buffy the Vampire Slayer* concluding its run on UPN, *Smallville* had grown into the centerpiece of the WB's schedule.

However, from the season three premiere in October 2003 until *Smallville* ended in 2011, the series methodically lost viewers, critical support, and most of its broader popular culture impact. During its last two seasons on the CW, *Smallville* aired on Friday nights, the proverbial death spot for television, and struggled to garner 3 million viewers.[5] Even cursory online research into the series' reputation among critics and viewers returns numerous negative screeds. Perhaps more damning is that when online television criticism exploded near the end of the 2000s, *Smallville* was often absent from the discussion altogether. One might argue that the series' declining Nielsen ratings were a byproduct of the struggling WB and later the nascent and stalled development of the CW, or that an aging project based on the world's most famous superhero was likely the perfect series to appeal to contemporary viewers watching in less traditional (and less legal) ways. At the same time, one might point to the long lines and jam-packed ballrooms at the San Diego Comic-Con as evidence of *Smallville*'s appeal, even until the end in 2011.

Yet for a series that produced more than 200 episodes over ten seasons and survived the aforementioned transition from the WB to the CW, *Smallville* has rarely received the attention that continues to be showered upon many of its contemporaries, including *Buffy*, *Angel* (1999–2004), *Firefly* (2002–2003), *Veronica Mars* (2004–2007), and *Supernatural* (2005–). Those series regularly appear on lists detailing the best "cult" television series, or even the best television series, period.[6] Fans regularly cry out for additional seasons or follow-up movies, and in the cases of *Firefly* and *Veronica Mars*, help those narrative extensions come to life. Although we do not intend to draw qualitative comparisons between *Smallville* and those series, the lack of acclaim and interest for *Smallville* is both notable and troublesome.

Perhaps most notable and troublesome is that *Smallville*'s absence in critical and fan discourse is replicated in scholarship as well, particularly in comparison to the aforementioned other series. Numerous book-length projects have explored the complexities of Joss Whedon's *Buffy*, *Angel*, and *Firefly*, and scholarly interest in the former two series led to the development of an entire field of research known as "Buffy Studies" and the academic journal *Slayage: The International Journal of Buffy Studies*.[7] Although not as prominent as

Buffy Studies, academic work on representation, genre, and fandom related to or in *Veronica Mars* and *Supernatural* has appeared in edited collections, journals, or at conferences quite consistently over the past decade.[8]

As of early 2014, very little scholarship has been published on *Smallville*. Melanie E.S. Kohnen's "The Adventures of a Repressed Farm Boy and the Billionaire Who Loves Him: Queer Spectatorship in *Smallville* Fandom" and Michaela Meyer's "Slashing *Smallville*: The Interplay of Text, Audience, and Production on Viewer Interpretations of Homoeroticism" explore the activity of the series' viewers, while Miranda J. Banks's "A Boy for All Planets: *Roswell, Smallville*, and the Teen Male Melodrama" examines how Clark Kent's early experiences subvert traditional generic expectations.[9] Along with these three pieces, the most notable scholarship on *Smallville* is 2011's *The Smallville Chronicles: Critical Essays on the Television Series*, edited by Lincoln Geraghty. The collection provides analysis on a range of topics related to the series, from its representations of gender and sexuality and engagement with politics and national identity to the pilgrimages and blogging of *Smallville*'s diehard fans.[10] Although we owe a great debt to this prior scholarship and nearly all of the essays in this book refer to or draw citations from it, there is simply still not enough academic attention paid to *Smallville*. We hope that this collection serves as another part of the much-needed ongoing dialogue about the series and its role within recent television and popular culture history.

What Makes *Smallville* Worth Studying?

In this section, we address some of the notable entry points into the series, its production, and its reception, but this list is far from comprehensive, nor is everything described here explored in detail throughout this collection. There is much to do with research into *Smallville*; the work here only scratches the surface.

Scholars have long been interested in the cultural role and impact of Superman as a heroic figure and in contemporary popular culture, superheroes and their origin stories dominate the big and small screens. *Smallville* provides the most developed and longest running live-action origin story for Superman—and for all superheroes. The series' version of Clark Kent (played by Tom Welling) regularly finds himself racked by self-doubt and an inability (or unwillingness) to embrace his superhuman abilities, traits much less prominent in other Superman stories. As such, *Smallville* is fundamentally a story about Clark Kent, not Superman. The series consistently (sometimes to a fault) illustrates how superheroes are made, not just born—and how humanity and human relationships shape characters who are decidedly not human.

The series makes similar strides in its representations of sympathetic villains, including Lex and Lionel Luthor (Michael Rosenbaum and John Glover respectively), Major/General Zod (primarily Callum Blue), and somehow even Doomsday (Sam Witwer). The television serial provides an outlet for further exploration of the villain's psyche, but *Smallville* thrives in exploring the dark and twisted pasts of some of Superman's most notable adversaries. Its treatment of the Luthor family, particularly in comparison to Clark's relationship with his parents Jonathan and Martha (John Schneider and Annette O'Toole), goes to great lengths to demonstrate the importance of family, the home, and personal responsibility.

Like *Buffy* and *Veronica Mars*, *Smallville* regularly combines a litany of different genres. The series grafts the conventions of the teen drama onto the superhero origin tale, mixing love triangles with special effects-driven action sequences. With the presence of Kryptonite-infected "Freaks of the Week" and later the inclusion of heroes from the DC Comics universe, *Smallville* raises questions concerning identity and difference. "Meteor freaks" and superheroes allow the series to turn these questions back to its most prominent characters, paralleling a given episode's Freak of the Week and Clark's struggles to find a balance between his humanity and his Kryptonian heritage.

More broadly, *Smallville* arrived on the WB's schedule in October 2001 at the dawn of a tumultuous era in American culture. Although it would be reductive to equate the pilot episode's destructive meteor shower with the 9/11 attacks directly, the series does demonstrate how such a momentous and deadly event can shape a community and its citizens for years to come. It regularly explores the dangers of foreign attacks, however small, on Middle America and traditional heteronormative values. Through the constant use of new technology and pseudo-science, *Smallville*, perhaps implicitly, also addresses Western society's turn toward increased surveillance and government black projects.

From an industry perspective, *Smallville*'s version of DC Comics characters, from Clark, Lex, and Lois Lane (Erica Durance) to the Toyman (Chris Gauthier) and Solomon Grundy (John DeSantis), illustrate how historical fictional figures are translated into a contemporary context, just as the series' alteration of notable Superman storylines displays the complicated processes of adaptation. Its strategic use of recognizable characters, storylines, and even performers reflects how individual media texts operate within the confines of both a larger textual universe and multinational media conglomerate. Furthermore, *Smallville*'s production in Vancouver, and how it made the Canadian city look like rural Kansas—and later the fictional Metropolis—on a seemingly ever-declining budget speaks to the production realities of contemporary television. The behind-the-scenes shuffling, with showrunner and actor departures and timeslot changes, elucidate the ways in which productions are forced to adapt on the fly.

Finally, though *Smallville* fans are not as known for their active reception like diehard viewers of *Buffy* or *Supernatural*, corners of the web are full of *Smallville*-related conversation and fan-made productions waiting to be investigated further. The dedication of *Smallville* fans kept the series on the air for a decade and their online activity provides compelling case studies related to participatory culture, gender, sexuality, and more.

Again, these are just a select few areas of interest. Possible future projects could further explore *Smallville*'s representation (or lack thereof) of race, its lack of non-heteronormative sexualities, its use of product placement, or any number of other avenues. With 218 episodes, hundreds of characters, and numerous instances of corporate synergy, *Smallville* is a text ripe for analysis. Both the minimal previous work on the series and our contributions here offer necessary and useful starting explorations, but there is more work to be done.

Structure of the Collection

This collection is broken down into four sections dedicated to broad categories: Clark's journey to Superman and the influence of his parents and the home; the role of the series' noteworthy female characters, including Lana, Lois, Chloe Sullivan (Allison Mack), Kara (Laura Vandervoort), and Tess Mercer (Cassidy Freeman); the series' representations of the Other, explorations of identity, and the ways in which Othered characters speak to Clark's own struggles; and finally, the audience reception of the series and its position within the larger Superman narrative universe.

Part One, "*Smallville*'s Decade-Long Mythical Journey," focuses on the series' central character Clark Kent and the influence of Campbellian and Jungian archetypes and relationships on his trajectory from farm boy to Superman. Although *Smallville*'s representation of Clark sometimes makes him appear far from super, the opening three essays elucidate how many of his bumps in the road are purposeful moments in developing the monomythic hero.

In "Mythicizing Clark Kent: Archetypes and Mythic Structures of *Smallville*," Daniel P. Compora draws upon the work of Joseph Campbell, Carl Jung, and Christopher Vogler to analyze the series' character archetypes and monomythic structures. Though the Campbellian influence is present, Compora postulates that Clark's journey more closely resembles sections of the twelve-step adaptation outlined by Vogler. Compora identifies numerous points of concordance between *Smallville* and the Vogler-Campbell hybrid approach to the heroic journey, to the end of articulating a simply stated but profound argument: *Smallville* was not just a television series whose stories and characters mimicked mythic structures and archetypes, but rather its utilization of these conventions should lead us to identify it as a truly American mythic series.

Where Compora traces the ways in which Clark moves from uncertain teen to Superman, James F. Iaccino's "The *Smallville* Destiny: The Superhero's Shaping by His Archetypal Fathers" focuses on two character types that influence his journey, the Wise Old Man (or mentor) and the Trickster. Utilizing Jung, Iaccino identifies how these figures, taken holistically, comprise the Father archetype—an assessment that he then expands to Clark's two father figures, Jonathan and Jor-El. Without dwelling on the ideas of nature versus nurture that are so prevalent in *Smallville*'s storylines, Iaccino details how Jonathan and Jor-El's conflicting parenting methods delay Clark's maturation process. Yet, as Iaccino suggests, Clark comes to "reconciliatory moments" with his fathers in the series' final season. In these moments, Clark realizes he needs both paternal influences to take flight—both figuratively and literally—and Jonathan and Jor-El come to understand their respective value in shaping the journey of their shared son.

In "'Always hold on to Smallville': Domesticity and the Male Hero," Bridget Kies provides a dissenting voice to Clark as the familiar archetypal hero. Kies argues that Clark's journey is less a masculine-coded gradual progression away from security and toward an uncertain future and more a feminine-coded series of events defined by time at home. In an examination of Clark's regular retreat to Smallville and the Kent farm, Kies demonstrates that his heroic deeds in the world outside of those spaces do not necessarily result in personal reflection and growth. Rather, these experiences push Clark to more fully appreciate his home and domestic life, ultimately defying gender expectations and underscoring cooperation and pluralism over the traditionally heroic values of individuality and striking out on one's own. For Kies, *Smallville* is as much about the titular town's impact on its hero as it is about the protagonist's impact on his town.

Although Clark's sometimes bumpy trajectory from farm boy to Superman dominates much of *Smallville*'s story, the series' female characters—Lana, Chloe, Lois, Kara, and Tess—provide more unexpected twists and turns. As such, Part Two, "Powerful Women," concentrates on these female characters, how they support Clark's journey, and perhaps most importantly, how they exist in roles other than as Clark's support system.

In "Sidekicks or Heroines? The Feminist Successes and Failures of *Smallville*'s Leading Ladies," Valerie Estelle Frankel explores whether Lana, Chloe, Lois, and Kara travel their own epic quests for salvation and adulthood, or remain in Clark's shadow. Frankel illustrates how Lana begins as the ideal woman for Clark, but ultimately remains largely defined through her relationships to men (Clark and Lex most notably). Comparatively, Frankel finds

Chloe's powers—empathy so strong it can heal and Brainiac-influenced super-intelligence—to be coded as traditionally feminine and thus she questions whether Chloe can act as superhero on her own. Frankel finds that Lois's most interesting source of growth occurs through roleplaying. As she tries on (often uncomfortable) costumes, Lois experiments with sexuality and power which Frankel claims is a way of confronting her unexplored shadows. Finally, Frankel argues that while Clark's destiny is on Earth, Kara's lies elsewhere; she suggests that Kara transcends her role as Clark's sidekick, developing into *Smallville*'s first true self-sufficient heroine.

Despite her initial role as one of *Smallville*'s ruthless antagonists, Tess grows into a more complex character as season eight progresses. Peter Melville's "Another Way: Tess Mercer as Ethical Hero," illustrates how Tess attempts to create the rupture that will transform Clark from small town hero to the savior of humankind—the event, in other words, that declares the birth of Superman. Taking responsibility for the legacy of destruction that her plan entails, Tess effectively sacrifices the integrity of her moral character for the good of her cause. She betrays humanity in the name of delivering to humanity its greatest hero, a gesture that associates her not only with Badiou's figure of the militant subject, but also Žižek's ethical hero. Melville also explores the ideological ambivalences of a normative popular text that opens the possibility of the militant ethical hero at the same time that it forcibly forecloses that possibility as a legitimate means of initiating change.

Offering a third framework to consider *Smallville*'s women, Tara K. Parmiter's "Girl Friday Power: Chloe Sullivan and the Hacker Sidekicks of Twenty-First Century Teen Television" investigates the female hacker character type embodied on the series by Chloe. Parmiter explores how Chloe serves as a reconciliation between the Girl Friday-esque support system and more contemporary hacking heroine. As Parmiter identifies, *Smallville*'s stories are frequently as much about investigation into the "Freaks of the Week" as they are about confrontation with same, and where research is concerned, Clark—not Chloe—is the sidekick. Even when Chloe develops superpowers Parmiter contends that she is more interesting without them—unlike Clark, she does not need a suite of superhuman abilities to give her a personality. However, Chloe's real contribution to *Smallville,* Parmiter ultimately argues, is not in being a cheerleader, or a hacker, or a shadowy Big Sister watching over all. Instead, Chloe is a fusion of heroine and sidekick, girl power and Girl Friday, someone too special to be pigeonholed into one stereotypical role.

In Part Three, "Bodies, Identities and Politics," the essays turn towards the series' representation of the Other. Meteor rocks pervade through *Smallville*'s geography, regularly infecting its inhabitants and ultimately creating non-normative bodies. As these essays illustrate, *Smallville* often uses meteor rocks as a storytelling device to discuss broader issues related to identity, from fitting in at high school to the United States' immigration policies. Furthermore, this section surveys how *Smallville* deploys Othered characters and how this deployment often serves as commentary on its most notable Other: Clark Kent.

With a thorough examination of the meteor freaks, in "Rummaging Through the Closet: (Un)Masking the Signified Other in *Smallville*'s First Four Seasons," Jonathan A. Austad postulates that while *Smallville* initially presents an essentialist perspective on good, evil, and marginalization of Others, later years introduce nuance and ultimately argue for the transcendence of overly simplistic, socially-constructed labels. Austad illustrates how the first two seasons fundamentally argue for a "one-drop rule" of Othered identities in connection to Kryptonite impurity, while seasons three and four introduce non-antagonistic and even sympathetic meteor infectees. This, Austad claims, presents a progression in the series' worldview, but also mirrors Clark's own coming of age and greater understanding of the world and non-human identities. The ignorant, inexperienced Clark of the early seasons encounters only villainous Others; with a few more years under his belt, Clark is capable of progressive thinking and considering how his identity, and the identities of those around him, are more complex than simple classifications of good and evil. For Austad, *Smallville* is ultimately about learning to accept differences and appreciate diversity.

Situating *Smallville*'s treatment of the racial Other within the historical context of the Superman character, Roger Almendarez's "Kryptonian Encounters: Model Immigration and Superman's Impossible Dream" proposes that the series addresses an overlooked aspect of the story: that Clark Kent is fundamentally an assimilating immigrant, and his journey to Superman is a tale of negotiating the visibility of one's outsider status in society. Almendarez reads Clark's heroic acts as participation in a cultural citizenship that connects him to his fellow Kryptonians, but consequently prohibits his full assimilation into the human race. This performance makes him both a hero and a pariah from the community that he strives to save, and he ultimately serves as a model immigrant who hides his labor. The presence of the Blur in later seasons demonstrates an ambiguous approach to immigrant inclusion as it shifts from being a source of valor to a malignant threat. Clark's refusal to publicly identify as the Blur, Almendarez claims, demonstrates *Smallville*'s model immigrant as one that must deny his/her ethnicity in order to assimilate and be accepted within society.

While the first two entries in Part Three address the ways in which the body of *Smallville* as a series reflects contemporary concerns about identity, Daniel Kulle's "Bodies as Unreliable Signifiers: The Inconsistency of *Small-*

ville's Character Construction" concludes this section with an examination of the inconsistencies within and threats created by the bodies of characters themselves. Drawing parallels between the use of visual effects to distort the on-screen image and the loss of self (be it self-control, self-discipline, sense of self, or all three at once), Kulle theorizes that the visual identity of the body is inextricably bound to the narrative presentation of character. When characters behave "out of character" and are visually incongruent in their appearance, they are villainous to the core, incapable of redemption. Yet when a character's appearance is left fundamentally unaltered but their behavior changes, the lack of visual signification of change is a diegetic free pass against any transgressions. A change rooted in the mind can be reconciled; a change reflected in the body, Kulle argues, is irreversibly damaging. Kulle contends that this presents a sort of moral lesson of conservative containment to be contrasted against Clark's repeated (psychologically-rooted but eventually overcome) "out of character" moments.

Smallville follows a long line of Superman stories across media and across decades. For viewers, this establishes specific expectations for character development and narrative outcomes. In Part Four of the collection, "Reception," two essays explore how history and expectations influence the audience's experience of watching the series, and in certain cases, what audiences may do if those expectations are not met.

In "Finding Clark Kent: Sites of Nostalgia and Affect," Gregory Bray and John Patrick Bray reflect upon the nature of *Smallville* as an adaptation of a preexisting material, a text, they argue, that is as much a creation as it is a recreation. The authors propose the concept "sites of nostalgia" to identify those elements that *Smallville* includes as an adaptation to exhibit loyalty to the source material and ultimately legitimacy, from John Williams's famous score to the casting of Christopher Reeve in a guest role. Bray and Bray theorize such creations as part of the "personal folklore" of Superman stories and their fans, whose inclusion then is meant to evoke a sense of authenticity-by-way-of-nostalgia. However, they are quick to note that sites of nostalgia are also double-edge swords. In casting performers from previous Superman stories to evoke a connection to the past, the authors acknowledge that *Smallville* puts pressure on itself and its cast and crew to live up to years of expectations.

But what about those moments where *Smallville* does *not* live up to expectations? In "'Chlark' Versus 'Clois': Shippers, Anti-Fans and Anti-Fan Fans," Cory Barker explores the history of online "shipper" conflicts in segments of the *Smallville* fandom, primarily those surrounding the Clark-Chloe and Clark-Lois pairings. Building upon Jonathan Gray's theorization of the "anti-fan" as one who strongly dislikes a text, Barker details the discourse and production of fans who love *portions* of *Smallville* (in this case, a specific romantic pairing) but strongly dislike others (competing romantic pairings), or what he calls the "anti-fan fan." Barker follows the tensions among anti-fans across message boards, social media, and countless comment threads to demonstrate how these long-running debates influence fan enjoyment of *Smallville*'s concluding seasons—and in the years after it concluded as well.

As we asked before: who cares about *Smallville*? Leaving aside that it remains the longest-running science fiction/fantasy teen drama on television to date (a remarkably well-populated genre in 2014), and the first post–9/11 Superman adaptation, who *really* cares? Perhaps more crucially: why should you, the reader, care about *Smallville*? The eleven essays by twelve authors outlined here provide you eleven different perspectives on the decade-long CW series, present eleven different lenses through which to view the series, and identify eleven different cultural impacts *Smallville* had. This collection illustrates how and why *Smallville* was worth the time and effort of eleven authors and three editors, and serves to answer the opening question with another question: Why did you not care about *Smallville* already?

Notes

1. Paul Simpson, *Smallville: The Official Companion Season 1* (London: Titan, 2004), 8–17.
2. Seth Gunderson, "Smallville, Kansas, the Biggest Little Town You've Ever Seen," *The Trades*, November 5, 2001, http://www.the-trades.com/article.php?id=908.
3. Erik Hedegaard, "Tall Tales from *Smallville*," *Rolling Stone #892*, March 28, 2002.
4. "Episode List: *Smallville* Season 2," *TV Tango*, Accessed March 3, 2014, http://www.tvtango.com/series/smallville/episodes?filters percent5Bday percent5D=&filters percent5B season percent5D=2&filters percent5Bbroadcast percent5D=No&filters percent5Bmedia percent5D=&commit.x=13&commit.y=13.
5. Robert Seidman, "Super Friday Night for The CW; Strategy of Pairing '*Smallville*'/'*Supernatural*' Again on the Night Paid Off," *TV by the Numbers*, September 25, 2010, http://tvbythenumbers.zap2it.com/2010/09/25/super-friday-night-for-the-cw-strategy-of-pairing-smallvillesupernatural-again-on-the-night-paid-off/65167/.
6. The noted series appear on some lists and not others (as is the nature with these kinds of lists), but for specifics see "The Best TV Series of the 2000s," *The A.V. Club*, November 12, 2009, http://www.avclub.com/article/the-best-tv-series-of-the-00s-35256; "26 Best Cult TV Shows Ever," *Entertainment Weekly*, March 14, 2013, http://www.ew.com/ew/gallery/0,,20741515_20620965_21199219,00.html; "The 50 Best TV Dramas of All Time," *Complex*, March 20, 2013, http://www.complex.com/pop-culture/2013/03/best-tv-dramas-of-all-time/.
7. For notable examples of scholarship on *Buffy* and *Angel* see Elana Levine and Lisa Parks, eds., *Undead TV: Essays on Buffy the Vampire Slayer* (Durham: Duke University Press, 2007); Lorna Jowett, *Sex and the Slayer: A Gender Primer for the Buffy Fan* (Middletown, CT: Wesleyan University Press, 2005); Anne Billson, *Buffy the Vampire Slayer (BFI TV Classics)* (London: British Film Institute, 2006). For more information on *Slayage*, visit the journal's web site: http://slayageonline.com/.
8. Recent noteworthy publications on *Supernatural* include Stacey Abbot and David Levery, eds., *TV Goes to Hell: An Unofficial Roadmap of Supernatural* (Toronto: ECW Press,

2011) and Lynn Zubernis and Katherine Larsen, eds., *Fan Phenomena: Supernatural* (Bristol: Intellect, 2014). Similarly, for work on *Veronica Mars* see Rhonda V. Wilcox and Sue Turnbull, eds., *Investigating Veronica Mars: Essays on the Teen Detective Series* (Jefferson, NC: McFarland, 2011).

9. For full explorations of this *Smallville*-related pieces, see Melanie E.S. Kohnen, "The Adventures of a Repressed Farm Boy and the Billionaire Who Loves Him: Queer Spectatorship in *Smallville* Fandom," in *Teen Television: Essays on Programming and Fandom*, ed. Sharon Marie Ross and Louisa Ellen Stein (Jefferson, NC: McFarland, 2008), 207–223; Michaela Meyer, "Slashing *Smallville*: The Interplay of Text, Audience, and Production on Viewer Interpretations of Homoeroticism," *Sexuality & Culture* 17.3 (2013): 476–493; and Miranda Banks, "A Boy for All Planets: *Roswell, Smallville*, and the Teen Male Melodrama," in *Teen TV: Genre, Consumption, and Identity*, ed. Glyn Davis and Kay Dickinson (London: British Film Institute, 2004), 17–28.

10. See Lincoln Geraghty, *The Smallville Chronicles: Critical Essays on the Television Series* (Lanham, MD: Scarecrow Press, 2011).

PART ONE:
Smallville's Decade-Long Mythical Journey

Mythicizing Clark Kent
Archetypes and Mythic Structures of Smallville

DANIEL P. COMPORA

When *Smallville* debuted in 2001, few could predict that it would enjoy a ten-year run and become the most successful televised adaptation of the Superman legend.[1] What was intended to be a portrayal of Clark Kent's teenage years at the Kent farm in Smallville, Kansas, eventually evolved into the story of the adult Clark's early days in Metropolis. The series' primary purpose was not to tell the story of a mature Clark Kent as Superman, but rather focus on the process and influences that lead to his becoming Superman. By design, this structure inevitably would represent an incomplete journey. Since most people already have a strong idea of who Superman is and what he represents, the outcome is already known: the emergence of an American superhero. *Smallville*, then, is more about the process than it is about the final product.

However, as the series evolved, and adulthood became impossible to ignore, Clark's heroic journey encompassed an entire decade. Perhaps it was the amount of time viewers spent watching the adolescent Clark grow into adulthood. Quite possibly, it was the repetition of countless moral lessons learned over this time. Perhaps it was the loss of his valued mentors, the struggles with interpersonal relationships, or his ultimate struggle with identity, but somewhere along the way, *Smallville* transcended the small screen and eventually embodied characteristics of myth. According to Joseph Campbell, "A whole mythology is an organization of symbolic images and narratives, metaphorical of the possibilities of human experience and the fulfillment of a given culture at a given time."[2] In this chapter, I illustrate how *Smallville* follows a mythic pattern of storytelling and employs the use of cultural archetypes to fulfill its role as an American myth.

The episodic nature of television actually contributes to the mythicizing of Clark. Rather than focusing on a series of repetitive adventures, this version of the Superman legend focuses more on a "series of epiphanies" for the developing hero.[3] *Smallville* spends ten seasons exploring this alter ego, transforming Clark into a heroic figure, even without the trademark red and blue suit. As Karin Beeler notes, "Though he is often reluctant to fulfill his destiny in the early part of the series, Clark assumes the role of mythic savior in multiple ways over the course of ten seasons while still providing a link to contemporary American culture."[4] In contrast to previous iterations of the Superman legend, *Smallville*'s approach is exceptional in that it mythicizes the alter ego of the character and not the much more familiar superhero. This familiarity with the superhero persona allows viewers to also see the adolescent Clark as a truly heroic figure. The pattern of an adolescent hero has always been popular, particularly in science fiction and fantasy based literature and film. Examples include the Pevensie children from five of the books that comprise C.S. Lewis's *The Chronicles of Narnia*; Ender Wiggin from Orson Scott Card's *Ender's Game*; and Paul Atreides from the first three books of Frank Herbert's *Dune* series. All of these adolescent characters help illustrate the appeal and enduring power of the adolescent hero, but none quite so strongly as that of Harry Potter. J. K. Rowling's famous hero debuted in 1998, with the first film appearing in 2001, right around the time *Smallville* began. Beeler supports this notion by stating, "*Smallville*'s use of familiar telefantasy or fantasy and science film character types and mythic patterns thus creates much of its social relevance for contemporary youth who may also be familiar with the cult phenomena of Superman films or comics."[5] Familiarity is indeed essential is establishing Clark as a mythical figure. In fact Clark, and his superhero persona Superman, have largely been entrenched in American culture as archetypal figures for decades.

The mythic nature of Superman is readily apparent. Dennis Dooley believes that Superman is "a myth worthy of the Greeks in its intuitive grasp of human aspiration confronted with self-knowledge. It reverberated with childhood fears and adolescent dreams revealed on many a Freudian couch. Yet it was a peculiarly American myth."[6] Superman has been sufficiently mythicized since his creation, but his alter ego has largely served as little more than a disguise. *Smallville* builds upon the mythic nature of Superman, and largely follows Campbell's mythic structure, known as the "monomyth," in constructing young Clark as a hero. The show declares its debt to Campbell declared this during the season seven's "Quest" (2008) in which *Daily Planet* photographer Jimmy Olsen specifically acknowledges Campbell's work. During a conversation with

Chloe Sullivan regarding an article, Jimmy says, "Well, it's all very Joseph Campbell—hero's journey and all that." The reference serves as little more than an inside joke; still, it is apparent that the creators of the series were well aware of the mythic nature of their protagonist.

The Hero's Journey

Campbell describes the hero's journey as occurring in a cycle consisting of three phases and seventeen steps. "The standard path of the mythological adventure of the hero is a magnification of the formula represented in the rites of passage: *separation—initiation—return:* which might be named the nuclear unit of the monomyth."[7] While the three phase-seventeen steps model is a bit cumbersome, Campbell succinctly describes this journey by focusing on its bare essentials: "A hero ventures forth from the world of common day into a region of supernatural wonder: fabulous forces are there encountered and a decisive victory is won: the hero comes back from this mysterious adventure with the power to bestow boons on his fellow man."[8] Every step in the process is significant and contributes to a greater understanding of mythic structure; however, Campbell's model was not specifically designed to discuss televisual media. A number of models of the monomyth have been derived from Campbell's framework. The most relevant to *Smallville* likely would be Christopher Vogler's adaptation presented in *The Writer's Journey*, a twelve-step journey that seems best suited to discuss film and television. This is not surprising, given that Vogler was once a story consultant for the famous Walt Disney Company.

The twelve stages of Vogler's model dovetail nicely with Campbell's three primary phases and include (1) The Ordinary World; (2) The Call to Adventure; (3) The Refusal of the Call; (4) Meeting with the Mentor; (5) Crossing the Threshold; (6) Tests, Allies, and Enemies; (7) Approach to the Inmost Cave; (8) The Ordeal; (9) Reward; (10) The Road Back; (11) Resurrection; and (12) Return with the Elixir.[9] While both authors provide solid reasoning for including each step in his model, for the purposes of this discussion, it simply is not necessary to examine either model in total. Analyzing the three primary phases of Campbell's model and selected steps from Vogler's work sufficiently contributes to a greater understanding of Clark's heroic journey.

During Campbell's separation phase, which he labels Departure, the hero is forced out of the familiarity of the normal world and is thrust into the world of adventure.[10] Defining the normal world for Clark, though, serves up its own set of problems. Does the viewer consider Clark's normal world to be that of Krypton? Or, is Clark's real world really the picturesque family farm in rural

Kansas? The answer to those questions is wholly dependent on the journey at hand. If one considers the series as a whole, then Clark's journey begins the moment he crash lands on Earth during the infamous meteor storm that occurred in the pilot episode (2001). Using this as the basis of the journey, the real world would be Krypton and the world of adventure would be Earth. The primary problem with this approach is that Clark does not willingly leave Krypton. He is an infant, incapable of making independent decisions. Krypton may have been the place he was born, but it is not home to the character viewers see every week.

From the viewers' point of view, Clark's home is the Kent farm. Each episode or event that takes Clark away from the farm and out into the hostile world establishes the Kent farm as his normal, safe world. As a result, though Clark is an alien by birth, he assimilates so well, and at such an early age, to the ways of Earth, he is viewed more as a Kansan than he is a Kryptonian. For all intents and purposes, one of Clark's journeys begins every time he leaves the Kent farm. As such, viewers do not see Clark as a Kryptonian hero visiting Earth; rather, they see a Midwestern farm boy with exceptional abilities as a possible savior. With America's long history of immigration, accepting Clark as a Kansan as opposed to a Kryptonian helps establish him as being truly an American hero.

Certain steps of the journey that would fit within this phase are specifically applicable to *Smallville*. The call to adventure is "the first stage of the journey ... signifies that destiny has summoned the hero and transferred his spiritual center of gravity from within the pale of his society to a zone unknown."[11] After a brief period in which the hero initially refuses the call, the challenge is almost always accepted. This call, followed by the refusal of the call, is such a familiar part of *Smallville* that it borders on cliché. For ten seasons, Clark struggles with choices, trying to balance a normal life with that of his superhero persona. While the refusal of the call is a necessary step to overcome, Clark overcomes this step on an almost weekly basis. Even as late as the tenth season, Clark has self-doubts about his destiny. In the season ten premiere "Lazarus" (2010), Clark is told by his Kryptonian father Jor-El that he is the impending evil that the world will face. Clark believes that he indeed has evil in him, but is reassured by the ghost of his earthly father Jonathan Kent that he is, indeed, capable of greatness.

During the initiation phase, "the hero moves in a dream landscape of curiously fluid, ambiguous forms, where he must survive a succession of trials."[12] It is during this stage where the hero is subjected to a series of tests and conflicts that help him define his character. Again, the episodic nature of a television series allows each individual episode to serve as a test, or mini-quest, which forms a pattern that helps make up the season, and ultimately the series.

Several steps of Vogler's model fit under Campbell's initiation phase, including the seventh stage of the journey, in which the hero must complete the "Approach to the Inmost Cave." During this stage, the hero prepares for the central ordeal or conflict.[13] While the reference to the cave is largely figurative, in the case of *Smallville*, it can be applied literally. During the early seasons of the series, especially before the Fortress of Solitude is constructed, Clark enters the Kawatche caves quite often. These caves running under the ground of Smallville provide a link to Clark's home world of Krypton in the form of cave paintings, many of which are historic, others prophetic. In later seasons, the Fortress of Solitude serves the same structural function as the Kawatche caves. Both sites provide Clark with information to assist him with the ordeal at hand.

Death and Resurrection

Fittingly, the eighth stage of Vogler's model is called "The Ordeal" and is the key to the heroic journey. This stage often presents the hero with a life or death situation that usually is resolved with a form of death experienced by the protagonist: "Heroes must die so that they can be reborn."[14] This death leads to a resurrection that allows the hero to emerge with a greater amount of wisdom or sense of purpose. Each individual episode of *Smallville* contains an ordeal that Clark must overcome. While it would be absurd to kill off a television program's hero literally in every episode, Clark does metaphorically die quite often during the series.[15] Every time Clark loses his power, it could be seen as a metaphorical death. Since his Kryptonian powers define much of Clark's persona, being separated from them, even temporarily, renders Clark powerless. The restoration of his power is also a restoration of his persona; hence it is a form of death and rebirth.

Furthermore, the death of his father Jonathan during season five's "Reckoning" (2006) could be construed as at least a partial death of Clark. Since Jonathan is Clark's primary mentor throughout the series, Clark's life changes dramatically once he is dead. The bond is so close that when Jonathan dies, a part of Clark dies as well. In addition, when Clark is dispatched to the Phantom Zone at the end of season five, only to return at the beginning of season six, this could easily be seen as a form of death and resurrection, as Clark is separated from his normal world and humanity. In fact, as a prison dimension created by Jor-El, the Phantom Zone represents a form of Purgatory or even Hell. As such, when Clark emerges from this terrible place, he has conquered a fate worse than death.

Yet *Smallville* does not just lean on metaphorical interpretations of this life or death ordeal. In the final episode of the ninth season, "Salvation" (2010), Clark allows himself be stabbed by a blue Kryptonite dagger, then falls with his arms outstretched in a pseudo-crucifixion pose, presumably to his death. Of course, since it was already known that *Smallville* would be returning for a tenth and final season, this death, though seemingly real at the time, is not permanent. The eleventh stage of Vogler's model is the "The Resurrection" and it is during this stage that the hero, having survived the ordeal, experiences a form of purification, or rebirth.[16] Appropriately, the opening episode of the tenth season is titled "Lazarus," a reference to the man whom Jesus Christ resurrected from the dead. Clark's death and resurrection at this point in the series is pivotal because it is the near the end of his ten-year journey.

Sharing of Power

The third phase Campbell presents is the return phase, in which the hero brings the benefits of his journey back to share them with his people.[17] Since *Smallville* by design presents a somewhat incomplete journey, it could be argued that Clark never fully achieves this stage, at least in the eyes of the viewers. He does not fully become Superman until the final minutes of the last episode, "Finale" (2011). In fact, even with the closing scene, viewers still see a close-up of Clark Kent. Although the Superman costume is present, the emphasis is on Clark's face—not his costume—before fading into a comic book image. Still, it is difficult, if not impossible, to view the ending scene as anything other than the fulfillment of a journey. Superman's journey is just beginning, but Clark's has just concluded. After years of conflict, moral dilemmas, countless deaths, literal and figurative, and copious amounts of teen angst, Clark finally gives America the benefits of what that struggle produced—a truly American hero who is there to protect them against the powerful and invading alien threat Darkseid.

Looking at each episode as a microcosm of the larger journey, Clark routinely shares the benefits of his adventures with others. Every time he saves someone or prevents a disaster, people experience the benefits of his journey. The lessons Clark learns are almost always shared at the end of each episode. Every sentimental, reflective talk he has after surviving yet another trial demonstrates growth and understanding that is only realized by sharing it with someone else. For example, near the conclusion of the fifth season premiere "Arrival" (2005), Clark, who is left vulnerable because of the loss of his powers, shares his understanding of what it means to be human with his parents. These reflections typically serve the narrative function of showing viewers what exactly Clark has learned; the process of sharing them touches the other characters, and they too enjoy the benefits of Clark's struggles. They do not experience the journey in full, yet they still reap some of the benefits of it.

More interesting is that Clark's Kryptonian powers are shared with others a number of times throughout the series. In the season one's "Leech" (2002), Clark's powers transfer to classmate Eric Summers, who takes them again in the third season episode "Asylum" (2004). Rudy Jones steals Clark's powers in the season eight's "Injustice" (2009), while Jor-El gives them to Lois for a day in the tenth season episode "Prophecy" (2011). These instances of power sharing are used in somewhat of an ironic sense. Sharing the benefits of a hero's journey is seen as a noble, even necessary element of the process, but giving heroic powers to someone who is not deserving of them is irresponsible and dangerous. These people have not experienced the same journey Clark has, therefore they are undeserving of this power. Also, the loss of power serves as a trial for Clark to overcome. In some instances, he is forced to deal with someone who, at the moment, possesses his Kryptonian powers; he himself is at a severe and unfamiliar disadvantage. These situations help fulfill this component of the journey, simultaneously making Clark even more heroic, since he succeeds without the use of his powers.

Archetypes

Not only does *Smallville* follow a mythic pattern, it also relies on familiar archetypes in developing its characters. Vogler builds off Carl Jung's theory of the collective unconscious to identify eight different archetypes central to the art of mythic storytelling. Jung defines archetypes as "forms or images of a collective nature which occur practically all over the earth as constituents of myths and at the same times as autochthonous, individual products of unconscious origin."[18] The eight major archetypal roles typically fulfilled in a heroic journey include the hero, mentor, herald, shadow, shapeshifter, ally, threshold guardian, and trickster.[19] *Smallville* employs all of these character archetypes at various points during its run, with certain characters fulfilling different archetypal roles at different times. Vogler states that "archetypes are amazingly constant throughout all times and cultures."[20] It is this familiarity with the archetypal forms that attracts viewers to these characters, illustrating how various characters in *Smallville* embody mythic characteristics. Of particular interest with regard to *Smallville* are the hero, mentor, the shadow, and trickster.

The most obvious archetype employed in *Smallville* is Clark as the hero. Campbell defines the hero as "a personage of exceptional gifts. Frequently, he is honored by his society, frequently unrecognized of disdained. He and/or the world in which he finds himself suffers from a symbolic deficiency."[21] Unlike legendary mythic heroes, and even the adult version of Superman popularized in the media, "[t]his young Superman wrestled with tough decisions and wore ordinary clothes."[22] The role of hero is practically forced on Clark. Even though he comes to Earth with tremendous power, Clark is not born a hero; rather, he is character with heroic abilities. The symbolic deficiency that Clark suffers from appears to be an absence of American values. This notion is supported by the fact that he really only becomes a hero because of the influence of his parents, Jonathan and Martha. They are the ones who teach Clark what it is to be truly American. They raise him with traditional Midwestern values, give him copious amounts of chores on the farm, and ultimately nurture him during his heroic journey. Without their influence, Clark would never have evolved into Superman.

Smallville's Clark, while not the Superman of previous generations, still embodies elements of the hero inherent within the character. He possesses larger than life abilities, even if they are not fully developed for much of the series. More so than his powers, his beliefs and values define Clark (and Superman), as being a truly American hero. Gary Engle argues, "Superman is the great American hero ... only Superman achieves truly mythic stature, interweaving a pattern of beliefs, literary conventions and cultural traditions of the American people more powerfully and more accessibly than any other cultural symbol of the twentieth century, perhaps of any period in our history."[23] The values of hard work, the love of his parents, loyalty, friendship, and the innate sense of right and wrong are Clark's truly heroic characteristics. In the *Smallville* universe, Clark is heroic not because he is Superman, but because he is not yet Superman. While he possesses great power, it is not his use of the power that makes him a hero; often it is how he reacts during the many times throughout the series when his powers are temporarily lost.

Mentorship

During the series' ten-year run, Clark seeks the counsel of a number of people, but the most prominent mentors are Jonathan and Martha and Jor-El. This is not surprising, given that the archetype of the mentor bears a close resemblance to the parental image.[24] The influence of the Jonathan and Martha is unmistakable. They raise the child on a Midwestern farm and teach him the value of hard work and personal responsibility. Even after his death, Jonathan still appears to Clark occasionally to provide insight and support. In "Lazarus," Jonathan warns Clark about an impending evil, yet also expressing faith in Clark. In this particular case, Jonathan serves two archetypal functions. By expressing his belief in Clark's heroism, he fulfills the role of mentor. When he warns Clark about a forthcoming threat, Jonathan also serves the function of a herald. According to Vogler, "Herald characters issue challenges and announce the coming of significant change."[25]

After Jonathan's death and Martha's ascension into politics, Clark turns to Lionel, who serves as an unlikely mentor for a short period. This is also not surprising, given that he is a strong, parental figure who has known Clark for a number of years. In addition, Lionel is one of the most interesting characters in the *Smallville* universe because he fulfills a number of archetypal functions. Early in the series, he is clearly a shadow figure. Later, Lionel attempts to step into Jonathan's fatherly role, even going as far as trying to romance Martha. In this regard, Lionel also represents the archetype of the shapeshifter, a character whose loyalty is always in question.[26] Despite the fact that Lionel appears to have Clark's best interest at heart, his past deeds and his relationship with Lex ultimately make his influence on Clark worrisome. If Jonathan fulfills the role of a noble father figure, then Lionel provides a stark contrast. In fact, this relationship is taken to a more literal level in season ten's "Luthor" (2010). In this alternate Earth, Clark finds himself the son of Lionel, not Jonathan. The Clark who emerges from that particular father-son bond is much different, and much darker, than the Clark to which viewers are accustomed.

To say that parental figures are the only ones to serve as Clark's mentors would be inaccurate. One of Clark's strongest mentors, especially during the first few seasons, is Chloe Sullivan. With her "Wall of Weird" and her investigative reporter instincts, she not only sets Clark on his career path, but also provides him with much needed acceptance. Later in the series, after she abandons her career as a journalist, she takes over control of Watchtower so she can, among other things, protect Clark. Other characters, such as John Jones (Martian Manhunter) and Oliver Queen (Green Arrow), provide support and guidance to Clark during his long journey.

Villains and Tricksters

Vogler discusses the importance of shadow figures, which represent evil and oppose the hero.[27] In most episodes, Clark encounters at least one villain who fulfills this archetypal role. Certain episodes contain a single villain who does not last very long, such as Cameron Mahkent (Icicle), who appears in season nine's "Absolute Justice" (2010). Other villains may be vanquished, but end up causing trouble during a later episode, like Winslow Schott (Toymaker) or John Corben (Metallo). Shadow figures may also be characters who endure a bit longer, like Davis Bloome (Doomsday), who serves as a menacing presence during the entire eighth season, or Milton Fine (Brainiac) and Major/General Zod, who spend multiple seasons tormenting—and in certain instances, befriending—Clark.

Undoubtedly though, the primary shadow figure in *Smallville* is Lex Luthor. Even when Lex almost entirely disappears during the last three years of the series, his specter continues to loom over Clark and the series. The great irony in the rivalry between Clark and Lex is the fact that the men share many similarities. Both of their lives were greatly transformed by the meteor shower that brought Clark to Earth. Clark was taken in by the Kents and began his heroic journey while Lex was left bald and facing insurmountable distance between him and his father. Both are destined for positions of great power due to their birthright. While Clark's Kryptonian powers will ultimately lead him to become the defender of humanity, Lex is the heir apparent to Luthor-Corp and his father's billions. Both men share a deep bond with Lana Lang, whose parents were killed during the meteor shower. If, as Vogler points out, that "shadows can be 'all the things we don't like about ourselves,'" then these similarities strengthen the hero-shadow relationship between Clark and Lex.[28] Without intending to do so, Lex serves as a constant reminder of what Clark may become if he fails to adhere to the heroic path he is following.

Clark faces shadow figures in every episode, and sometimes for entire seasons or off and on for a number of years. Lex is the primary external villain of *Smallville*, and in Superman lore in general. However, one of the strongest shadow figures Clark faces is himself. Most of Clark's struggles are internal and are often resolved by the end of an episode, but external variants of Clark's dark side are present in *Smallville*. Bizarro (or Bizarro-Clark) is a Phantom Zone escapee who steals Clark's DNA and poses as him at different moments during the sixth and seventh season. Clark Luthor (Ultraman), introduced in the tenth season episode "Luthor," is Clark's alter ego in the alternate Earth universe. Like Clark, he is Kryptonian, but in this universe has been raised by Lionel. These externalizations of villainous Kent personas illustrate that regardless of who or what Clark is fighting at the moment, his own potential dark side is always part of the conflict.

The trickster is one of the most intriguing archetypes, largely because it "embodies the energies of mischief and desire for change."[29] A trickster may actually be an ally or an adversary posing as an ally. While the trickster is somewhat of a shadow figure, its role is often a bit more defined, and the relationship is often much more complicated than that of the hero-shadow. According to John R. Van Eenwyk, "The figure of the trickster in folk tale and myth is one of the most important and ubiquitous of the archetypal shadow. It symbolizes the shadow side of ideals and beliefs about the nature of reality."[30] Many characters that Clark encounters over ten seasons could easily be labeled tricksters, including Lionel and Lex. In fact, nearly every villain succeeds in tricking Clark at some point and could be seen as fulfilling this role on an episode-by-episode basis.

However, of all the characters in the *Smallville* universe, no character fulfills this role, as defined, more consistently than Jor-El. As Clark's father from a dead world, Jor-El's belief about reality simply does not coincide with Clark's. While Clark is Kryptonian by birth, he has been raised, and truly embodies, the characteristics of an all–American teenager. Clark embraces his humanity while Jor-El fights against it. In fact, Jor-El strips Clark of his powers during season five's "Arrival" as a punishment for disobeying him. He pulls the same trick on Clark by transferring his power to Lois in the season ten's "Prophecy." Although some may view these actions as part of parental mentoring, the fact that Jor-El puts Clark and others in danger, even allowing Clark to die at the end of the ninth season, simply to prove a point makes this more mischief than mentoring. Throughout the course of ten seasons, Jor-El often serves as more of an obstacle that Clark must overcome during his journey rather than a figure for Clark to emulate. While he does at times fulfill a mentorship role, Jor-El's prime function is to get Clark to achieve his destiny, even if he has to trick him into doing it, such as when he introduces a fake version of Clark's Kryptonian cousin Kara in season three's "Covenant" (2004) to draw Clark into the Kawatche caves.

Conclusion

Smallville clearly follows a mythic pattern of storytelling and employs the use of familiar archetypes to create an American myth. As a series that focuses on the early life of a well-known cultural icon, viewers know that the journey, while complete to a certain point, remains largely unfinished. The ten-year run of *Smallville* represents Clark Kent's journey from a small town farm boy into the big city hero Superman. The series is not designed to portray the exploits of a fully realized superhero; it is about the process of a young man becoming such a figure. The stages of the mythic elements and archetypes can be found in every episode, in every season, throughout the entire series. The paradigm of an episodic television series allows viewers to see a multi-layered journey. Each episode sees Clark confront problems, solve them, and learn from them. Each season uses these experiences to build season-long story arcs that represent longer variants of the journey. Finally, the series in total uses all of these elements to form the basis of Clark's transformational journey. *Smallville* can easily be described as a mythic series, comprised of mythic seasons, and made up of mythic episodes.

Notes

1. Grant Morrison, *Supergods: What Masked Vigilantes, Miraculous Mutants, and a Sun God from Smallville Can Teach Us About Being Human* (New York: Spiegel and Grau, 2011), 324.
2. Joseph Campbell, *Thou Art That: Transforming Religious Metaphor* (Novato, CA: New World Library, 2001), 1–2.
3. Stan Beeler, "From Comic Book to Bildungsroman: *Smallville*, Narrative, and the Education of a Young Hero," in *The Smallville Chronicles: Critical Essays on the Television Series*, ed. Lincoln Geraghty (Lanham, MD: Scarecrow Press, 2011), 3.
4. Karin Beeler, "Televisual Transformations: Myth and Social Issues in *Smallville*," in *The Smallville Chronicles: Critical Essays on the Television Series*, ed. Lincoln Geraghty (Lanham; MD: Scarecrow Press, 2011), 31.
5. Ibid., 26.
6. Dennis Dooley, "The Man of Tomorrow and the Boys of Yesterday," in *Superman at Fifty*, ed. Dennis Dooley and Gary Engel (New York: Collier, 1987), 19.
7. Joseph Campbell, *The Hero with a Thousand Faces* (Novato, CA: New World Library, 2008), 23.
8. Ibid., 30.
9. Christopher Vogler, *The Writer's Journey: Mythic Structure for Writers*, 3d ed. (Studio City, CA: Michael Wiese Productions, 2007).
10. Campbell, *The Hero with a Thousand Faces*, 41.
11. Ibid., 48.
12. Ibid., 81.
13. Vogler, *The Writer's Journey*, 143.
14. Ibid., 155.
15. According to the *Smallville* wiki, Clark lost his powers ten times throughout the series' run, and found himself temporarily powerless in other circumstances as well. See "Clark Kent's Power Loss," *Smallville Wikia*, http://smallville.wikia.com/wiki/Clark_Kent percent 27s_power_loss.
16. Vogler, *The Writer's Journey*, 197.
17. Campbell, *The Hero with a Thousand Faces*, 167.
18. Carl Jung, quoted in Campbell, *The Hero with a Thousand Faces*, 342.
19. Vogler, *The Writer's Journey*, 26.
20. Ibid., 23.
21. Campbell, *The Hero with a Thousand Faces*, 29–30.
22. Morrison, *Supergods*, 324.
23. Gary Engle, "What Makes Superman So Darned American?" in *Superman at Fifty*, ed. Dennis Dooley and Gary Engel (New York: Collier, 1987), 80.
24. Vogler, *The Writer's Journey*, 40.
25. Ibid., 55.
26. Ibid., 59.
27. Ibid., 65.
28. Ibid., 65.
29. Ibid., 77.
30. John R. Van Eenwyk, *Archetypes and Strange Attractors: The Chaotic World of Symbols* (Toronto: Inner City Books, 1997), 99.

The *Smallville* Destiny

The Superhero's Shaping by His Archetypal Fathers

JAMES F. IACCINO

Approximately one month after the September 11, 2001, tragedy, the world was ready to embrace one of its most famous superheroes once again, in yet another television series. But unlike its previous incarnations, such as *The Adventures of Superman* (1952–1958) and *Lois and Clark: The New Adventures of Superman* (1993–1997), *Smallville* (2001–2011) focuses on the early life of Clark Kent before he becomes the Man of Steel.

This teen drama reflects the concerns and worries of a number of societies that are trying to carve out their destiny in the midst of impending war and global turmoil. Popular culture analyst Lincoln Geraghty notes that *Smallville*'s development parallels the creation of the original Superman figure by Jerry Siegel and Joe Shuster who wanted to provide people with a much-needed hero at the time of a Great Depression and World War II.[1] Similar to the comic book prototype, *Smallville*'s live-action lead character fulfills the monumental, almost superheroic goal of providing new generations of viewers with inspiration and hope for a brighter tomorrow.

The evolution of the superhero into a strong and self-assured leader of the people is not an easy task to accomplish.[2] It took a full decade for *Smallville* to relate that transformation of everyday human into powerful god on the small screen, and one of Clark's greatest challenges in becoming that Hero is incorporating (as well as reconciling) two pivotal paternal figures into his overall psyche.[3] Of course, those parents are none other than his Kryptonian birth father, Jor-El, and his adopted father from Kansas, Jonathan Kent. While both men loved their son, they are frequently at odds due to their differing views of what Clark's destiny should entail. This essay will therefore examine Jor-El and Jonathan's combined influence on the development of Clark into Superman. Particular archetypal themes will be referenced in order to provide a theoretical foundation for the overall analysis as well as demonstrate how many mythic tales involve continual struggles with parents so that a realization of the Hero's potential can eventually be achieved.

The Hero Archetype

According to Carl Jung, all tales of the Hero archetype begin with the character as a "divine child" (or *puer aeternus*) who is "smaller than small, [but] bigger than big."[4] What this definition essentially means is that the child is not yet ready to undertake heroic tasks because of his/her small size, coupled with the lack of psychological maturity. However, the child also possesses a superhuman, almost godlike nature; it is this "semi-divine" state that will allow him/her to accomplish great things throughout the lifespan. Jung likens the child to a seed that, once planted, will develop into a miraculous organism full of life and beauty.[5] *Smallville*'s *puer aeternus* is none other than Kal-El/Clark who arrives on Earth via a spaceship amidst a meteor storm that devastates the town of Smallville to its very core. Out of this destruction, the young and innocent Kal-El emerges from his vessel and meets up with Jonathan and Martha Kent, whose lives are forever changed by the encounter. It is Martha who states that the boy found them, recognizing the divine qualities of this youngster almost immediately; Jonathan's silence as he looks up at the sky is his affirmation to what Martha has said. And so the pilot episode (2001) of *Smallville* begins, along with the development of its Hero.

Joseph Campbell expands upon the work of Jung by elaborating on some of the salient characteristics of the Hero archetype.[6] The "child of destiny" has obscure and mysterious origins, and is often raised by guardians other than his/her biological parents. It is only in his/her later adolescence or adulthood that s/he realizes who s/he is and, just as importantly, who his/her parents are.[7] Interestingly, it takes almost a full two seasons of *Smallville* for Clark to learn what his real name is (Kal-El), and that Jor-El is his biological father. In the season two episode "Exodus" (2003), Clark encounters the spaceship that the Kents have kept hidden in the storm cellar. As it begins to glow, the voice of Jor-El relates that while the man has died on Krypton along with everyone else, Jor-El's "memory and will" are still being kept alive through his home world's technology.[8] Jor-El reveals that he is meant to guide Kal-El on his journey and make him fulfill his destiny on Earth. Clark begins to realize that his reason for existence has taken on more "heroic" proportions than ever he (or Jonathan) thought possible.

The Hero's Journey

It is also important to discuss the stages of the Hero's journey so that one understands the complexity of each of the phases and why it takes Clark/Kal-El a significant number of years to reach the end-point of that overall cycle. Campbell summarizes the Hero's journey as a story that can be divided into three phases: Separation, Initiation, and Return. More specifically, "a Hero ventures forth from the world of common day into a region of supernatural wonder (the Separation Phase); fabulous forces are there encountered and a decisive victory is won (the Initiation Phase); the Hero comes back from this mysterious adventure with the power to bestow boons on his fellow man (the Return Phase)."[9] Each of these phases can be broken down into a number of subcategories, many of which are included in every Hero's story. I will examine only those that directly relate to Clark's journey in the *Smallville* series. It should be mentioned that he spends a good deal of his time in the Separation and Initiation phases of the journey, and that the final stage of Return is only completed in the closing minutes of the series' concluding episode "Finale" (2011), when he dons the familiar cape and tights and becomes the legendary figure of Superman.

The Separation Phase consists of the following elements: the Call to Adventure, Refusal of the Call, Supernatural Aid, and the Crossing of the First Threshold. The adventure first starts with the Hero receiving a call to head off into a strange and new world, sometimes of his/her volition (and sometimes not). Initially, the Hero does not want to heed that call, but wants to remain in his/her comfortable surroundings. What convinces the Hero to eventually venture into the unknown is a magical talisman or artifact, entrusted to him/her by some otherworldly agent, which provides the means to cross that threshold and move him/her into the next phase of the journey.[10]

The closing episode of the second season, "Exodus," will now be explored with respect to this Separation Phase and how the two fathers play an instrumental role in Clark/Kal-El leaving Smallville and heading toward the big city of Metropolis.[11] When Clark hears Jor-El's "call" to embrace his destiny, he refuses to follow that guardian's directive and instead blows the ship up with a Kryptonite key that he steals from Lionel Luthor. Not only does a section of the farm get blasted away, but the explosion also results in Martha losing her unborn child and Jonathan expressing disappointment that Clark took this reckless course of action. Frustrated by both fathers who clearly want to see him pursue a particular direction to his life, Clark chooses to wear a red Kryptonite ring (an object fashioned from a special type of rock from his home planet) that allows him to become a more "liberated" and carefree individual who is not burdened by familial concerns. His new persona is further reflected in the sunglasses and leather jacket that he puts on, plus the motorcycle that transports him away from the safe confines of Smallville (as well as his two fathers) into the relatively new territory of urban existence.

The second phase of the Hero's journey, the Initiation (or immersion in that lifestyle), features a number of elements, including the Road of Trials, Atonement with the Father, Apotheosis, and the Ultimate Boon. To elaborate on each, the Hero undertakes a series of tests or ordeals, some of which s/he will fail at in the first outing. But it is the Hero's endurance and persistence that primarily characterize this "road of trials." The Hero's transformation continues by reconciling with a significant Father figure in his/her life and then undergoing a death of his/her current self so that a rebirth can be attained. This phase ends with the Hero achieving the goal of the quest; this coveted boon is typically something transcendent such as the elixir of life or the Holy Grail.[12]

Returning to the first *Smallville* journey, the start of season three's "Exile" (2003) illustrates that Clark has been initiated into quite a different lifestyle in Metropolis for the past three months. He has a lavish apartment, drives expensive cars, holds beautiful women on his arm, and calls himself "Kal" (which is an abbreviated title for the more formal Kal-El, with just the same familiarity to it as Clark's adopted name). Of course, Kal is able to maintain these extravagances by committing numerous robberies with his superpowers. Clearly, he is failing to live up to his true potential by giving in to such materialistic wants and desires. Even Jor-El occasionally reminds Kal that he is meant for a greater destiny by causing the Kryptonian symbol burned on his chest to glow fiery hot. (The symbol was a mark with which Jor-El branded his son when his offspring defied him in "Exodus.") Rather than listen to his biological father, Kal continues to deal with his numerous "trials" by succumbing to temptation instead of mastering those weaknesses of the flesh. While it looks like Clark has undergone a "rebirth" into Kal, it is certainly not the apotheosis of the Initiation Phase as the transformation is letting the dark side of Kal take over while restraining his good side.

Interestingly, both fathers are able to work together to bring Clark back to Smallville before his journey leads him down the path to possible self-destruction. Jonathan makes a deal with Jor-El whereby he is given superpowers equal to Clark. And after a lengthy, fierce battle between father and son (which extends into the next episode, "Phoenix" [2003]), Clark "snaps" out of his Kal state when he smashes the red Kryptonite ring rather than kill Jonathan with his bare hands. Interestingly, the Kryptonian symbol disappears from Clark's chest, suggesting that he has successfully passed his first major test on that Hero's road of trials. Paul Simpson reflects in the *Season 3 Companion* that Clark has been "healed" in the process of engaging in that life-and-death struggle with his parent.[13] The episode even includes mini atonement with the father when Clark holds Jonathan with affection. When both return to Smallville, Clark further relates to both Jonathan and Martha that "he is so sorry for everything" that has occurred, seeking their forgiveness that they gladly give him. Clark's return to his hometown marks the interruption of his Initiation Phase, preventing him from completing the Hero's journey. I will still discuss that end-point of the cycle so that we are able to familiarize ourselves with all aspects of the Hero's developmental cycle.

The third and final phase of the Hero's journey, the Return, is marked by the following: Rescue from Without, the Magic Flight, the Crossing of the Return Threshold, and Master of Two Worlds. Just as the Hero needs supernatural guides to set off on the quest, s/he requires powerful "rescuers" to bring him/her back home (i.e., the origin point). And if the Hero has his/her blessing, then the flight back becomes something miraculous and magical. To complete the adventure, the Hero has to cross a threshold back into the known world while retaining the wisdom that was gained on the quest. Finally, and most importantly, this figure has to attain a balance or "mastery" between his/her inner and outer self so that a truly integrated psyche can be achieved.[14]

Similar to Campbell's "mastery of two worlds," Jung refers to this psychic wholeness as an archetypal Self that represents the "God-image" within the human soul.[15] The Return Phase of Clark's journey will be considered in the closing pages of this essay, and it will be placed in the context of his finally obtaining reconciliation with both of his fathers. It should be noted that the birth of Superman represents that completed figure of a human who has reached a divine level of existence. Thus, Superman is a realization of Jung's Self depicted within the *Smallville* universe, right down to the uppercase "S" in his name that denotes his actualized identity or Selfhood.

The Father Archetype

Now that I have presented a description of the Hero archetype and the critical stages of the Hero's journey, a more in-depth focus will be provided on Clark's two guardians: earthly farmer Jonathan and Kryptonian scientist Jor-El. To begin the discussion, Jung defines the Father archetype as a powerful figure who rules his household "with an iron fist" (sometimes referenced as "the hand of God"), while still displaying feelings of love and affection toward those family members.[16] Jung further indicates that the Father embodies characteristics of two central and complementary characters within Hero tales: the Wise Old Man and the Trickster. As a Wise Old Man, the Father shares his knowledge and insight that he has accumulated over the years with his offspring, assisting them in their development.[17] Conversely, as a Trickster, he can also disrupt his children's autonomy with his judgmental (and prejudicial) views toward others as well as the strict, and sometimes irrational, control that he continually exercises over their lives.[18] This ambivalent parent archetype is clearly displayed in *Smallville*'s two fathers; in fact, the argument can be made that each father represents half of that archetypal personality, with Jonathan typifying more of the nurturing, guiding side and Jor-El signifying more of the domineering and repressive side. It then becomes Clark's major (and definitely Heroic) task to synthesize these conflicting father "halves" into his overall personality. Let us examine each of these fathers as well as their differing styles of parenting in more detail.

Jonathan Kent

First and foremost, Jonathan is a loving father who is not afraid to show his feelings toward Clark. Throughout the first five seasons of the series prior to his death, Jonathan hugs the teenager over and over again, accepting him for who he was—in spite of the many mistakes Clark makes. According to *Smallville*'s executive producer Brian Peterson, actor John Schneider did not hold back from touching Clark: "It [that contact] was very important as Clark could not physically touch his own father [Jor-El]."[19] Paul Simpson would add in his *Season 1 Companion* that Jonathan was not only the backbone of the Kent family unit, but that he also played a vital role in the development of Clark into Superman, specifically by showing his son how much he loved him and always acting within his best interests.[20] Jonathan's unconditional love even transcends his own physical death when he reappears several times in the remaining seasons and continually reminds Clark how proud he is of him. It is those words of encouragement that moves Clark along into becoming the superhero he is meant to be.

Jonathan is also very protective of Clark, ensuring that no one finds out about the teenager's identity. Several episodes showcase this quality of the father. In the first season story "Rogue" (2002) when a crooked cop from Metropolis, Sam Phelan, finds out about Clark's special abilities and exploits them, Jonathan physically attacks him at the Talon out of frustration at being blackmailed by the man. While Phelan is killed in a gunfight with law officials at the end of the episode, Jonathan informs Clark that he should never "cross the line" and take a human life, even one as despicable as Phelan's, as there is no going back to normalcy once that happens. In a similar storyline that extends from season one's "Tempest" (2002) into season two's "Vortex" (2002) Roger Nixon, journalist for the *Metropolis Inquisitor*, not only learns about Clark's powers, but also videotapes them so that the whole world can find out about "the most amazing being on Earth." Naturally, Jonathan prevents this from happening and pursues the man out into a raging tornado that tears through Smallville. The two get trapped in a crypt and while Jonathan destroys the incriminating evidence, Nixon is ready to kill Clark's father, explaining that he will do anything to get his story published. Fortunately, Lex Luthor arrives and shoots the reporter dead. Once again Jonathan explains to Clark that not killing a human was the hardest thing he ever did. While Jonathan appears hotheaded in these episodes, it is not because he has an inherently bad disposition. Rather, it is because Jonathan "feels he knows the bad side of people ... and he wants to protect his family [especially Clark] from that [those negative influences]."[21]

Jonathan's strong, loving, and protective nature further enable him to perform the ultimate sacrifice on more than one occasion, namely, the willingness to give up his life for Clark. When Jonathan discovers in the season three finale "Covenant" (2004) that a Kryptonian survivor Kara is in reality a Smallville resident possessed by Jor-El in order to reunite Clark with his biological father, he is not afraid to confront the devious parent—even if it means suffering Jor-El's wrath in the form of powerful tendrils of energy which strangle him close to the point of death. Jonathan is subsequently pronounced brain dead and Martha decides not to remove him from the hospital's life support system for the next three months. Instead, she takes it upon herself to save Jonathan as well as Clark in "Crusade" (2004) by freeing her son from Jor-El's influence with a chunk of black Kryptonite rock, which subsequently breaks Jonathan's comatose state and allows him to sufficiently recover. More than anything else, this storyline portrays how powerful the Kents' love is for their adopted son, to the point where Jonathan will risk his very life so that Clark will not be controlled by Jor-El, but rather have the freedom to choose his own destiny.

Not only does Jonathan stand up to Jor-El, but he also faces another patriarch, Lionel Luthor (the father of Lex), who slowly learns that Clark is an extraterrestrial with amazing superpowers. Over the course of the series, Jonathan engages in a number of life-and-death battles with Lionel to prevent the man from using Clark for his own selfish purposes. Before one of these dangerous fights ensues in "Legacy" (2004), Lionel lectures Jonathan on how a father should really parent their children: "If you'd raise your son the way I raised mine, maybe you wouldn't have to protect him.... Weakness isn't something you're born with. You learn it. And Clark learned his from you." Lionel's words have a familiar ring to them; it is almost as if Jor-El assumed physical form and is saying these words. These fathers embrace more Nietzschean, self-motivated values and want Clark to rule the world simply because he has the power to do so.[22] Conversely, what Jonathan instills in Clark is compassion and respect for other humans, qualities that are regarded as weaknesses by both Lionel and Jor-El.

Things come to a head in the one-hundredth episode of the series, "Reckoning" (2006), when Lionel obtains photographic proof of Clark's otherworldly abilities and threatens Jonathan with that evidence. As noted in "The Making of" DVD special feature for the episode, Lionel is positioned strategically above Jonathan in the barn loft so that his adversary has to look up at him to acknowledge his superior status. In addition, Lionel antagonizes Jonathan with his sarcastic words, all the while remaining calm so that Jonathan's temper gets the better of him.[23] The end result is that Jonathan starts pummeling Lionel, yelling out that he will not let the man destroy his family. But the strain on Jonathan's heart is just too great (especially after the aforementioned bout with Jor-El in "Covenant"). He finally collapses in a Christ-like posture into the arms of Martha and Clark, dying, as Lionel skulks off. Consistent with previous storylines, Jonathan will do anything to protect his son, even sacrifice himself, so that Clark can fulfill his destiny. John Schneider felt it was necessary for his character to die so that "Clark would have to become Superman in order to fill that void [left by his passing] ... [and so that Clark] would know the world needed him as Superman."[24]

But this would not end Jonathan's presence in the series. He continues to provide a pivotal influence in Clark's life as a spiritual guide and Jungian Wise Mentor, sharing his knowledge and insights on the human condition with the young man. His very first appearance as this "larger than life" supernatural father would be just five episodes later in the appropriately titled "Void" (2006). A Kryptonite-based serum concocted by two medical students that allows the test subject to have a near-death experience enables Clark to interact with Jonathan. Unfortunately, a deleterious side effect of the drug is its powerful addictive quality. When Clark saves Lana from repeatedly taking the dangerous substance, he is forced into the death-like state by one of the med students who injects the serum directly into his heart. While under the drug's influence, Clark is visited by Jonathan who tells him to protect Martha and his closest friends from the dangerous Lionel (who knows his secret). Jonathan also explains that it is not Clark's time to die, but that he is "going to touch the lives of so many people, not just as a man, but as a symbol of peace... and justice." He further hugs Clark and says that he will always be watching over him before departing, inspiring the budding Hero to return to the land of the living, armed with the knowledge about Lionel and what his own future path will entail.

Another encounter between Jonathan and his son occurs in the final season's "Lazarus" (2010) after Clark undergoes a rigorous set of almost impossible tests created by a clone of Lex. The young Kent is dejected, as Jor-El does not praise him for his accomplishments; instead, Jor-El warns Clark that he will never be "Earth's savior" so long as doubt exists in his heart regarding his destiny. Forlorn and demoralized, Clark returns to the farm and sees Jonathan doing one of his many mundane chores (repairing a broken fence). When his dad notices him, they embrace and immediately Jonathan gets him out of his negative state by saying he is so proud of everything that Clark has done and that he will be "the greatest hero the world has ever known." While there might be many trials ahead, Jonathan believes Clark is up to the challenge. His words are in stark contrast to Jor-El's; in fact, Jonathan advises Clark to do what he does best—to prove Jor-El wrong. Even in spirit form, Jonathan is able to motivate the Hero like any Wise Old Man, spurring him on with all the love and support he can provide. As Schneider remarks in *The Son Becomes the Father* DVD special, his character is definitely a great role model for any son to have.[25]

Jor-El

If Jonathan is a loving, protective, and self-sacrificing father, Jor-El is more of a commanding and demanding one. These negative qualities can possibly be attributed to Jor-El's non-human, alien nature coupled with his biased view that the human species needs to be dominated and led by a superior individual like Kal-El.[26] Since Jor-El is represented throughout most of *Smallville* as a voice (delivered by Terence Stamp) emanating from the spaceship, one of the Kawatche cave walls, or within the Fortress of Solitude, it is important to analyze his statements when he is conversing with Kal-El. Just as importantly, we will look at the actions that follow his words, which are designed to correct the "wayward" course that his son is following.

When Jor-El makes his first appearance in "Exodus," he informs Kal-El that it is time to leave the humans and let go of his past life to embrace his Kryptonian destiny. He gives Kal-El until sundown to make that choice, but when the teenager opposes him, the father says in a strident tone, "You will obey me!" Jor-El then forces Kal-El up against a corner of the storm cellar and brands a fiery Kryptonian symbol on his chest to remind him, in as painful a manner as possible, that he does not originate on this planet and to point to where his continued defiance will lead (namely, more torture as seen in "Exile"). A later season five episode, "Hidden" (2005), provides some insight into Jor-El's punitive actions. He informs his son that it is only through such "lessons of pain" that inner strength and conviction can be attained. While this might appear harsh by our standards, Jor-El does not want his son to be weakened by human emotions and feelings; rather, he wants those components to be purged from Kal-El's body (via that "blazing brand" which he reactivates again and again on Kal's chest) so that his true Kryptonian nature can be actualized.

While it might be the case that Jor-El believes he is working in the best interests of Kal-El, his disciplining technique is far from perfect and leaves little room for independent thought or autonomous behavior on the part of his offspring. This is clearly demonstrated within the season three finale "Covenant" where Jor-El does not even ask for Kal-El's permission as he forcibly takes him through a portal within the Kawatche caves into an otherworldly dimension and "reprograms" the boy to fully activate his Kryptonian side. The father proudly announces that his son "will [finally] be reborn!" Upon Kal-El's return in "Crusade" he is totally changed; now he is more alien, divorced of all feeling, and almost puppet-like, following the orders of Jor-El without question. Kal-El is also able to do something that he could never do when burdened down by his human persona, namely, achieve the power of flight. Fortunately, Martha saves the day by restoring her son back to normal with black Kryptonite, which splits Kal-El into two entities, with the Clark side eventually winning out over his non-human half.

To put these episodes in context, Jor-El waits throughout season three for Kal-El to come to him. One of the conditions of his pact with Jonathan is that at some point in time the man will relinquish "ownership" of Kal-El so that he would be returned to his rightful parent. That day finally arrives, but human intervention once more prevents the union of the son with his birth father. Is it any wonder then that Jor-El lashes out at Jonathan or seizes Kal-El against his will at the conclusion of "Covenant?" The frustrated father simply wants his boy to leave the Kents, join him, and realize his destiny of being a Superman to rule over all the imperfect mortals on the planet. This would appear to be a "tall order" since Jor-El does not yet comprehend just how much Kal-El values the human condition and prioritizes it over his alien nature.

By season five, a noticeable change occurs in the relationship between Jor-El and Kal-El. This is primarily due to Kal-El creating the Fortress of Solitude, where he trains under the tutelage of Jor-El. And for a while, things are proceeding nicely until, in "Arrival" (2005), Chloe Sullivan breaks the psychic connection between father and son by calling on Clark to rescue her before she freezes to death in the Fortress. Jor-El allows Kal-El to save her, but informs him that if he does not return before sunset, there will be grave consequences. "Do not fail me!" warns Jor-El as his son leaves him to bring Chloe to the nearest hospital facility that will treat her injuries. Unfortunately, two Kryptonians who have come to Earth to enslave humanity distract Kal-El. He is able to dispose of the pair by imprisoning them within the Phantom Zone, but because he does not return to Jor-El at the designated time, his powers are removed. Jor-El considers this punishment a just one, as Kal-El always wanted to be fully human. Thus, the father provides Kal-El a valuable lesson to learn: by being human, he will eventually understand that there are unexpected weaknesses and vulnerabilities that will prevent him from ever reaching that Heroic level in his development.

It does not take long for Kal-El to register that his "gift" of humanity is, in actuality, a curse. Within a mere two episodes in "Hidden" (2000), Kal-El/Clark manages to get himself fatally wounded while Smallville lies on the brink of destruction by a deadly missile attack engineered by a computer geek who wants to rid the town's population of its "meteor freaks." Jor-El manages to bend the rules of time and space by resurrecting Kal-El from the dead with all of his superpowers intact, thereby allowing him to protect Smallville from almost certain doom. However, the natural order of things has to be restored, and so someone very close to Kal-El has to be sacrificed—and very soon. Of course, that person is none other than Jonathan.

It is important to consider what Jor-El has done here for his son. He is willing to sacrifice another so that his own flesh and blood can live again. He even states matter-of-factly that he will always love his son, no matter what transpires between them. This is one of the few scenes where Jor-El shows his strong feelings toward Kal-El, and it is because he has possessed the human body of Lionel to voice these sentiments. It is no coincidence that Jor-El uses Lionel as his vessel since both fathers believe that the destinies of their sons can only be achieved through the exercise of sheer "will."[27] Craig Byrne relates that actor John Glover (who played Lionel) wanted to reprise Marlon Brando's performance of Jor-El from the *Superman: The Movie* (1978), and it worked beautifully.[28] Thusly, the sequence between Lionel/Jor-El and Kal-El in the Fortress of Solitude turns out to be one of the most "touching" moments between the Kryptonian father and his son within the entire series.

There are times, though, when the friction between the two resumes in later seasons, and it is because Kal-El continues to act on his human emotions instead of using his superior logic. In "Blue" (2007) Kal-El does not heed his father's warning that his mother is gone forever, and when the opportunity presents itself, he uses his cousin Kara's crystal to bring back an almost perfect version of Lara (referred to as a "replicant") whom he can hold and love. What he does not know is that a copy of Jor-El's evil brother, Zor-El, has also come through the gateway and shortly after his arrival, the relative casts the sun in a deadly eclipse that will destroy all life on our planet. Kal-El is able to stop him by breaking the crystal, which causes Zor-El and (sadly) Lara to fade out of existence. But Jor-El cannot permit another instance of his son's flagrant disobedience to him due to those "damnable" human feelings he keeps on expressing, and so the father literally places the teenager "on ice" within one of the pillars in the Fortress of Solitude. This is not as harsh as removing Kal-El's abilities, yet it still serves as a reminder that what the boy does has serious repercussions—not just for himself, but for the entire human race.

Yet, soon after in "Persona" (2008), Jor-El breaks Kal-El out of his frozen tomb so that he can deal with Phantom Zone escapee Bizarro, who has cloned his DNA, taken his identity, and caused all sorts of mischief in Smallville. That Jor-El rescinds the penalty illustrates that he cannot stay angry at Kal-El for long and is still hoping that his son will follow the right path toward his Heroic destiny. It looks like Kal-El is on track to becoming the Man of Steel when he decides to abandon his friends and complete his training with Jor-El in the season nine opener, "Savior" (2009). But when Lois Lane returns from an unexpected journey into the future, Kal-El becomes distracted and loses interest in his Kryptonian education. Jor-El advises him to say goodbye to Lois, but the son cannot comply with the elder's request. Consequently, Kal-El disappoints Jor-El yet again, since it is clear that his love for the earth woman is stronger than his desire to become a Hero for all of humanity. At this point, Jor-El apparently takes a different approach to dealing with Kal-El. Now that he is a man and no longer a teenager, Jor-El attempts to reason with him instead of continuing to use physical means (e.g., inflicting pain, brainwashing, or imprisoning him) to make a case for why Kal-El should pursue his destiny.

This does not mean, however, that the father will treat others so tactfully—especially Lois. When Lois enters the Fortress of Solitude in "Abandoned" (2010), and demands an audience with Jor-El, he lifts her up in the air and holds her in a vice-like grip until Kal-El arrives and forces him to put her down. Or in "Prophecy" (2011), once Kal-El informs Jor-El that he plans to wed Lois, the patriarch bestows (or more appropriately, imposes) upon Lois all of his son's superpowers for one full day as a test to see if the two can maintain the serious relationship they have developed. As expected, the couple comes to near fatal blows, and a very distraught Lois breaks off her engagement to Clark. We might empathize with Lois at these times, but Jor-El should also be acknowledged here. After all, Kal-El was not sent to this planet simply to love one of its inhabitants and do nothing more with his life. Thus, Jor-El's presence is inserted at critical moments to provide Kal-El with that focus and direction he is lacking. Unfortunately, Lois prevents him from fully accomplishing his mission, and that is why Jor-El treats her the way he does in these storylines.

If one examines the two *Smallville* fathers, Jor-El typifies the classic Jungian archetype of the "loving and terrible" parent much more so than Jonathan, to the point where if his "terrible" side dominates, then a much more satanic

Trickster nature emerges.[29] For instance, he makes pacts with both Kal-El and Jonathan and when the conditions of those contracts cannot be met (which is typically the case), all sorts of disastrous outcomes occur, including the "deaths" of those characters. Moreover, like the mythical devil, Jor-El has incredible mental powers and possesses a number of individuals, forcing them to do things against their will. Ones that fall under his influence include not only Kal-El, but also Smallville teenager Lindsey Harrison who believes she is Kara from the planet Krypton in "Covenant," and Lionel, who becomes Jor-El's oracle for several seasons beginning with "Hidden."

There is definitely a loving side to Jor-El as well, and two episodes in particular depict the more positive features of the Kryptonian scientist. Interestingly, both episodes provide a more tangible, corporeal form for the space father (i.e., his own body) instead of the usual portrayal of the cold, disembodied voice. In an early season three episode "Relic" (2003), the storyline concentrates on Kal-El finding a Kryptonian medallion in the Kawatche caves and then receiving images of the time that Jor-El came to Earth in human form.[30] Apparently Jor-El was not the model son (like Kal-El), and so he was sent there as a "rite of passage" to interact with the Smallville residents, in particular Lana Lang's aunt, Louise, for whom he has strong feelings. When the time comes to leave Louise, Jor-El experiences deep regret, but ultimately obeys his father and returns to Krypton a changed individual.

"Relic" is very interesting from a number of viewpoints. First, Kal-El obtains a much clearer perspective on who Jor-El really is. He is not "the monster" who simply dictates orders to his son; rather, he is very human-like and shares the same emotions that Kal-El does.[31] Secondly, and even more importantly, Kal-El realizes that his father faced a number of trials in his life as well, and had to endure those tests in order to become an effective leader of his people. As a result, the events of "Relic" provide motivation for why present-day Jor-El drives Kal-El so hard. He wants his son to accomplish so much more than he could ever do, and (in his view) human feelings only get in the way of attaining those successes. The adage "like father, like son" comes to mind when viewing the series of flashbacks with Jor-El in "Relic."

In an episode situated closer to the end of the series, "Kandor" (2009), Kal-El is finally able to interact with Jor-El for the first time, thanks to technology developed by his father. Fearing that Krypton might one day be destroyed in a global war, Jor-El placed his DNA along with other leaders in an Orb that would allow clones of themselves to be released well after the catastrophe was over, thus continuing of their race on Earth. Upon his emergence, Jor-El (now played by Julian Sands) begins his search for the Kent farm and quickly discovers that his son has matured and has been using his powers for the benefit of mankind. Like Jonathan, he even sacrifices himself so that

Kal-El's secret identity is protected and dies in the arms of his offspring, telling him how proud he is of what the young man has achieved before expiring. Kal-El is, at last, able to differentiate the "real" Jor-El from the "recreated voice" within the Fortress of Solitude. The one in the flesh is so much like his adopted father—warm and intimate. Conversely, the spectral version of Jor-El features none of his biological father's feelings and emotions, but rather operates solely on logic and willpower. That Kal-El arrives at this distinction is an important one, because he no longer rejects Jor-El. He has come to learn that his father has done so much for him—including creating a computerized presence that monitors him throughout his development on Earth—for better or for worse. "Kandor" shows that Jor-El loves Kal-El very deeply and is willing to do practically anything for his son's quest toward greatness.

The Hero's Atonement with His Two Fathers

As evidenced in the last section, both Jonathan and Jor-El have played a significant role in shaping Clark's evolution from a teenager into an adult. It is time to reflect on those "turning points" with both fathers that enable Clark to take those next steps into truly becoming that legendary superhero icon. All of these reconciliatory moments occur in the tenth and final season of *Smallville*.

The atonement with both fathers follows a particular sequence, starting with each figure admitting his faults and weaknesses to Clark. In "Lazarus," the spirit of Jonathan explains to Clark that his hatred for the Luthors, in particular Lionel, was so strong that it grew inside of him like a malignant cancer until his heart could not handle it anymore. Jonathan's disclosure of this "dark stain" on his soul is intended to show Clark that no one is perfect, least of all him. Like the archetypal Wise Elder, Jonathan wants his son to reflect on what he is saying so that Clark can acknowledge any deficiencies within himself that might impede him from moving forward on his Hero's journey.

Jor-El reaches a similar point of self-divulgence when Kal-El is ready to turn his back on him and make a life for himself with Lois in "Abandoned." The Fortress "voice" plays a holographic recording of both himself and his wife Lara who are ready to send Kal-El away from their dying planet in the spacecraft programmed to reach Earth. As both Kryptonians wish their son safe travels, Jor-El reveals that he is sending the boy a crystal which contains all of his knowledge, but none of his own frailties (i.e., emotions and feelings) so that Kal-El will be able to live up to his potential—unlike himself who has failed to save his home world. Kal-El sees that Jor-El blames himself for the death of his race and further, that he wants to spare his son that terrible burden while he attained adulthood on Earth. It would appear that both fathers, Jonathan and Jor-El, are able to share their personal "demons" with Clark only after they have died. Perhaps entering the spirit world like Jonathan or being recreated in the Fortress like Jor-El provides these parents with sufficient distance from their bodies to more objectively perceive the defects that reside within their own psyches.

Whatever the reason for these introspective intervals, Clark has to integrate the two (more alike than disparate) paternal sides into his personality, but this task proves to be a very challenging one. He decides to remove himself from their influence by no longer heeding their advice. In "Prophecy," Kal-El disconnects the crystal that contains Jor-El's persona from the Fortress control panel, and early in "Finale" (2011) Clark ignores Jonathan's ghost at the Kent gravesite, reflecting that he cannot lean on either father in the upcoming battle with his greatest adversary, Darkseid. When previously confronting Darkseid in "Supergirl" (2010), Clark was forced to rely on Kara, as his self-doubts limited his abilities. In his next (and final) outing with this creature, Clark does not want to make the same mistake again. Thus, he pushes those who are closest to him away in order to keep focused on defeating the enemy at all costs.

But like so many Heroes who have made the wrong choice by not listening to their elders, Clark is encouraged by his closest friends as well as adopted mother Martha to seek out his fathers in this time of crisis. It is then that Jonathan appears in the Kent barn to tell Clark that he will need Jor-El's help in the upcoming fight with Darkseid. This is a significant admission on Jonathan's part as he has always seen Jor-El as a competitor for Clark's love and affection. All that has now changed since Clark will require the assistance and encouragement of both parents to get him through this ultimate test. Listening to Jonathan, Clark retrieves the crystal and is able to communicate with Jor-El in what is probably the first harmonious exchange between himself and his biological father. Jor-El causes Kal-El to experience a series of visual flashbacks on every trial he had to endure throughout the last ten years, and he then mentions that Kal-El is ready to "seize his destiny." These words are what the Hero definitely needs to hear. The "ogre aspect" of Jor-El, which Kal-El has envisioned his father to be for quite some time, has been replaced with a more positive image of a comforting and helpful presence.[32] Through his atonement with both fathers, "Clark-El" finally obtains their support that will enable him to navigate through any monumental obstacle, including his impending face-off with Darkseid.[33]

The "apotheosis" of Clark/Kal-El into Clark-El comes right at the time that Darkseid (in the body of alternate universe Lionel) intrudes into the barn and tries to crush the Hero with his deadly powers. However, Clark-El gains a newfound strength and confidence; after shrugging off the physical blows, he rams himself through Luthor, destroying the physical shell of Darkseid and sending the entity back to his otherworldly dimension. The determined look shown on Clark-El's face when vanquishing the stunned Darkseid indicates that he has attained the stature of a true leader and become a father figure so much like Jonathan and Jor-El. As Campbell indicates, the apotheosis of any Hero involves a "dawning" realization that the father always co-existed inside of his/her self: "we in Him [with emphasis] and He in us."[34] In achieving his destiny, Clark-El at last comes "full circle" and transforms into the dual fathers whom he so admires and loves.

The Hero's Ultimate Boon

Since every Hero obtains that "ultimate boon" at the end of his/her journey, what is Clark-El's? It can only be the Superman suit and cape, which has isolated in a holding chamber by Jor-El within the Fortress of Solitude until the time is ready for his son to assume the mantle of responsibility. The suit represents a synthesis of Clark-El's two worlds: his Earth mother Martha has sewn the costume while the S-shaped insignia displayed on the chest is the Kryptonian symbol of the House of El. Clark-El could never put the outfit on as he really did not think he was worthy of ever wearing it.[35] Upon his entering the Fortress, however, Jor-El opens the chamber and allows the presence of Jonathan to hand the garb over to him. Both of them are of one mind, believing Clark-El is ready to don those Heroic clothes.

As he accepts the precious boon, his two fathers send him off with words of inspiration. Jor-El tells Clark-El that he is truly a Hero, and it is chiefly because of that loving relationship he has had with Martha and Jonathan for all these years. Jonathan adds that Clark-El should never forget Smallville as he forges ahead, since his past has made him into the man (or more appropriately, Superman) he is today. One might regard both Jor-El and Jonathan as those Campbellian "supernatural forces" that assist Clark-El on the start of the Return phase of his Heroic journey back to Metropolis.[36]

The Hero's Attainment of Flight and Beyond

Obtaining the blessings of his parents, Clark-El is able to change into his attire and "soar" for the first time out of the Fortress with purpose and conviction. It should be pointed out that Joseph Campbell does not literally mean that the Hero has acquired the power of flight within the Return phase; rather, the archetypal "magic flight" has to do more with the Hero fleeing obstacles and impediments that the antagonist has placed in his/her way to interrupt the journey back home.[37] Clark-El's ability to fly is something even more Heroic than Campbell originally envisioned, as he is clearly not avoiding any enemy. He is flying entirely of his own volition, a task he could never do before, and this is a remarkable acquisition on his part, in keeping with his recent apotheosis.

Paraphrasing my comments on Clark-El's flying in *The Son Becomes the Father* DVD special, previous to this moment our Hero was not able to lift himself up because he was being weighed down by a significant number of "burdens," with the most prominent one being his inability to reconcile with both fathers. Clark-El believed he was not living up to their expectations and so the resultant guilt contributed to his inability to fly of his own accord. But once he successfully experiences atonement with Jor-El and Jonathan, he is able to actualize that elusive, god-like power and accomplish some amazing feats in the closing minutes of the series finale. Darkseid has sent his home planet, Apokolips, on a collision course with Earth. As the gigantic mass approaches, it is responsible for a number of disasters including smashed skyscrapers and fierce weather anomalies. Fortunately, Clark-El zooms in to prevent further destruction. He also manages to save his fiancé Lois by getting her malfunctioning plane back onto a safe course. Finally, with Herculean strength he manages to push Apokolips completely out of our solar system, thereby saving the world from Darkseid's attack. Thus begins the first chapter in Superman's adventures.

Smallville ends with a time jump several years later where Clark and Lois are living together in Metropolis and still working at the *Daily Planet*. The new Clark is much more comfortable with his responsibilities as Earth's savior, plus he is getting ready to undertake even greater ones by marrying Lois. As the two lovebirds engage in some small talk, a bomb threat is called in and Lois tells Clark to "take off." Reaching the rooftop, Clark-El peels off his shirt to reveal the Superman suit directly underneath, and he ascends into the skies with a natural ease to stop the latest terrorist attack against the city. Evidently, he has reached a level of contentment being a Hero for the entire human race. It is inferred that he has further assumed the leadership of several superhero organizations like the Justice Society of America, which lost Carter Hall (aka Hawkman), in an earlier battle with one of Darkseid's soldiers, General Slade, in "Icarus" (2010). One might say that Superman is not only the "father" to others with special abilities, but also that he comes to be the patriarchal figure of the world's millions who have entrusted their lives to him. It has not been a simple evolution for our Hero, and he could only have done it with the guidance of those loving and caring parents in his life who he has decided to emulate.

Closing Remarks on the Hero's Destiny

Smallville is the first Superman story that satisfactorily explores the father-son dynamic as it related to all three phases of the archetypal Hero's journey, from the Separation to the Initiation to the Return. Without the presence of his two fathers, Jonathan and Jor-El, Clark-El would not have completed his development as a Hero. Because of these significant individuals, he is able to effectively synthesize his roots from two very different worlds and attain a well-balanced psyche that incorporates elements of both his Kryptonian heritage with his Kansas upbringing. As Carl Jung remarks about the father figure, he "influences the psychic life of the child so enormously that we must ask ourselves whether we may attribute such magical power to an ordinary human being at all."[38] Both Jonathan and Jor-El have such an effect on Clark-El's life that even death does not stop them from reaching out to their son when he was in most need of their support. Perhaps Heroes are born to remarkable, "superhuman" fathers who possess those same Heroic tendencies like their offspring. After all, Heroes learn from the best role models, and certainly Jor-El and Jonathan fit that designation. There is little doubt that Clark-El will be able to tackle new Heroic trials in the (post-series) years ahead as Superman for he has finally realized his Smallville destiny, thanks to both of his fathers who raised quite an extraordinary son.

NOTES

1. Lincoln Geraghty, "Introduction," in *The Smallville Chronicles: Critical Essays on the Television Series*, ed. Lincoln Geraghty (Lanham, MD: Scarecrow Press, 2011), x.
2. For more details on the superhero myth, see my essay "Superman and Batman: The Divided Superhero Archetype" in *Jungian Reflections Within the Cinema: A Psychological Analysis of Sci-Fi and Fantasy Archetypes* (Westport, CT: Praeger, 1998) and my DVD feature, "The Son Becomes the Father," included on *Smallville: The Complete Tenth Season*, Warner Home Video, 2011.
3. The capitalization of Hero throughout this piece refers to the Jungian archetype and its presentations.
4. Carl Jung, *Collected Works, Volume 9, Part 1: The Archetypes and the Collective Unconscious*, trans. R. F.C. Hill (Princeton: Princeton University Press, 1990), 158.
5. While "The Psychology of the Child Archetype" in *The Archetypes and the Collective Unconscious* provides a good base for describing the origins of the Hero, a deeper analysis of the Hero archetype is provided in *Collected Works, Volume 5: Symbols of Transformation*, trans. R. F.C. Hull and Gerhard Adler (Princeton: Princeton University Press, 1977).
6. I am using Jung's definition of archetype, namely a pattern (or image) of psychic perception common to all humans, in reference to the Hero and all of its associated manifestations.
7. Joseph Campbell, *The Hero with a Thousand Faces* (Princeton: Princeton University Press, 1973), 39.
8. I will refer to the voice of Jor-El as Jor-El himself throughout this essay since his consciousness is embedded within that "recreated" persona.

9. Campbell, *The Hero with a Thousand Faces*, 30.
10. Ibid., 49–89.
11. There are far too many journeys undertaken by Clark/Kal-El to address within the scope of this essay. Therefore, I have selected the specific journey in which he leaves Smallville for the first time, depicted at the conclusion of season two and the start of season three. I would like to note two other significant quests in the *Smallville* series. The first involves Jor-El taking Clark away from Smallville in the season three finale, "Covenant" (2004), and then reprogramming him as "Kal-El" in the season four opener, "Crusade" (2004). The second one is where Clark decides to embrace his Kryptonian heritage after one of his friends, Jimmy Olsen, dies in the season eight finale "Doomsday" (2009) and then begins his training with Jor-El in earnest within the Fortress of Solitude in the season nine opener "Savior" (2009).
12. Campbell, *The Hero with a Thousand Faces*, 97–192.
13. Paul Simpson, *Smallville: The Official Companion Season 3* (London: Titan, 2005), 20.
14. Campbell, *The Hero with a Thousand Faces*, 193–243.
15. Carl Jung, *Collected Works, Volume 9, Part 2: Aion: Researches into the Phenomenology of the Self*, trans. R. F.C. Hull (Princeton: Princeton University Press, 1990), 31.
16. Carl Jung, *Collected Works, Volume 4: Freud and Psychoanalysis*, trans. R F.C. Hull (Princeton: Princeton University Press, 1990), 314.
17. Jung, *The Archetypes and the Collective Unconscious*, 220–222.
18. Ibid., 255–56.
19. "The Son Becomes the Father," *Smallville: The Complete Tenth Season*, Warner Home Video, 2011, DVD feature.
20. Paul Simpson, *Smallville: The Official Companion Season 1* (London: Titan, 2004), 140.
21. Ibid., 142–143.
22. Both Lionel and Jor-El embrace many of the values advocated by German philosopher Friedrich Nietzsche, especially the Will to Power which is a powerful, driving force that enables one to overcome hurdles, accomplish goals, and attain the highest possible position in life—all through the exercise of sheer will.
23. "The Making of a Milestone: *Smallville*'s 100th Episode," *Smallville: The Complete Fifth Season*, Warner Bros. Home Video, 2006, DVD featurette.
24. Craig Byrne, *Smallville: The Official Companion Season 5* (London: Titan, 2007), 132.
25. "The Son Becomes the Father."
26. Clark will be referred to by his Kryptonian name, Kal-El, throughout this section of the essay since it deals with his interactions with Jor-El, who shares that kindred (i.e., Kryptonian) nature with him.
27. See note 22.
28. Byrne, *Smallville: The Official Companion Season 5*, 27.
29. Jung, *The Archetypes and the Collective Unconscious*, 82; For the purposes of this essay, I am relating the "loving and terrible" description which Jung exclusively uses for the Mother archetype to the Father image.
30. Tom Welling, the actor who plays Kal-El, also portrays a young version of Kal-El in "Relic" to show viewers there are more similarities than differences between the father and his son.
31. Simpson, *The Official Smallville Companion Season 3*, 37.
32. Campbell, *The Hero with a Thousand Faces*, 129–30.
33. Clark-El represents the synthesis of both the earthbound and Kryptonian personalities of Clark Kent and Kal-El. This new name is my way of indicating that the Hero has transformed himself into a more balanced individual who is no longer at odds with his two-sided nature. While this name might not be liked by some *Smallville* fans and scholars, it is

intended to show the growth of Clark and Kal-El into the superhero who is more than just one of these former selves; in fact, he has become the completed Self, Superman.

34. Campbell, *The Hero with a Thousand Faces*, 161.

35. Clark-El's reluctance to don the Superman suit was in keeping with the "rule" established by series creators Alfred Gough and Miles Millar that there would be "no tights and no flights" until *Smallville*'s final episode aired; Simpson, *The Official Companion Season 1*, 12.

36. Campbell, *The Hero with a Thousand Faces*, 216.

37. Ibid., 201.

38. Jung, *Freud and Psychoanalysis*, 315.

"Always hold on to Smallville"

Domesticity and the Male Hero

Bridget Kies

Over the course of its ten-season run, *Smallville* meticulously depicted Clark Kent's coming of age journey and his ultimate acceptance of his superhero identity. While this narrative arc emphasized Clark's physical and emotional growth, the title of the series focused on location, rather than character. Smallville, Kansas, is the site of a meteor shower that brings Clark to Earth and gives strange powers to some of the town's residents; it is Clark's job to stop them from using those powers for evil. In addition to this mythological reason for staying in Smallville, Clark is the son of farmers—a profession more rooted to the land than any other.

Because he is fixed in one place, Clark is different from other male science fiction and fantasy heroes. The male hero's journey, as chronicled by Joseph Campbell, begins with a call to adventure, a requisite departure from home.[1] Darwinian notions of gender identity, in which males venture out to compete for resources, support Campbell's monomyth. While some recent scholarship questions these claims, the wandering male hero remains an ever-present trope in popular culture. As a male hero who mostly stays in one place, Clark is therefore an important, anomalous figure.

Clark's story begins with an intergalactic journey from Krypton to Kansas, but after the Kents adopt him, he remains in Smallville for nearly the entire series. Rather than traveling around in a spaceship or a cool car, Clark nests. Luke Skywalker of the *Star Wars* trilogy, by contrast, travels across the galaxy to fulfill his destiny as a Jedi knight. Clark's heroism is thus more closely aligned with that of female protagonists. In *The Wizard of Oz*, Dorothy has Technicolor adventures after leaving Kansas, but what she learns from the experience is that "there's no place like home." Although saving the world from crime may occasionally take Clark away from Smallville over the course of a particular episode, he, like Dorothy, always returns home in the end. I will argue that given its reconfiguration of the Superman myth as a domestic story, *Smallville* defies gender expectations and upsets the monomyth of the male hero.

> "Well, it's all very Joseph Campbell—hero's journey and all that."— Jimmy Olsen, "Quest" (2008)

In order to understand the extent to which Clark's rootedness is unusual, I will briefly introduce Darwinian sex roles and Campbell's monomyth, which draws upon those roles. In the mid-nineteenth century, Charles Darwin and his colleagues noticed a pattern across various species: females often tended to the young while the males were engaged in obtaining food, fighting off competition, and traveling in search of other females so they could produce more offspring. Darwin concluded, "males of almost all animals [have] stronger passions than females" because "it is the males that fight together and sedulously display their charms before the females; and the victors transmit their superiority to the male offspring."[2] In contrast to the male's passions, the female "plays coy" and is careful about selecting a sexual partner because she is the one burdened with caring for any offspring. Females typically remain in one place with their offspring, while the males of the species are the seekers—of food and other resources, of females, of sex.[3]

Although Darwin's ideas are deeply ingrained in the cultural psyche, spawning the fields of evolutionary theory and evolutionary psychology, some contemporary critics, such as Christopher Ryan and Cacila Jethá, believe it is shortsighted to claim that "our thoughts and feelings are as hard-wired in our genetic code as the shape of our heads or the length of our fingers."[4] They argue that Darwin's findings were influenced by Victorian age "erotophobia," the moral restriction of sexual energy in order to improve productivity in the industrial age.[5] While Darwin's sex role distinction holds true for many species, Ryan and Jethá argue that scientists often retroactively apply modern sexual morality to prehistoric humanoids. Rather than examining evidence of polyamorous females and rooted males (for example), these scientists perpetuate the myth that the Darwinian division of the sex roles is and always has been a standard way of life. Furthermore, evolutionary psychology suggests that "contentious issues such as love, jealousy, mate choice, war, murder, rape, and altruism" are all linked to these sex roles—a claim which denies the influence of environment on personality.[6]

Regardless of these recent criticisms, Darwinian images of the wanderlust male and nesting female persist across popular culture texts. Consider, for instance, this 1975 explanation Tristram Potter Coffin offers for the passive role of women in folklore: "As Mother Nature had blessed her own sex with the privilege of carrying and nursing infants, and as the men enjoyed no such blessing, it made sense not to assign tasks that involved raid, escape, fisticuffs and the like to those members of society who were often too swollen to handle them."[7] The earlier examples of Dorothy and Luke Skywalker reflect the sex role division as well. Both characters are orphans taken in by an aunt and uncle, and both have a fantastic adventure in which they defeat some force of evil. The lessons they learn, however, are disturbingly different: Dorothy concludes that she draws strength from loved ones at home, but Luke learns that wherever he goes, the force will be with him.[8]

The sex role division has repercussions for the mythic hero as well. In his foundational work, Joseph Campbell divides the hero's journey into three parts: the hero "[1] ventures forth from the world of common day into a region of supernatural wonder; [2] fabulous forces are there encountered and a decisive victory is won; [3] the hero comes back from this mysterious adventure with the power to bestow boons on his fellow man."[9] Although Campbell begins with the explanation that the hero may be male or female, other scholars of heroic myths like Carol Pearson and Katherine Pope point out that Campbell is quick to only look at the heroic male and "to define the female characters as goddesses, temptresses, and earth mothers."[10] While the male hero has the supernatural journey, the female characters he encounters along the way are relegated to supporting—and often location-bound—roles.

Andrew Gordon calls Campbell's hero "a dream-figure who stands in for an entire culture."[11] For Pearson and Pope, this is a problematic identifier, given that the hero is usually a white, upper-class male. The hero's journey excludes women and minorities, who are often the obstacles standing between the hero and his destiny.[12] Because of the sex role division in Campbell's monomyth, the implicit message is that men should "develop their individual identities" while women strive to be "selfless helpmates to husband and children."[13]

There are occasionally female heroes in popular culture. Coffin offers the example of the female folk hero who, after losing her lover, "poses as a cabin boy or a warrior, even captains ships, fights victorious battles, and wins back her boyfriend or gets herself a higher-ranking bunkmate."[14] While this female hero does indeed make a journey away from home, it is only to win back her lover in order to secure her position as the beloved. Coffin acknowledges that in these stories, "[it] is not so much that [the heroine] is heroic (often she cries and seeks the aid of the captain): the interesting thing is that she has been unorthodox."[15] Thus, like Dorothy, these female heroes only venture out for the sake of reaffirming the value of remaining home. Rather than engaging in an adventure quest, the female hero's journey is one of self-discovery, in which she is taught not to sacrifice herself for others, unlike the male hero. For Pearson and Pope, this mission is a double-edged sword: because she has not acted for the good of others, the female hero does not become a leader; however, she does defy "female sex role conditioning which teaches a woman to be selfless."[16] Although the male hero's journey is largely oedipal, the female hero "demythologize[s] the patriarch" and learns that everything she has been taught by him is false, that the distinctions "between male and female, mind and body, spirit and flesh, self and Other, are artificial dualities that distort her perceptions of the world."[17]

Smallville's Clark Kent embodies certain qualities of these female heroes. His journey defies the typical three stages outlined by Campbell, and his character development throughout the series indicates self-discovery. Clark is not, however, merely emulative of the female hero; his mythological role is still as self-sacrificing savior. He is never "brought back from his supernatural adventure" because the place where Clark is initiated as hero and the place that benefits from this heroism are one in the same: Smallville, or, more simply, Earth.[18] In the season two episode "Rosetta" (2003), Clark first learns that he is Kal-El, the mythic alien whose mission is to deliver the people of Earth from an unspecified evil. The episode begins with Clark lying in the street with his arms extended in an image of crucifixion. Similarly, during a scene in a cemetery in the pilot episode (2001), Clark is framed standing in front of a statue of an angel, so that he appears to have wings. The messianic imagery and overtones throughout the series suggest that, unlike Pearson and Pope's female heroes, Clark will ultimately sacrifice himself for humanity. Indeed, Clark forfeits friendships and a love life for the greater duty of heroic acts. Yet his journey is also one of self-discovery. It is as much about the adventure and sacrifice as it is about transformation of his worldview. Clark therefore exists somewhere in between the archetypal male and female.

If, as Campbell and Gordon claim, the hero is the stand-in for humanity, what does it mean that Clark branches outside traditional sex role divisions? Although he is biologically Kryptonian, Clark is in many ways a typical American teenager. He worries about being popular and getting the girls of his dreams (first Lana Lang, then Lois Lane). He watches his parents worry about their finances. Although he is not, technically speaking, American—or even human—his alienness might best be understood as the feeling of otherness experienced by all teenagers, rather than a racial or ethnic identifier. This blending of "self and Other" is one additional way in which Clark resembles Pearson and Pope's female hero. His position in between the archetypal male and female offers a new breed of masculinity in the twenty-first century.

"You put the 'Smallville' in Smallville, Smallville." —Lois Lane, "Homecoming" (2010)

This new masculinity coincides with the repositioning of the Superman myth into a domestic story. Stan Beeler notes *Smallville* is "more concerned with developing [Clark's] human life" than any previous version of the Superman story.[19] Airing on the WB and later the CW, *Smallville*'s primary audience was young women.[20] Miranda Banks argues that *Smallville* and its short-lived contemporary *Roswell* (1999–2002) are examples of teen male melodramas: a subversion of the genre in which the male protagonist is "motivated to action by enlightened dreams for an equal partner, emotionally fulfilling relationships and a sense of duty to the community."[21] Although the series' science fiction aspects traditionally entice a male audience, Banks believes that the central characters' "willingness—often even eagerness—to be reflective and emote without losing control" attracts a wider (female) audience.[22]

Other series on the WB/CW also pair emotional melodrama with action and adventure, but what distinguishes *Smallville* is the relationship between masculinity and home seen within the series.[23] Like *Smallville*, narrative elements of *Buffy the Vampire Slayer* (1997–2003), *Charmed* (1998–2006), and *Supernatural* (2005–) include the deaths of parents, superpowers, and the sacrificial death of the hero to avert an apocalypse. In spite of common themes, the series can be separated along gender lines. The female heroes of *Buffy* and *Charmed* remain in specific towns, while the male heroes of *Supernatural* travel the country. With a male hero who rarely ventures out, *Smallville* complicates the Darwinian pattern seen in its contemporaries.

For the female heroes of *Buffy* and *Charmed*, home is where the fantastic occurs. As the lone vampire slayer of her generation, Buffy Summers must stay in Sunnydale to guard the Hellmouth, a portal between hell and Earth situated underneath the town's high school. Although she has designs to go away to college, she comes to understand that she must fulfill her destiny by staying put. The Halliwell sisters of *Charmed* all live in their grandmother's Victorian mansion because their magic is more powerful when they work together. Two sisters get married during the course of the series, but their spouses (and eventually children) move into the mansion with them. The Halliwells share a domestic space where they can tend to the needs of family and magic all at once.

The male heroes of *Supernatural*, however, roam the great American landscape in search of demons and other monsters. The Winchesters' mobility affords them the opportunity to save a more diverse population of victims than Buffy or the Halliwells. Each week, they leave behind grateful civilians and a legacy of heroism as they drive off toward their next case. While the Winchesters, like Clark, are "unabashedly emotional and decidedly masculine" all at once, their story affirms the Darwinian sex role division.[24] Among these three series, the characters' missions as heroes are therefore derived from well-established sex roles: women occupy the domestic space and guard the young while men venture out.

Unlike the itinerant Winchester brothers of *Supernatural*, Clark belongs in Smallville. In the pilot episode, a group of football players ties him to a stake in a cornfield with the Superman crest (an "S") emblazoned on his chest. Although the "S" in this case could stand for "scarecrow," Karin Beeler argues that for the football players it "signifies Smallville and functions simultaneously as their desire to brand Clark with their collective school identity."[25] When Clark creates the same "S"-design in his metal shop class at school in season two's "Dichotic" (2002), he tells his teacher: "'S' for Smallville." For viewers familiar with the Superman mythos, these moments are humorous references to the traditional costume. Since Clark has not yet assumed the Superman identity (and never fully does until the closing moments of the *Smallville* narrative, becoming instead the Red-Blue Blur and later just the Blur), these early encounters with the Superman crest do not brand him as a hero so much as demonstrate how Clark and Smallville are one in the same.

Lois's affectionate nickname for Clark ("Smallville") also conflates the person and the place and reiterates the series' emphasis on the domestic storyline. Clark is not Superman, nor Metropolis; he is the small town where he was raised. When Lois and Clark attend a high school reunion in the final season's "Homecoming" (2010), the differences in their respective relationships to the town are exaggerated. As a self-described military brat, Lois never stayed in one place for very long; her week at Smallville High was a significant stay for her (though, comically, no one remembers her). Although Clark was often an outcast during the four seasons the series focused on his high school life, he has a glorious return in which everyone remembers him. Lois sums up Clark's position as the small-town hero by declaring: "You put the 'Smallville' in Smallville, Smallville."

Several season finales explore the possibility of Clark leaving Smallville. Each of these incidents, however, lead to some form of tragedy, after which Clark's return sets things right. At the end of the second season in "Exodus" (2003), Clark flees to Metropolis while he is under the influence of red Kryptonite. By the third season premiere "Exile" (2003), Clark has begun to work for the leader of an organized crime syndicate. He steals, lies, and avoids contact with his friends and family in Smallville. A bartender reveals that he also drinks and goes out with a different woman every night.[26] When Clark finally returns to Smallville, friends and family immediately forgive his transgressions. He is home, where he belongs, and it is understood that the departure was the result of the red Kryptonite—and therefore unintentional.

Other unintentional departures from Smallville demonstrate how critical Clark's relationship to home is. At the end of the third season in "Covenant" (2004), Jor-El places Clark in a fetal state out of time. Although Jor-El claims this "training" is necessary so that Clark may be reborn a hero, his absence in Smallville is cause for panic. Jonathan Kent is unconscious, possibly dead; Chloe Sullivan and her father are presumed dead in an explosion; Kryptonian symbols appear in flames around the farm; Lionel Luthor succumbs to madness; and Lex Luthor keels over after being poisoned. At the end of the fifth season in "Vessel" (2006), Clark becomes trapped in the Phantom Zone, another liminal space, while the world riots and burns. Whereas the third season finale demonstrates the necessity of Clark remaining home so his loved ones will not suffer, the fifth season takes that further: Clark needs to remain at home (in this case, both Smallville and Earth) or else the entire world will collapse.

Although these episodes reinforce Clark's nesting, as a teenager Clark expresses desire to explore the greater world. In the first season episode "Kinetic" (2002), Chloe is hospitalized after falling out a window at Luthor Manor. Because he is suffering the effects of "meteor rocks" (Kryptonite), Clark is not able to stop the fall. He expresses his remorse to Chloe and adds, "Sometimes I wish I could just leave this town and get away from meteor rocks." His desire to leave in this moment is tied up with his failure to help Chloe, an indication that Clark sees his heroic duties and his domesticity at odds. In that same episode, Whitney mocks Clark for wanting to take over the family business one day, but Clark tells him diplomatically: "I'm not sure that's the life for me." Both incidents demonstrate a young man struggling with what he feels is the yoke of small-town life and his fated duty as the next manager of the Kent farm.

Nevertheless, when Clark is given the chance to leave Smallville after graduating high school, he opts instead to live at home and commute to a nearby college. Jonathan and Martha, the farmers, are the ones who leave: Jonathan dies, and Martha assumes his job in the state legislature before becoming a United States senator. The departure of his parents is understandable from a metatextual perspective; the hero of the monomyth has to learn to overcome the father figure (either through an oedipal defeat or a demythologizing), and the protagonist of a teen melodrama must lose his parents through some narrative device in order to continue his development.[27] Yet even Clark's peers move on: Chloe goes to Metropolis for college and work, Lana spends a summer in Paris and later marries Lex and travels around the world. Clark, the male hero, is the only one who remains firmly rooted in Smallville.

In later seasons, Martha returns briefly for visits, often prompting discussions about Clark's connection to the family homestead. Before she begins her term as a senator, Martha admits to Clark in "Phantom" (2007), "I always thought you'd be the one to leave the farm first." This confession speaks to her expectations for their sex roles. As the mother, Martha believes her place should be at home, and Clark should fulfill the hero's journey by leaving. However, Clark explains to her, "This farm, it's my home," as if leaving is anathema to his worldview. This change of heart from his earlier comment to Whitney reflects his emotional growth. As an engagement present to Clark and Lois, Martha puts the deed to the farm in their names in "Kent" (2011). His ownership of the farm further solidifies Clark's position as nester, and the itinerant Lois becomes rooted with him.

Ultimately, Clark decides to sell the farm and move to Metropolis, but he admits he is afraid of letting go of Smallville. Reconciling the past and the future remains a theme throughout the tenth season, until Clark decides in the series finale (2011) that his past is what makes him the hero he is. When Martha learns the farm has been sold, she expresses her disapproval and insists Clark does not "have to let go of the past to move on." After a visit to his father's grave and a talk with his friend Oliver Queen, Clark comes to understand that Smallville is what makes him who he is (a closed loop back to the "scarecrow" from the pilot). Although Lois and Clark eventually relocate to Metropolis, Clark learns that he does not need to let go of his roots in order to move forward with his life. In fact, Jonathan's ghost reminds him to "always hold on to Smallville" in the moments before Clark finally dons the Superman suit for the first time.[28] This connection with the past, specifically with his adoptive hometown, inverts the hero's journey, where the experiences *away* from home shape the hero.

> "It doesn't matter what you wear or what name you go by, because you'll always be my son." —Martha Kent, "Beacon" (2011)

Clark's relationship with Martha, which deepens after Jonathan's death, is another way in which Clark redefines the role of the male hero. For Campbell, the hero's journey is oedipal; any encounter with a woman is a meeting with a goddess who is also a mother-bride, and the hero must learn to defeat his father figure in order to achieve his destiny.[29] Throughout the series, though, Clark's paternity is in question. After Clark's spaceship activates the memory of Jor-El, there are numerous discussions about Clark's father. Is Jonathan his "real" father or his adoptive father? Is Jor-El his "real" father or his biological father? That particular question is complicated by the multiple versions of Jor-El encountered in the series: the brain memory in the ship and later in the Fortress of Solitude, the clone seen in "Kandor" (2009), and the flashback version from "Relic" (2003). For a brief moment in "Lineage" (2002), Lex even thinks that *Lionel* is Clark's biological father and, in an alternate universe seen first in season ten's "Luthor" (2010), Lionel does adopt Clark.

Although Clark's paternity is tested and challenged throughout the series, his maternal line is never a mystery. Clark's biological mother Lara is released from a crystal in season seven's "Blue" (2007). Unlike the discovery of Jor-El, though, Clark's awareness of Lara's existence never complicates his sense of identity. He calls Lara his mother just as he does Martha, with no concern over the qualifications "biological," "adoptive," or "real." Both women can fulfill the role of mother at the same time without jeopardizing or challenging each other's position. While Clark's role as the son of any given father is disputable, his connection with his mother(s) never is.[30]

Clark's respective relationships with Lara and Martha are different from the relationship Campbell's hero typically has with his mother. It is also a reinvention of the relationship seen in teen male melodramas. Banks argues that mothers in these series are largely ineffectual, that they can "offer little beyond affection" and are "not the type of women who could have given birth to such emotionally well-rounded young men."[31] Her application of this claim to Martha, she concedes, may be due to the time of writing (the second season). In fact, following Jonathan's death in the fifth season, Martha's role becomes more significant than Jonathan's does—if much less obvious.

Jonathan, as well as Jor-El and Lionel, function as patriarchs who offer Clark guidance even as he learns to demythologize them. Clark visits Jor-El in the Fortress of Solitude for matters as simple as intelligence on particular villains; at other times, he seeks wisdom in matters of life and death. Jor-El sometimes offers hope but often reminds Clark and the audience of his patriarchal authority. Jonathan guides Clark through the dramas of daily life. He discusses the severity of playing on the high school football team in "Hothead" (2001) and reassures Clark when his burgeoning sexuality begins to interfere with his superpowers in "Heat" (2002). Lionel is invested in ensuring Clark's safety—though this role is complicated by Lionel's own self-interest. Like most male heroes, Clark loses these father figures, but not as the result of an oedipal struggle.[32] The deaths of these men, Jonathan in particular, open up possibilities for exploring Clark's affiliation with his maternal line.

Although Banks rightly notes that Martha was conspicuously quiet in the first season, Martha's character evolved, as did her backstory. While Jonathan was born into a family of farmers, Martha came from a world of privilege and education. It is her job as Lionel's assistant in the second season that keeps the family financially afloat; it is her father's wealth that serves as an emergency back-up plan for the Kents in "Redux" (2002). As Martha rises in political power, her role in the series mythology also grows. In "Hostage" (2010) she is eventually revealed to be the Red Queen, a figure whose covert tactics protect Clark from a secret government operation. Even after Annette O'Toole departed as a series regular, Martha's role in Clark's life was never in question. In "Beacon" (2011), she uses her political power to speak against the Vigilante Registration Act, which puts superheroes like Clark at risk from zealots and covert military operations. Rather than being an absent, ineffectual woman, Martha is an important figure, both emotionally and mythologically.

Because of her, Clark is reinvented from a modern Oedipus to a hero who appreciates certain qualities associated with the Darwinian female sex role. When Clark and Lana care for an abandoned baby in season four's "Ageless" (2005), Lana comments on Clark's natural talents with the child. Although the child, whom they name Evan, ages rapidly and dies in that same episode, he has the opportunity to call Clark and Lana his parents. Perhaps the most important example, though, is the discovery a genetically-engineered "son" named Conner, whose DNA is half–Clark Kent, half–Lex Luthor. In "Scion" (2011), Clark enrolls Conner at Smallville High and invites him to live on the farm, thus establishing Clark's maternal responsibility to nest and guard his young.[33] Although Clark is male, he undertakes certain duties traditionally relegated to the Darwinian female sex role.

> "I want our first time to be as special as you are." —Clark Kent, "Mortal" (2005)

The complex characterization of Clark is further manifest in his virginity, a theme traditionally common to female characters. Stan Beeler argues that *Smallville* is "the only adaptation of the mythos that explicitly thematizes the sexuality of the hero," but that theme is one of prolonged repression.[34] Part of the delay for his deflowering is the character's age; season one begins, after all, when he is only a freshman in high school. A part of the repression is, no doubt, the convenience of avoiding a canonical explanation for "how Kryptonians do it."[35] More significantly, though, is the way in which this rewrites the male hero. Rather than trying to copulate as often as possible, Clark "plays coy" like the females Darwin observed.

As the last remaining virgin among his peers, Clark stands apart from the norm, in his narrative world and in terms of popular culture's expectations for the male hero. Chloe, for instance, reveals in "Unsafe" (2005) that she lost her virginity during a summer internship when she was in high school. Oliver is known to be something of a playboy, and as Clark discovers in "Bound" (2004), Lex has a propensity for one-night stands. On the particular issue of sexuality, then, most of the characters in *Smallville* are rather worldly—except Clark. As a new breed of male hero, Clark values courting long-term relationships, rather than wantonly spreading his seed.

In spite of mixed messages from earlier episodes, it is made clear in the fifth season episode "Mortal" that neither Clark nor Lana has had sex before; Clark tells Lana that he wants their first time to be special. The series codes his continued virginity as indicative of his true love for her. However, they are only able to consummate their relationship because Clark has temporarily lost his powers. Two years later, in "Wrath" (2007), Lana absorbs Clark's powers through a quirk of lightning and meteor rock, and they are finally able to have sex again. At this point in the narrative, Lana has already married and divorced Lex, thus when she and Clark have such enthusiastic sex that the earth shakes, the deflowering is entirely Clark's. His repeatedly delayed sexual awakening is another way in which the series subverts the role of the male hero.

Although he has very brief flings with Alicia Baker in "Obsession" (2004), "Unsafe," and "Pariah" (2005), the only other woman with whom Clark has a true sexual relationship is Lois. How exactly this is achieved is only briefly explained as the result of Clark's extensive training with Jor-El to suppress his strength. It is not important that the series offers an explanation of how the sex act happens; what is significant is that Lois and Clark are committed to each other. Both of Clark's sexual relationships are in the confines of monogamous, long-term relationships.

Superman's sexuality has fascinated fans for decades. Lincoln Geraghty notes that Christopher Reeve's *Superman* films "moved Kent's relationship with Lois Lane front and center."[36] Ian Gordon agrees that the "sexual tension and attraction between Superman and Lois formed an important element of the movies."[37] The series *Lois and Clark: The New Adventures of Superman* (1993–1997) put the relationship between the two characters at its forefront, as the title indicates. DC Comics' Les Daniels calls *Lois and Clark* "a romance novel with pictures."[38] Both title characters in that series were established as virgins, which Gordon argues made their first time together a "virtuous connection of love."[39] Since Lois and Clark were both titular characters, it was a romance of seeming equals. Although the notions of virginity and sexual virtue are also seen in Clark's relationships in *Smallville*, the series title takes the emphasis off any particular person or pairing. Just as the titles of the various incarnations shift focus from *Superman* (the lone hero) to *Lois and Clark* (the heterosexual romance) to *Smallville* (the community), the character Clark Kent shifts from dominant, to equal, to blushing virgin.

Conclusion

If, as Joseph Campbell says, the hero is an identifier for all of humanity, or, as Lincoln Geraghty says, Superman is "an icon of American idealism," then we must consider what values *Smallville*'s Clark Kent perpetuates.[40] Certainly the series' debut post–9/11 shaped its narrative. Geraghty suggests that the "regression back from the big city (Metropolis) to small-town life (Smallville) attests to the major impact 9/11 had on the American psyche."[41] I would also add that the emphasis on the town, rather than the mythic hero, demonstrates post–9/11 valuing of cooperation and pluralism. Although Clark does fulfill the role of heroic savior, he does so among other heroes and helpers—Chloe Watchtower, Oliver/Green Arrow, and so on. The narrative's emphasis on Clark as one of a community is in contrast to other incarnations of Superman, Campbell's monomyth, and Darwinian sex roles.

Clark's slow rise to his role as the Blur, the series title, the character's sexuality, and the differing roles of Clark's various parental figures all indicate that the ideal superhero is one who is able to transcend expectations for his expression of masculinity. Rather than affirming Darwinian notions of the competitive, wandering male, whose philandering can be forgiven because of his heroic sacrifices for humanity, the new male hero is one who commits himself—to a matriarchal line, to a community, and to a monogamous relationship. Clark's journey shows that being a hero is not about abandoning home. It tells us that heroism can take place among family and community and that men can fulfill functions typically attributed to women. *Smallville*'s Clark is a newer breed of hero, one that "always holds on to Smallville" even as he flies through space to save the planet.

Notes

1. Joseph Campbell, *The Hero with a Thousand Faces* (Princeton: Princeton University Press, 1968).
2. Charles Darwin, *The Descent of Man and Selection in Relation to Sex* (New York: Merrill and Baker, 1874), 216.
3. Ibid., 217–218.
4. Christopher Ryan and Cacila Jethá, *Sex at Dawn* (New York: Harper Collins, 2010), 37.
5. Ibid., 28–29.
6. Ibid., 37.
7. Tristram Potter Coffin, *The Female Hero in Folklore and Legend* (New York: The Seabury Press, 1975), 1.
8. A more extensive comparison of Dorothy and Luke Skywalker can be found in Andrew Gordon, "*Star Wars*: A Myth for Our Time," *Literature/Film Quarterly* 6.4 (1978): 314–326.
9. Campbell, *The Hero with a Thousand Faces*, 30.
10. Carol Pearson and Katherine Pope, *The Female Hero in American and British Literature* (New York: Bowker, 1981), 4.
11. Gordon, "*Star Wars*," 320.
12. Pearson and Pope, *The Female Hero in American and British Literature*, 4.
13. Ibid., 6.

14. Coffin, *The Female Hero in Folklore and Legend*, 190.
15. Ibid.
16. Pearson and Pope, *The Female Hero in American and British Literature*, 14.
17. Ibid., 225.
18. Campbell, *The Hero with a Thousand Faces*, 207.
19. Stan Beeler, "From Comic Book to *Bildungsroman*: *Smallville*, Narrative, and the Education of a Young Hero," in *The Smallville Chronicles: Critical Essays on the Television Series*, ed. Lincoln Geraghty (Lanham, MD: Scarecrow Press, 2011), 3.
20. Lincoln Geraghty chronicles *Smallville* as a replacement for *Buffy the Vampire Slayer* in the network's lineup. See Lincoln Geraghty, "Introduction," in *The Smallville Chronicles: Critical Essay on the Television Series*, ed. Lincoln Geraghty (Lanham, MD: Scarecrow Press, 2011), xiv. For additional information about the WB/CW's network brand and target audience, see Valerie Wee, "Teen Television and the WB Television Network," in *Teen Television: Essays on Programming and Fandom*, eds. Sharon Marie Ross and Louisa Ellen Stein (Jefferson, NC: McFarland, 2008), 43–60.
21. Miranda Banks, "A Boy for All Planets: *Roswell*, *Smallville*, and the Teen Male Melodrama," in *Teen TV: Genre, Consumption, and Identity*, eds. Glyn Davis and Kay Dickinson (London: British Film Institute, 2004), 18.
22. Ibid., 22.
23. *Roswell*, with a series title emphasizing the town, works in the same way, but its potential impact was reduced by its short-lived run. Also, because the Superman myth is so ingrained in the American cultural psyche, the new characterization of Clark in *Smallville* makes for a more important case study.
24. Banks, "A Boy for All Planets," 20.
25. Karin Beeler, "Televisual Transformations: Myth and Social Issues in *Smallville*," in *The Smallville Chronicles: Critical Essays on the Television Series*, ed. Lincoln Geraghty (Lanham, MD: Scarecrow Press, 2011), 29.
26. The bartender also reveals that Clark does not have sex with any of these women. While much of the episode works to establish the "bad boy" persona that is Clark under the influence of red Kryptonite, the preservation of his virginity works into my later argument about Clark's subversion of male sexuality.
27. For instance, Banks describes how the Walsh parents of *Beverly Hills, 90210* "became superfluous" to the central narrative and "conveniently moved overseas," in "A Boy for All Planets," 2.
28. Ibid.
29. Campbell, *A Hero with a Thousand* Faces, 110–111.
30. In "Lineage" (2002), a woman claims to be Clark's birth mother, but the viewers, as well as the Kents, know this is impossible. While Lex and others may see this as a moment of confusion over Clark's maternal line, the viewers know the plot will eventually reveal how the woman arrived at such a case of mistaken identity. In that same episode, viewers learn that "Clark" was Martha's family name—further solidifying their mother-son ties.
31. Banks, "A Boy for All Planets," 25–26.
32. Lex is the classic oedipal character in *Smallville*, not Clark. A deleted dream sequence from "Scare" (2004) shows Lex preparing to marry his mother, and in "Descent" (2008) Lex murders his father.
33. Clark's role as guardian is admittedly short-lived. Conner does not appear in later episodes, though there are brief mentions that he has gone to live first with Chloe and Oliver, later with Martha. Because of this disappearance, I do not argue that Clark is Conner's "mother," but rather a father with certain maternal qualities.
34. Beeler, "From Comic Book to *Bildungsroman*," 21.
35. Several references in later seasons indicate that Clark has to learn how to restrain his abilities so that he does not harm his partner—an acceptable if vague explanation. Fans,

it should be noted, are often happy to suggest their own more detailed explanations in fan fiction, vids, and metatextual essays.

36. Geraghty, "Introduction," xii.

37. Ian Gordon, "Nostalgia, Myth, and Ideology: Visions of Superman at the End of the 'American Century,'" in *Comics and Ideology*, eds. Matthew P. McAllister, et al. (New York: Peter Lang, 2001), 185.

38. Cited in Gordon, "Nostalgia, Myth, and Ideology," 187.

39. Ibid.

40. Geraghty, "Introduction," ix.

41. Ibid., vii.

PART TWO:
Powerful Women

Sidekicks or Heroines?

The Feminist Successes and Failures of Smallville's *Leading Ladies*

VALERIE ESTELLE FRANKEL

There is no doubt that Clark Kent is on the hero's journey, a classic coming-of-age pattern that sees him facing his dark opposite in Lex Luthor, Doomsday, and a number of other villains. But what of the heroine's journey? Do the women of *Smallville* travel their own epic quests for salvation and adulthood, or do they fail to step out of their roles as sidekicks? The epic hero faces his shadow side, all the rejected qualities he could become if his life had been just a bit different. These often take the form of alternate selves, or sometimes the patriarch he is destined to be. At last, the hero faces the ultimate shadow–death–and is reborn stronger than before with new wisdom. Clark undergoes this quest in each season's arc and many individual episodes; Lex and Oliver Queen (Green Arrow) too follow this pattern. But again, what of *Smallville*'s many women? Do they face their dark sides and revive as strong, independent heroines? Or do they only follow their roles as Clark's sidekicks, protectors, and inspirers?

An examination of the heroines of *Smallville* will reveal whether they have storylines, futures, or destinies outside of Clark's journey. Lana Lang evolves from Clark's fantasy woman to his menacing trap, but every moment of her story arc relates to the men in her life, as she attempts to discover, aid, or revenge herself on Whitney Fordman, Clark, Jason Teague, and Lex. Chloe Sullivan's story is that of a perpetual sidekick; even when she selfishly turns to the dark side, it is a rebellion against the too-good persona she keeps up with Clark and Jimmy Olsen. As Watchtower, she grows into a mistress of information and technology, but uses it all to aid her team. Her eventual husband

and career are in fact Clark substitutes as she goes off with a superhero to train a future Justice League. Lois Lane is self-sufficient and capable against a legion of evildoers. However, by the final seasons, she is most often seen giving speeches to inspire Clark or persuade the world to have faith in superheroes. Her mission as reporter and public figure is wrapped up in Clark. Only Kara, Clark's Kryptonian cousin, when offered the choice to be Clark's earthly sidekick forever or to let him face his destiny, leaves on her own mission. However, hers is a small arc among the women of *Smallville* who never lose sight of their hero in red and blue. This essay breaks down the journeys of *Smallville's* primary female characters and describes how many of them are closely connected to and supportive of Clark and his journey.

Lana and Clark

Lana of the early seasons is the ideal woman for Clark, the generally unattainable focus of all his attention. She is a fairy princess beyond Clark's reach (as she identifies herself in her first episode, complete with wings and wand). However, she eventually transforms into the poisoned maiden and femme fatale. In fact, she is a type of Kryptonite even before her last episode (where she is *literally* full of the alien poison), radiating pain and angst for Clark whenever he comes too close and costing him too many loved ones. From the series premiere onward, he finds himself stumbling, clumsy, and pained when he approaches her Kryptonite necklace and the complex emotions she inflicts. She is treated more as a liability that needs protecting than as an equal partner. As an action heroine, she is most often seen knocked on the head and tied up, awaiting rescue. In the second season episode "Precipice" (2003) she trains to become an instant martial arts expert, but her skills are almost never used after this. She lacks the research skills, let alone fighting ability, to back Clark up.

Worse, she is always defined through her relationships to Clark and Lex (and earlier, Whitney), reacting to the men rather than toward her own goals. Her relationships with mostly older guys (Whitney, Jason, and Lex) are similar to her relationship with Clark—they have all the power and secrets; she has none. When she does have secrets, such as Isobel's possession in season four and the spaceship she sees in season five, she confides in Clark, and thus has even more reason to be hurt when he does not trust her in return. Lana is up on the "Wall of Weird" because she lost her parents in the meteor shower. Thus while she is literally powerless (except for the Kryptonite around her neck), she and Clark are linked from the beginning. However, when Lana's with someone else, Clark is jealous and miserable. When she is with him, he determinedly keeps secrets and pulls away to protect her, finally dumping her for her own good. They never have a happy relationship for more than a few episodes and she turns from girlfriend to inspiratrice or occasional villainess with no other identity on the series.

Lana's Shadows, Lana's Descent

As Chloe notes in season five's "Hypnotic" (2006), "Every single one of us has gone through some sort of an identity crisis at one point or another. It's like a rite of passage in Smallville." All these crises represent descents into the shadow self; just as Clark is replaced by his Bizarro side or acts out on red Kryptonite, the heroines of the series are possessed, drugged, or replaced, allowing them all to sample untapped sides of themselves and learn from the descent into darkness before return. These shadow selves offer hidden wisdom, often reminding the adolescent of his or her untapped potential. This is Joseph Campbell's monomyth pattern. In fact, Campbell describes facing this shadow as "destruction of the world that we have built and in which we live, and of ourselves within it; but then a wonderful reconstruction, of the bolder, cleaner, more spacious, and fully human life."[1]

Early on in season one, Lana discovers that her mother hated cheerleading and wanted a very different life for herself and her children. This is one of Lana's first steps to stop conforming and find her own path. In the same episode, "X-Ray" (2001), shapeshifter Tina Greer morphs into Lana and kisses Clark, embodying the buried side Lana that has never acted on that longs for the outcast boy rather than Whitney the jock. Tina, appearing as Whitney, tells Lana deep truths, pointing out that she has too good a life to be always mourning in the graveyard. Later in "Nicodemus" (2002), under the influence of the Nicodemus flower, Lana channels her bad girl side again, much like Clark on red Kryptonite. In a black miniskirt and boots, she coaxes Whitney to play hooky and goes swimming with Clark. She tries to seduce Lex and steals his car, and then climbs the windmill she has always been too afraid to scale. "You spoke your mind and you did what you wanted. Kind of an alpha Lana," Clark explains. This is what descending into the shadow means—the bad girl side, but one with power and strength rather than literal evil. At the end of the episode, Lana and Clark climb the windmill together and gaze off at the Metropolis skyline, their potential future away from Smallville. Emily Dinsmore, the clone of Lana's dead childhood friend, acts as another shadow for her in the early seasons. While Clark puts Lana on a pedestal, Emily drags her off it and reminds her that she is terribly flawed, tormenting her with survivor guilt. In season three's "Forsaken" (2004) Emily imprisons Lana before she can leave for Paris. Emily is the scared voice inside Lana who hesitates as

Clark courts her and then hesitates again as she considers flying off to Europe. Both times, Lana weathers the crisis with a new resolution.

More than the others, season four represents a heroine's journey arc for Lana. Like Clark, who discovers his powers in a terrifying instant, Lana absorbs her ancestress's spirit and turns from a normal girl to one with a back tattoo and a mission to find the three mystic stones. Lionel Luthor acts as a mentor on her quest, giving Lana one stone and the map to find another because she, as he claims in "Forever" (2005), is "the chosen one." Lana also develops superpowers in season four, thanks to the spirit of her ancestress. Countess Isobel is Lana's dark, vengeful, powerful side, which emerges to protect Lana when she is in danger, like when she is tortured in China in "Sacred" (2005). Jung notes that everyone has a "Countess Isobel" side, one far more savage and powerful than most people realize:

> The change of character brought about by the uprush of collective forces is amazing. A gentle and reasonable being can be transformed into a maniac or a savage beast. One is always inclined to lay the blame on external circumstances, but nothing could explode in us if it had not been there. As a matter of fact, we are constantly living on the edge of a volcano, and there is, so far as we know, no way of protecting ourselves from a possible outburst that will destroy everybody within reach.[2]

Season four's "Spell" (2004) represents Isobel's first and most thorough takeover. The new shadow-possessed Lana is "aggressively sexy" as Clark puts it, a bad girl who dresses in black and casts powerful spells on her friends. She also has far more perception than Lana the "good girl." Under her influence, Lana (whose memories exist somewhere within Isobel) can do all the things she has never allowed herself: she sees Lex is lying to her and casts a spell to control him forever; she realizes Jason is not as nice as he seems; and she comes on to Clark. She also discovers Clark's abilities and uses a kiss to force the truth out of him, something Lana has longed for and yet been unable to do. After Isobel temporarily departs, Lana makes it clear she has grown from the journey. Still dressed in black, she channels a little of her bad girl side to tell an overprotective Lex, "I'm old enough to decide who I want in my life, and who I don't."

Yet, later in "Sacred," she also confides her terrible secret about Isobel to Clark:

> **Clark:** Seeing you speak Latin and throw those guys around the room like toothpicks is kind of weird. And even when Isobel's gone, sometimes I look at you, and there's a part of you that I don't recognize anymore.
> **Lana:** I'm sorry. It's just that...Do you know how funny that sounds coming from you?

Isobel's superpowers—from a different origin than Clark's but just as mighty—make Lana a match for him, and the two bond over their common situation:

> **Lana:** Ever since that tattoo appeared, I feel like I've been walking around with this huge secret. Like, everybody only knows what's on the surface, but there's something inside of me that's so much more powerful.
> **Clark:** And you're afraid if people know about that part of you, they'll see you differently.

Nonetheless, Isobel's powers are used for selfishness and revenge, casting her as Clark's nemesis (and foreshadowing the superpowered Lana of season seven). Furthermore, both teens are pawns in the treasure hunt for the stones as Jor-El and Isobel direct them. As Clark tells Lana in "Sacred," "It must be scary to think that someone out there has a plan for you, but you don't know what it is yet." At season's end, Lana's Isobel side kills the evil matriarch Genevieve Teague, who has been scheming against Lana and over-controlling her son Jason all season (Lionel calls her "a woman without a heart"). Facing down the wicked queen is the prototypical female journey, a quest to accept her dark side and reintegrate it into the psyche. The innocent Cinderella figure "must face her stepmother and learn how to dominate a household, give orders, [and] acknowledge her own suppressed cruel streak. She needs the shadow's dark vicious strength, and the shadow craves her innocent happiness. They will have to find a way to reintegrate."[3] Lana does this by letting Isobel take her over and save her from Genevieve, thus allowing Isobel to complete her mission and depart, leaving Lana shaken but still wiser. Following the murder, Lana faces another death, her helicopter hurtling from the sky to throw her, badly injured into a new world, one where alien spacecraft have landed. This prepares her for a new identity and quest as a college student—one determined to expose the alien invaders.

When she starts college, Lana is briefly bitten by vampires in "Thirst" (2005) and again enters a shadow phase. Dark Lana is much like Isobel, "aggressively sexy" and rather scary. As with other episodes, Lana's powers are a match for Clark's abilities, and she even absorbs some of his when she bites him. In her black cat suit, she flirts with other men and blows off Clark, channeling the Lana of the episode's beginning, who is uncertain where their relationship is heading. When Clark protests that this dark side is not her, she responds, "Maybe it is. Maybe I've been hiding it from you all along, just like you were hiding who you really are from me." Jung notes, "Everyone carries a shadow, and the less it is embodied in the individual's conscious life, the blacker and denser it is....if it is repressed and isolated from consciousness, it never gets corrected."[4] To this point, Lana is so determined to be a good girl and a good girlfriend that she neglected her powerful, dark sexy side, which is struggling for an outlet. In fact, Lana's dark side is her emotional strength; under its influence, Lana passionately defends Clark, vaporizing the vampire leader Buffy Saunders (an obvious reference to another teen series) with heat vision to protect him and vowing to spend her eternal life with him. After her recovery, Lana admits that she loves and misses him, and they reach a new closeness. Nonetheless, Clark does not fight to hold onto her. After he sees her "die" because she knows his secret and ultimately loses his father reviving her in "Reckoning" (2006), he pulls away and finally breaks up with her.

After the break up, Lana takes an experimental serum that kills her and brings her back so she can see her parents again in "Void" (2006). Surrounded by their love and support, she learns from her descent into (literal) death and vows she will never be so dependent again. This episode is notable because she seeks what *she* wants, not using her descent to show Clark her bad girl side or learn his secrets. Yet she soon falls for Lex and allows him to control every aspect of her life. While Lana and Clark begin season five in love and surrounded by sunlight, it ends in "Vessel" (2006) with her committing to an evil, Zod-possessed Lex. As they kiss, both in ominous black clothing, blood red light shrouds them and spooky music plays. Metropolis is destroyed below them, emphasizing the caustic nature of their love. Young girls are taught to be "nice," to smooth away differences, and accept people rather than being revolted by their less-than-appealing behaviors. As such, Lana dates untrustworthy men but does her best to ignore these unattractive traits, focusing on Whitney's flattery, Jason's self-sacrifice, Clark's kindness, Lex's benevolence, rather than their callousness and secretiveness. As she ignores the instincts that warn her about committing to unequal and disturbing relationships, she blinds herself to seeing her lovers' dark sides, so the lesson presents itself more forcefully. She willingly gives herself to Lex, the ultimate predator-as-boyfriend, and then finds herself struggling to escape his control. As Clarissa Pinkola Estés argues, "Many women have literally lived the Bluebeard tale. They marry while they are yet naive about predators, and they choose someone who is destructive to their lives. They are desperate to 'cure' that person with love."[5]

Understanding the predator means leaving behind one's childish naiveté and growing into someone who understands evil as well as goodness, and this is precisely the journey Lana takes. Early in season six, Lana volunteers to murder a possessed Lex to save the world, something Clark cannot bear to do. She also tells Lex it is all right if he is experimenting on meteor freaks, because she is afraid of them and thinks they are dangerous. She admits to spying on Lex and controlling him for his own good and blackmails a researcher and his family in "Arrow" (2006). "Apparently Lex has finally found his equal," Lionel muses. At Lex's costume party in "Wither" (2006), he and Lana go as Caesar and Cleopatra, conquerors whose epic love changed the world ... and then led to painful tragedy and death. Lana's imaginary shadow in "Labyrinth" (2007) is the "good" Lana in a pretty country girl blouse and jeans, the one who loved Clark since kindergarten and visits every week while he is in a mental institution. Lana as Lex's wife dresses far more adult, with upswept hair, satin bathrobes, and formal suits. There are more black and red color patterns as she becomes stronger and more ethically compromised. While she occasionally portrays innocence with a sweet and wholesome look, her kindness is now the act. "Nice Lana" is no longer the Lana that is in control; dark Lana is running the show, and she wears the "good girl" like a deceptive mask.

After her marriage, she is even more firmly a Luthor. In season seven, Lana steals ten million dollars from Lex and uses it to spy on him. She keeps Lionel chained in the woods with a bear trap on his hand and sits calmly, calculatingly behind a desk, holding back the information that would save Lex's life. The Luthors have taken control away from Lana, and she takes it back through equal deviousness and cruelty. And when she and Clark restart their relationship in season seven, she keeps all of this secret. However, once more, her attainment of power relates to the men in her life.

When she gains superpowers in "Wrath" (2007), Lana turns on Lex, leading Clark to realize that she is a far darker girlfriend than he had imagined. However, unlike her more personal battle with Isobel, this decent into darkness is framed as a quest for Clark to save her. "Lana, I can live with you changing, I just need to accept the fact that I'm responsible for it," Clark tells her, taking all agency from her. The episode depicts her as the monster Clark has caused her to be. As Lex smirks to Clark, "I wasn't the first person to teach her about betrayal, now was I? It's hard to face what you've created, isn't it?" Everyone else also views Lana's descent in terms of Clark. Chloe and Lionel worry that Lana will bring down their hero. Lex warns Lana not to become a killer, not for herself but because "Clark would never look at you the same way again." Even Lana explains that she is courting darkness to protect Clark, hurting Lionel and Lex because they are a threat to him.

"Action" (2007) sees a superhero fan try to kill Lana to change Clark's life. This, in an episode about comic book heroes, echoes the "women in refrigerators" trope of a heroine who is violently murdered only to affect the hero. The *Encyclopedia of Comic Books and Graphic Novels* explains:

> Another element too often found in superhero comics is the use of the death or injury of women characters as a plot device to stir the male hero into action. In 1999, a group of comic fans created a Website titled "Women in Refrigerators," a term coined by writer Gail Simone, to list and criticize the death and dismemberment of women in comic books.[6]

This theme reappears far more poignantly when Brainiac infects Lana later in season seven. On the surface Lana's coma could be a death-and-rebirth, like Clark's in most season premieres; however, both Brainiac and the series' writers victimize her to hurt Clark, who breaks down in tears. Furthermore, this bodily possession that takes over Lana and sometimes Chloe hints that they have no control over their wayward female bodies, and indeed, reduces them to little more than bodies. When both are taken over by Brainiac, they can only lie passively, awaiting Clark's rescue.

After Lana returns from her catatonia in season eight, she quests for superpowers. The episode in which she gets them—the aptly titled "Power" (2009)—is described in popular press interviews as the female empowerment show. As the episode's director Allison Mack (Chloe) noted:

> For Lana, this episode is really about rising from her former self and saying...I'm going to go understand what it means to be independent, I'm going to go understand what it means to be myself. ...It parallels from a very female perspective the same sort of journey that we were on with Lex and Clark and I think that we really got to see that exemplified from the feminine point of view.[7]

In the episode Lana's trainer tells her, "I'm not training you to be like someone else. I'm training you to be Lana Lang, to rise from the ashes of your previous life, stronger, more powerful ... fearless." In fact, she *is* questing to be like someone else—a second Clark, gaining superpowers to fulfill his mission of helping others. She wants to be his equal partner, someone who does not need protecting. But because this is her goal, she still defines her life in terms of him.

Worse yet, her story is minimized in Clark's larger arc; the series, too, is defining her quest in terms of how that quest relates to Clark. Executive producer Todd Slavkin notes, "One thing we wouldn't do [with the episode] is to compromise the show and the complexity of the show."[8] He insisted on telling Lana's story only as a flashback episode—Lana is not *Smallville*'s hero, so the story of her training and personal growth happens only in the past. Her trainer reveals it to Clark, and *his* reactions are central. In fact, Lana is the helpless, motionless object of most of this episode, as Clark seeks to rescue her from her apparent kidnapping. Only at the end of "Power" is it obvious that Lana has orchestrated it all. Her quest for power is a quest to be a second Clark and make him truly happy, and as such it is a failure. In "Requiem" (2009), Lex takes his revenge on them both by poisoning Lana forever; infecting her with the Kryptonite she has worn through the series, emphasizing her nature as a poisonous influence on Clark. She ends the series still a pawn and now a deadly one, significant only in how Lex uses her to hurt the story's real hero.

Chloe and Clark

In the latter half of the series, Chloe is indeed Clark's "Watchtower," keeping an eye on the city and helping lost heroes find their way home. Protecting Clark's secret and acting as his errand girl hurts her relationships, leads to her termination from her dream job at the *Daily Planet*, and even gets her arrested for terrorism. Yet she continues, perfectly willing to be taken for granted. She comments in "Charade" (2010) that she and Oliver will always put supporting Clark ahead of their own lives because, as she says, "We both understand that our relationship comes second to a higher calling." As such, Chloe too fails as an independent heroine.

Chloe's meteor powers are traditionally feminine: empathy (triggered by crying in fact) so strong it can heal and Brainiac-created superintelligence even greater than Hermione Granger's. As such, she is a figure of support rather than of superheroics. She saves Lois with her powers in "Phantom" (2007) and almost dies in the process, so Clark later forbids her to save Lex with them and insists on risking himself instead in "Fracture" (2008). Clark is meant to be the hero of the story, not Chloe. While Clark uses his gifts to help others, Chloe is punished with near-death for doing so, and resolves not to take the risk. She is far more secure in her sidekick role. Her early-season hopeless schoolgirl crush on Clark, like Lois's later infatuation with the Blur, makes her appear weak and fawning. Clark has all the power in both relationships.

Chloe even fails to have a significant romantic relationship until her season six pairing with Jimmy Olsen. Clark and Chloe occupy a world of secrets from which Jimmy is completely cut out, until Jimmy is genuinely surprised to discover Chloe is not still in love with him. In "Bride" (2008), Clark even gives Chloe his freshman spring dance boutonniere to carry in her wedding bouquet. Though Chloe protests she loves Jimmy completely, both Lois and Davis Bloome voice skepticism about the depth of her feelings. Before and after Jimmy, Chloe's love life is rocky, to say the least. In season two's "Rush" (2003), a parasite pushes to Chloe act out-of-control and make out with Clark, and when he falls ill a short time later in "Fever" (2003), she reads him her touching, selfless crush letter. Two seasons later in "Devoted" (2004), a Kryptonite-laced sports drink turns Chloe into Clark's personal cheerleader complete with uniform to support her football hero. "Look, Clark, as much as I'd like to blame the pom-pom juice for this, I obviously still have those feelings in me somewhere," she confesses. After seeing what her life would be like as Clark's love slave, she agrees to a "just friends" agreement. Season nine's "Warrior" (2010) sees Chloe falling for a kid in an adult's body. Not only is he nonthreatening, preferring Xbox to anything romantic, but also his powers are identical to those of a Kryptonian. Her naive, superpowered new boyfriend is in fact another Clark fantasy. At the same time, as she and Clark both wear dark business clothes at a fantasy convention, the boy convinces her to loosen up and enjoy life. She soon realizes how foolish she has been and shows up at Oliver's place. As she strips down to her tank top, drinks scotch, and fires his bow, his hand over hers, she seems ready to let go of her own childhood fantasies and devote herself to an adult relationship.

However, Oliver, with his secret identity and heroism, is a substitute Superman for the women of the story. Lois and Clark share their first kiss when Clark pretends to be Green Arrow. This disguise, like Oliver himself and the Blur, is something of a practice superhero for Lois. In "Toxic" (2008), she even calls Oliver "an icon; the man of tomorrow," and herself "Lois Lane, the girl who writes about him," both references to her future relationship with Superman. As such, Chloe's eventual marriage to Oliver means settling for a second Clark. In "Escape" (2010) and again in "Fortune" (2011), Chloe and Clark toy with the relationship that never developed between them: the former sees a possessed Chloe coming onto Clark in a towel and the latter features the two of them confusedly suspecting that they got married the night before. In both instances, Chloe commits more deeply to Oliver after her moment of "might have been" with Clark. Yet up until nearly her last episode, Chloe's relationship with Clark is shown to be the most all-consuming of her life. During her first engagement in "Instinct" (2008), she tells him, "Clark, what you and I have, I will never share with anyone else." Perhaps Jimmy is right to protest that she never says these things to him.

Chloe's Shadows

Chloe's weakness has always been knowledge, from her first moments with the Wall of Weird and her attempts to discover the mysteries of Smallville and particularly her best friend Clark. In season three's "Truth" (2004) when a temporary ability means no one can lie to her, she presses her advantage by raising questions she knows people do not want to answer, from asking Lionel if he killed his parents to pressing the Kents about Clark's secret. Despite watching her friends flee the room, knowing she has destroyed a family, Chloe does not stop her relentless pursuit of the truth. Before Clark's meteor-infected flame Alicia Baker dies in "Pariah" (2005), she gives Chloe a great gift—the knowledge of Clark's secret. Alicia, Chloe's shadow, embodies everything Chloe is not: she is dating Clark, she has powers to equal his, and she knows his secret. Of course, she is also insane and occasionally murderous, in contrast with Chloe, who mostly follows the rules. Alicia torments Chloe about Clark, noting that "Chloe Sullivan ... ace reporter. You write all these articles about the people you call 'freaks,' and you don't even realize that someone close to you is one of them. Why are you ignoring what's right in front of your face, Chloe? Don't you want to know the truth about Clark Kent?" Through this revelation, Chloe realizes that she has been harming the teens around her by labeling them as "freaks" and exposing their secrets. In horror, she dismantles the Wall of Weird and commits to protecting Clark's secret until he decides to tell her himself.

Of course, this pursuer of secrets is hiding a secret of her own. Chloe meets her worst fear as a straightjacketed woman in "Scare" (2004). Though she initially believes it to be her mother, it is actually herself, warning that she too will someday go insane. After she comes through her crisis, Chloe confesses to Clark that she has found her mother, who has been locked away with a hereditary mental disease Chloe may inherit. A year later in "Tomb" (2006), Chloe apparently attempts suicide. "Sometimes a person has a secret they feel they can't share," her psychiatrist warns. While Chloe is not actually psychotic or suicidal, only possessed by the ghost of a murdered girl, this possession makes her face this great fear. After revealing her mother's secret, Chloe finds the courage to go see her in the asylum.

As "Progeny" (2007) illustrates, it turns out Moira is another shadow of Chloe. Chloe (apparently) is the girl with no superpowers, one who can only watch others' heroic feats. However, Moira can control all the meteor-infected, and by doing so (unwillingly) endangers Chloe's life and enables Lex's secret projects. Although Chloe occasionally compromises her ethics by making deals with the Luthors in exchange for information, Moira chooses nonexistence and catatonia, all for the love and safety of her child. Thus, Chloe discovers that her mother, whatever her mental condition, is a figure of incredible heroism and love, rather than a source of terror. Chloe commits to go after Lex and end his tyranny, just as Moira vanishes from Chloe's life. However, this experience teaches Chloe to be the girl who protects superheroes from the sidelines like her mother, something she masters as Watchtower.

Chloe's Descent

As I write in *From Girl to Goddess*:

The underworld ... is the realm of the unconscious, of magic, of desires made manifest with a wish, and, yes, of death. This is the woman's traditional sphere of power—the world of emotion and spirit. Yet too long a stay will transform princess to death-crone, Kore to Persephone. Thus the heroine must finally ascend, richer for her underworld knowledge, and yet committed to the world of life.[9]

In "Phantom," Chloe faces death—in this case, Lois's death—and taps into her superpowers for the very first time. Wiser since learning about selfless love from her mother, Chloe no longer holds back from her gift but instead gives herself over to it utterly, even dying, to gain the healing powers that can save Lois. Chloe dies, but soon returns stronger than before. While the sixth season sees her controlled by her powers, the seventh season shows her mending her relationship with Jimmy and saving Clark by using her gifts instead of *being used by them*. Chloe has other heroine's journeys, especially her (apparent) death in the safe house of season three's "Covenant" (2004) and her possession by Brainiac throughout season eight. Each of these descents into the underworld matures Chloe by bringing her in contact with death and its power.

The greatest of these experiences comes in the season seven finale "Arctic" (2008). As she explains, "I passed out, and when I woke up, I was different." Infected by Brainiac, she becomes her greatest dream—the ultimate researcher and hacker. No puzzle is safe from her enormous mental powers. "My hunger's never satisfied. Knowledge is what fuels me," she notes in "Legion" (2009). Though she is black-eyed and infected by Brainiac, there is truth to her words. As with most shadow stories, there is an element of wish fulfillment, of acting on one's forbidden impulses present with Chloe's story. She brings the entire planet to a standstill, endangering everyone in it as she drains the information from every head. "I'm happy to be Brainiac-free. But my evil upgrade was really ... convenient," she confesses in "Bulletproof" (2009). Her need for knowledge remains an obsession after Brainiac is long gone, as she is caught up in the power of Watchtower and the secrecy of the Justice League's heroic missions. Chloe embodies this desire, as, in a blood-spattered wedding dress, she becomes the ultimate seeker of knowledge, no longer searching for it with her clever curiosity but leaching it from people's brains. "To restrain the natural predator of the psyche it is necessary for women to remain in possession of all their instinctual powers," Estés explains, listing among them, intuition, tenacious loving, intuitive healing and creativity.[10] These all correspond to Chloe's empathic healing power that is ultimately revealed in "Cure" (2007) to be centered in her heart. Brainiac wipes this power from her, even as he threatens to consume her entire self. She trades human empathy for a supercomputer of a brain.

It is significant that as Brainiac takes her over, she loses her memories of her loved ones and replaces them with photos and notes—using data in place of emotion. As she tells Clark in "Abyss" (2008), "I've forgotten almost everyone, Clark. And I'm having to fake my feelings more and more with people. Pretty soon, there isn't gonna be any 'I, Chloe.' Just... an I.Q," she worries. She becomes stripped of emotion, leaving only the pertinent information behind. Caught up as she is in the intellect, it is easy for a predator to consume her entire life, which contains only her role as sidekick and advisor to the superheroes of her life. She loses her job at the *Daily Planet* and spends her days at the Isis Foundation as Lana's fill-in, left to watch from afar while her heroes save the day. She branches out from her constant sidekick role with kind, sweet Clark to love kind, sweet Jimmy and reassure them both constantly. Her superpower is also one of caring, letting her give up her life to save others in the ultimate helpless sacrifice. Yet she craves something more, something just for her. A life of all goodness and proper behavior is eating away at her.

Season eight marks Chloe's true test, torn as she is between Jimmy, the male daylight voice of reason and caring and her darker impulses—Brainiac, the greed for knowledge, and Doomsday, her seething need to lash out. As Allison Mack explained in an interview with *TV Guide*:

> On the one hand, she's still doing work with Clark and getting married to Jimmy and doing her lovely, good-girl Chloe thing, and on the other hand she's struggling with this "pull" towards Davis and these dark, evil tendencies and a want to destroy things, which is very much Brainiac. She has a massive pull between these two sides of her that she's struggling to suppress until she learns to understand it.[11]

Estés notes that a woman who loses her joys and creative outlets will channel them into dark, disturbing paths like addictions and secrets: "Because a woman feels she cannot in daylight go full-bore at whatever it is she wants, she begins to lead a strange double life, pretending one thing in daylight hours, acting another way when she gets a chance."[12] In season eight, Chloe keeps more secrets than she needs to: her engagement, her new brainpower, and a kiss with Davis. Doomsday (the evil Kryptonian monster within Davis) kidnaps her from the wedding, taking her from the too-good husband Jimmy in "Bride." When he carries her to the Fortress, Chloe becomes evil, black-eyed, bloodstained, and immeasurably powerful. Her meek bride days are over. Clark turns her back into the "kinder, gentler Chloe" in "Legion," but she is already on the path for another descent.

The basement is the dwelling-place of the subconscious, of the things one cannot consciously face that lurk beneath the surface. As Chloe hides the monstrous, unstable Davis there, he becomes her secret identity, her twisted ugly secret she cannot share. Above, she pretends everything is normal, even over-normal as she bakes and reassures her friends. But at night, she is busy dumping body parts in trashcans and caring for Davis, murderous Beast to her Beauty. As Clark protests "Beast" (2009), "Davis must have done something to her. Chloe would never have lied to me if she weren't trapped. ...She'd never choose Davis over her friends." But Chloe is tired of subsuming all her needs in theirs and being taken for granted. She quickly turns from being the one waiting by the phone for Clark and Oliver to call to being the one with her own secrets who cannot return their messages. She's found a new mission:

> **Davis:** You wouldn't be able to say goodbye to anyone, not even Clark. Can you do that? Can you honestly tell me that I am the most important person in your life?
>
> **Chloe:** Davis, I would do anything for you.

Chloe dreams of a Phantom of the Opera-style romance with red roses, candles, and Davis, marred only by a trail of blood. She follows it, like Bluebeard's wife, and discovers he has killed Clark. In her dream, Chloe breaks out of the beautiful veneer in which she and Davis are playing house. She opens the forbidden door and sees the secret concealed behind it—Davis is a murderer. She can hide from the truth, convince herself he is innocent, ignore what is going on in front of her, but there in her dream, it is waiting. Davis came to Earth to murder her best friend.

As I write in my heroine's journey study, *From Girl to Goddess,* "The Bluebeard tale is a challenge for the psyche. Will the girl come to realize that her lover is a murderer before it is too late?"[13] This test of perception tears at the conflicted Chloe. Though the predator is gaining power over her life, part of Chloe is insisting that she look deeper, accept the darkness within the predator and flee before it is too late. All her friends, acting as the voices of consciousness and sanity, offer to rescue her. However, Chloe is not yet ready to leave her exploration of the dark side to return to her empty life. Dr. Emil Hamilton notes in "Beast" that "Sometimes, dramatic changes are caused by intense emotions—love, hate, obsession." Though he is discussing Davis, this has also grows to apply to Chloe who directs all her priorities to fit her new obsession. She finally has something that is only hers, something she does not have to share with a team of better-qualified superheroes. "I think she's starting to understand what *she* wants separate and aside from Clark, and she is building her own relationship with herself and her own life, and proactively going after all of that instead of just running around and doing whatever she thinks Clark needs. She's grown into her own woman," Mack commented.[14]

Chloe eventually insists she is running off with Davis to save Clark, putting her needs aside to help him yet again. She may even believe it. But what she really wants is the Phantom of the Opera moment of her dream—a world of sensuality and darkness. She wants the Beast all for herself, so much so that she is willing to give up her whole life for him. They discuss her feelings in "Doomsday" (2009):

> **Davis:** How could you do this? I loved you. You're the only one... who ever loved me. Why? Why?!
>
> **Chloe:** I thought I did. Okay? But really, what I wanted to do was save you.

The cry of the wounded man clinging to her as his hope of salvation is terribly compelling, drawing Chloe to Davis as Lana is drawn to Lex. After Jimmy dies from Chloe's misplaced trust, she shuts herself away in Watchtower, committing to the intellectual world of research. Once again, she handicaps herself, shutting off so many sides of her personality that they may rise up and take her over, as they did with Brainiac and Davis. As Jung warns, "If it comes to a neurosis, we invariably have to deal with a considerably intensified shadow. And if such a person wants to be cured it is necessary to find a way in which his conscious personality and his shadow can live together."[15] By denying her rage and misery, Chloe channels them into a double life of devious, unethical behavior. She steals from Oliver and stockpiles Kryptonite weapons. She also reads her friends' email and watches them through spy cameras. As Chloe becomes controlling, even monstrous, another dark shadow arrives to echo her descent. Amanda Waller, leader of Checkmate, is the evil queen of the story, wearing purple silk shirts and dark jackets, a force of feminine power. Much like Chloe, Waller strives for more information (and control of it). However, she is a shadow figure, determined to tear down all Chloe stands for. As Mack noted in an interview:

> Chloe plays a very proactive role in the relationship between Clark and Amanda Waller, mainly because she's a threat to her league. As part of her duties as Watch Tower, [sic] she is very protective of her league and what they represent and stand for. She's very aggressive about trying to figure out who Checkmate is, what it's about and how to stop her.[16]

As Waller paces Chloe in a literal castle in "Checkmate" (2010), she moves chess pieces around the board like the people she dominates. Waller is often very manipulative and threatens her employees, "Fear is what prompts us to protect ourselves. And studying fear gives us insight to others' phobias." She over-controls her environment—superheroes must all work for her, unmasked and instantly obedient, or die.

Waller's myriad of screens and monitors echo Chloe's own Watchtower headquarters, as does her need to know and understand everything. Each sits in her base of operations, advising the superheroes out in the field. As Waller murders, calling it "strategy," this behavior is an extreme form of where Chloe is heading, a wake-up call for the young Watchtower that she is once again playing with fire.

Chloe's other shadow in the later seasons is Tess Mercer, also a collector of secrets and hidden projects. As such, Tess is the only one able to get through to Chloe. In "Sacrifice" (2010) the two are trapped in Watchtower as Tess confronts Chloe with what she is becoming: "This entire building was programmed to prevent anyone from getting close to you." As they talk, Chloe realizes why she's been keeping Oliver at a distance, dominating everything, even as she criticizes the same impulses in Tess.

> **Tess:** I just wanted to save the world.
> **Chloe:** That's funny—last time I checked you were just trying to get rid of everyone in it.

Although Tess has indeed trespassed, Chloe begins to see an echo of herself. The episode ends with Chloe temporarily killing Tess to help her escape Checkmate and dragging her back from death, forcing them both to face their mortality and grow from the journey. Chloe at last destroys Watchtower, valuing their human lives over her stronghold of information. With this, she turns a corner in "Hostage" (2010), accepting what she has become and deciding to change:

> I'm sorry. You know, I got tangled in my own little world wide web, and I just lost track of what was important. Clark, when you disappeared from my life, I retracted into Watchtower. And as I became Big Brother, I—I guess more like Big Sister. It's easy to think that having all the information is the same as having all the answers. But I can't be the eye in the sky anymore, Clark. And now that I have Ollie, I, I want to plug in to the real world. Virtual reality bites.

Chloe continues battling her addiction to knowledge, even dangerous knowledge. In season ten's "Collateral" (2011) Clark and Oliver have visions of a mad scientist version of Chloe experimenting on them, though it turns out they are trapped in a virtual world and she is attempting to save them. The real Chloe (as opposed to the treacherous one in their visions) uses her knowledge to gain great power, taking over Waller's Suicide Squad and commanding godlike powers in the virtual world. Once again, her shadow represents a possible future for her.

In "Absolute Justice" (2010), Doctor Fate tantalizingly warns her that she walks the same path he does–seeing so much she risks madness. "It could mean she's the next Doctor Fate. It could mean that she will soon be ridiculed and put in the hospital for being insane, like her mother, sort of a throwback to Chloe's fear of adopting her mother's mental illness," Mack explained.[17] However, when later Chloe risks wearing the Helmet of Nabu in "Lazarus" (2010), she does it for love of Oliver rather than love of information. This becomes clear when she offers her life for his in a moment of touching sacrifice. Her quest for understanding finally guides her to protect the one she loves.

In season ten's "Masquerade" (2011), Chloe travels into Desaad's club, where she faces a final set of temptations: a vision of Clark asks her for a kiss, Oliver asks her to run away with him, and Lois tries to provoke her envy as they channel the deadly sins. At last, Chloe faces herself as the white-coated Chloe avatar from "Collateral" who chides her for her pride and isolation. Chloe is finally facing her shadow, not as the information predators Waller, Doctor Fate, or Brainiac, but simply as herself. Afterwards, Chloe searches to define herself under all her personas and find "Chloe 1.0," the clever high school reporter she once was. She also offers to define herself as Oliver's girlfriend.

Chloe ends the series by moving away from Metropolis and Clark. Though she claims to choose her own path, her mission of training young heroes is awfully close to her role as Clark's sidekick. She even follows Clark's lead with a "double identity" as she puts it. Like Lois and Clark, she becomes a reporter by day and works with superheroes by night. Though she finds a job at another paper and marries Oliver, she is still Watchtower inside.

Lois's Shadows

Lois's most interesting source of growth is roleplaying: she dresses as an ancient witch, stripper, prison guard, vixen fighter, French maid, superheroine, golden bunny girl, and dominatrix. As she tries these (often uncomfortable) roles, she experiments with skills outside her usual arsenal. Lois is defensive and frightened of relationships; so many of her costumes are sexy and revealing, showing a side that is the opposite of her personality (and a gratuitous treat for fans, one assumes). This is her particular way of confronting her unexplored shadows. Her costumes, like her investigative skills and powerful self-defense, take the place of powers, so much so that in "Stiletto" (2009), she becomes a superhero—even saving Clark—without any superhuman abilities.

Although Lois has been a "bad girl" before her first appearance on the series—she mentions smoking cigarettes just to defy her father—she has also dealt with her mother's death, a rebellious little sister, and a distant father. She is hardly as damaged as Lex, but Lois experiences more trials than the innocent school-girlish Lana and Chloe. As such, Lois never becomes the all-too-good girl possessed by a monstrous shadow for entire seasons. She is more balanced, deliberately channeling her dark side's rage and power to attack the series' many villains. Particularly with her countless guises, Lois shows herself to be controlling her shadow descents and her own destiny.

In season four, her two costumed appearances (as a powerful witch in "Spell" and Clark's pink-clad prom date in "Spirit" [2005]) are both cases of possession, emphasizing the shadow nature of her terribly out-of-character disguises. However, the first time she proposes a costume for an investigation, she does not wear it herself. Instead, she dresses *Clark* up in a bathing suit and he is the sexy distraction while she investigates in "Devoted." A similar scene occurs in "Recruit" (2005) when Clark visits Metropolis University as co-eds come on to him and Lois spies from the closet. She tries her own subsequent personas as she weighs her feelings toward the other characters, battling Clark in a fight ring in "Combat" (2007) and dressing as Oliver's Maid Marion in "Wither."

In season seven, however, surrounded by couples Chloe and Jimmy and Lana and Clark, Lois wears drabber disguises like that of a maintenance worker. She does not toy with being sexy and desirable but invisible, a role she feels reflects her real life. She is busy dating her boss, Grant, a relationship everyone counsels her is a bad idea even before they discover his secret (he is a clone of Lionel's long-dead son Julian). Thus, the inner Lois is not seductive but wary, trying to caution her.

As Lois weighs her feelings for Clark in the following season, the evil Kryptonian Faora takes over her body in "Bloodline" (2008). While ruthless and immeasurably powerful, Faora is also determined and passionate enough to stab her beloved son Davis and leave him bleeding, knowing he will rise again, invulnerable. For Lois, unsure that she can love enough to have a relationship and children, this Kryptonian woman is the ultimate shadow. Furthermore, in season nine's "Warrior," Lois and Clark's relationship is still tentative and developing. She wears a fully concealing stormtrooper costume to a convention, and when Clark walks off with Zatanna, the look on her face shows that she feels as unglamorous as her outfit suggests. Soon after, she changes into a skin-baring Amazon costume that has Clark staring at her just the way she wants. He finally offers to take her to a fantasy ball and says that he understands the need for fantasy considering that his dream is to be with her. As the relationship progresses, she later quits her job to dress as a 1950s-era homemaker and try on Martha's wedding gown under the effects of Kryptonite in "Persuasion" (2010). Her sexy bunny costume when she and Clark compete on a story in "Charade" and the entire rack of lingerie she brings on their bed-and-breakfast trip in "Escape" indicate how eager she is to look desirable for her new boyfriend. Of course, in the latter episode her real disguise is the man-slaying banshee who takes over her body. Once again, her dark side is cautioning her to be wary of men, especially Clark, who may still have lingering feelings for Chloe.

When she returns from Africa in season ten and shyly tells Clark they are only work partners, Lois also disguises herself as a naughty dominatrix in a sleazy club, seducing the villain into compliance. While she is willing to be Clark's friend and work partner, she is clearly hungry for more. Shortly after, in "Isis" (2010), she decides to commit completely to love and tell Clark that she knows his secret. At the same time, she transforms into her gala costume, a superpowered goddess with abilities like Clark's. The goddess Isis is wholly committed to love but questions the depth of Clark's feelings for Lois, voicing her host body's worries about why Clark will not reveal his secret. In goddess form, Lois finally tells Clark that if he cannot commit and give up the world for her, he should die.

Lois: Have you given this woman your heart?
Clark: She knows how I feel.

Lois: But you hold yourself back from her, hmm? If you will not risk your heart completely then I will.

With those words, she attempts to rip his heart out (unsuccessfully obviously). The next episode "Harvest" (2010) also features human sacrifice, but this time Lois's, not Clark's. While in the previous episode they were both superpowered, this time they must escape their enemies while mortal. Lois takes charge, insisting Clark wear a disguise and picking the locks so they can escape. "Sometimes even the hero needs a guardian angel, Clark," she notes. Her last and permanent role is being his equal partner, one that will continue through the final season. Aside from a humorous throwaway moment as a showgirl (featuring Oliver in feathers by her side) in "Fortune," she is done with disguises, just as Clark finally tells her the truth.

Lois and Clark

In her earliest episodes in season four, Lois is presented as incredibly strong and self-sufficient, an equal partner for Clark. On separate investigations to find Chloe in "Gone" (2004), she and Clark turn up the same clues and arrive in time, destroying Chloe's assassin in tandem. Chloe leaves with an arm around each of them, melding them into a trio for the rest of the series. On Lois's first journalistic investigation in "Façade" (2004), she is stripped to her underwear and strapped to a table. Nevertheless, Clark is incapacitated with Kryptonite and she ends up rescuing them both with martial arts. In "Tomb," a terrified Lois hurls a knife at the serial killer who has tied her to a chair and again saves the day, rescuing Clark, Chloe, and herself. She remains incredibly independent, dismissing the need for college or romance. In later seasons, however, Lois replaces Lana as the most likely character to be helplessly knocked on the head or kidnapped. Like all Superman stories' Lois, she is best defined by her cluelessness as she fails to guess Clark's secret, and on *Smallville*, she is quite literally the last character to learn it. As she seems oblivious to the secret meetings between Chloe, Oliver, Clark, and Tess, Lois appears even more of the clueless female. Her friends even use chloroform and memory wipes to keep her uninformed.

In "Hostage," Lois saves Perry's life as Clark watches on proudly. As she says afterward, "I realized I don't have to go anywhere to find my higher calling. I just, I needed to find the hero inside myself." However, like Lana, Lois becomes a superhero just like Clark in this episode, fulfilling his destiny rather than hers. By grabbing Perry as he dangles off a roof, Lois saves him in the same way Clark saved her in an earlier season nine episode. She ends the season seeking a purpose and runs off to be a reporter in Africa. Yet once there, she only obsesses over Clark. She leaves and returns with no sign of having done any career-boosting journalism, only taking a pause to reevaluate her relationship.

Many characters tell Lois she must stay with Clark to keep him grounded and help him achieve his destiny. In season ten's "Supergirl" (2010), she says that her "worst fear in the world is to be alone in the world without heroes." In that same episode, her faith in the Blur, Clark's alter ego, is proven to be all consuming, blocking her from all doubt and darkness. Similarly, in "Idol" (2009) Lois is willing to sacrifice her life to preserve his secret identity. She gives a stirring speech to the crowd, reminding them that the Blur is "A light in the darkness. A symbol for us to believe in when all other hope is lost." Even though she is unaware of it, Lois's speech saves Clark from bowing to political pressure and revealing his identity to the world. As Erica Durance, the actress who plays Lois, stated in an interview, "She just has this absolute loyalty for what is good and right and just, and it parallels what Superman is and what he embodies."[18] "Collateral" sees Lois pledge to help the Blur at any expense, selflessly offering to be kept in the dark to protect his secret. Trapped in a virtual world, Lois saves his life and leads Clark to fly through her faith and inspiring speech. After, he comments that she will help him fly in the real world someday. In "Beacon" (2011) Martha, Lois, and Chloe all campaign across the web to save Clark. He, in turn, is apathetic about his future until he sees how much support the women have found for him.

When Lois gains Clark's powers before their wedding in "Prophecy" (2011), she sacrifices herself to save him, much as Clark frequently does when she is in danger. This leads to a greater sacrifice, as Lois realizes that she is holding Clark back from saving the world and insists on setting Clark free to pursue his great destiny. In the series finale, Lois uses her research, her smarts, and her military knowledge to figure out what the president is planning and sneak onto his plane before he can launch a nuclear assault. However, once she is there, she saves the day by pleading for the country's leaders to put their faith in superheroes. Once again, her primary act of heroism is being Clark's cheerleader. She snatches a video camera and gets the scoop that likely launches her career. But it is the Superman scoop. As shown through future glimpses, she will become a great journalist, but always one devoted to making sure her superhero looks great in headlines. Both their journalism careers will never be more than fronts for his heroism.

Kara and Clark

Kara, Clark's Kryptonian cousin, first appears to Lex in "Bizarro" (2007) as a beautiful angel, and that image sticks. In fact, she comes to Earth to be

Clark's guardian angel (though he spends plenty of time teaching her to be human as she starts her own teenage quest). Kara is also interesting because unlike Clark, her destiny is not set. Her first episodes in season seven display a repetition of Clark's journey. Her desire to show off as Miss Sweet Corn is compared to Clark's time as quarterback. Similarly, Lex meets Kara, like Clark, when she pulls him from in his submerged car, and he begins the same crusade to unravel her secrets, telling her in "Fierce" (2007), "Twice I've been pulled back from the brink of death, and both times it was by a member of the Kent family. I'm not a man who believes in coincidences."

Clark, of course, is seen taking his parents' role as he struggles to teach her to hide her abilities. "She's a young teenager ... she's a little rebellious," noted Laura Vandervoort, who portrays Kara. "She knows what she wants and she goes after it."[19] Kara is eager to use her powers while Clark is cautious and "uptight." While her red pageant bikini seems like a disturbing moment for female empowerment, there is a precedent in nineties girl power heroines like Buffy and Xena:

> Girl power heroines, while strong, are also thoroughly feminine, wearing short skirts and makeup not to please society but *because they want to*. This era of feminism has been designated "third-wave": Unlike the 1970s second-wave demands for equality, third-wave feminism believes in choice, in multiple paths to feminist empowerment.[20]

Adds *Smallville* co-creator and executive producer Alfred Gough, "Today's women can be strong and sexy and they don't have to apologize for it."[21] This is what Kara tries to tell Clark as he begs her to cover up her bikini; if she wants to be a gender-clichéd beauty queen as he was an equally stereotyped quarterback, that is her choice.

Nonetheless, Clark soon acknowledges that though she does things differently from him, she is just as skilled, and they grow into a more balanced relationship. When he is downed by Kryptonite in several episodes, she shoots it from a distance with heat vision, providing a wiser, more calculating solution to the problem. Of course, like the other women of Clark's life, she believes in him with all her heart. In season ten's "Supergirl," she explains that while Clark doubts himself, her own faith in him is "pure" and unwavering, so she can fight the darkness but he cannot. As such, she temporarily takes over his role as Earth's protector.

Kara's Shadows

Through her first and only complete season, Kara offers herself to Brainiac to save Lana and resolves to kill her evil father to save Clark. As she faces down these murderous patriarchs as Lana does the Luthors, Kara grows stronger and wiser through the journey until she finally chooses her own path. Taken over by Brainiac, she appears to still be Kara, just an overprotective, violent version. Chloe points out in "Arctic" that the power to kill has always been part of Kara, as most Kryptonians have ultimately proved themselves cold-blooded murderers. Brainiac makes Kara tap that side of herself, which "good Kara" never explores. Possessed Kara teams up with Lex, as the good Kara wanted to do when she had amnesia earlier in the season. When she is in an altered state, Kara seemingly feels drawn to the bad boy rather than the good one (Clark).

Rediscovered in the Phantom Zone during season eight's "Bloodline," Kara valiantly sacrifices herself for the good of humanity, refusing to escape because that will release monsters to attack Earth. While Clark yields to his heart and insists on saving Lois, Kara advises him to consider the big picture, acting as the wiser voice of his conscience. In fact, Clark brings back not only gentle Kara but also the monstrous Faora. Kara banishes this evil matriarch with the Phantom Zone crystal, like the magic mirrors and gems so many fairytale heroines wield. The valiant daughter has returned.

The series' penultimate episode "Prophecy" offers Kara a choice: to be Clark's earthly sidekick forever "risking the future of this planet" or let him face his destiny. She has been seeking the shining silver bow of Orion, allegedly to help Clark, though she admits she has gone off on her own without informing him. A silver bow is a feminine symbol, like those wielded by Artemis or *The Hunger Games*' Katniss Everdeen. As Kara seeks it, she is imprisoned for a time in a withdrawal from the world, like the temporary deaths or comas so many characters face on their journeys. Upon her release, she chooses a new destiny for herself—not Clark and the bow but her own future. Jor-El even admits she is too strong to need him anymore and that her destiny is written in another place and time. She takes the Legion of Super-Heroes ring, another feminine symbol like the rings of so many fairytales. Grasping it, she goes to find her own people and lost Kandor. She transcends her role as Clark's sidekick to seek her own destiny, developing into *Smallville*'s first heroine to be more than a partner for its hero. She, among all of Clark's associates, finds a quest that is truly hers.

Conclusion

Kara is Clark's link to Jor-El, Chloe his eyes on camera, and Lois the journalist who improves his public image. All of them, even Lana on her wedding day to Lex, consider protecting Clark to be their greatest mission. The series' three main female characters—Lana, Chloe, and Lois—fall in love with Clark at some point and the three female leads that do not—Martha, Kara, and Tess—still prioritize him as their last remaining family member and/or hope for humanity's future.[22] Lois begins as a warrior maiden and equal partner for the hero, but she soon fades into the damsel to Clark's "knight in shining armor."[23] Chloe and Kara are Clark's guardian angels, watching over him on his quest, but through it all, Clark is undoubtedly the hero of *Smallville*'s tale. Whether it be Lana remaking her entire body to be Clark's partner or Chloe admitting that her marriage to Oliver is second to her mission, the series' female characters arrange their lives around one central figure: the man who will be Superman.

Notes

1. Joseph Campbell, *The Hero with a Thousand Faces* (Princeton: Princeton University Press, 1973), 8.
2. Carl Jung, *Collected Works, Volume 11: Psychology and Religion: West and East*, ed. Herbert Read and Gerhard Adler, trans. R. F.C. Hull (Princeton: Princeton University Press, 1968), 25.
3. Valerie Estelle Frankel, *From Girl to Goddess: The Heroine's Journey in Myth and Legend* (Jefferson, NC: McFarland, 2010), 134.
4. Jung, *Psychology and Religion: West and East*, 131.
5. Clarissa Pinkola Estés, *Women Who Run with the Wolves* (New York: Ballantine, 1992), 50.
6. "Feminism," *Encyclopedia of Comic Books and Graphic Novels Volume 1*, ed. M. Keith Booker (Santa Barbara: Greenwood, 2010), 261.
7. "In the Director's Chair: Behind the Scenes and Calling the Shots with Allison Mack," *Smallville: The Complete Eighth Season*, Warner Home Video, 2009, DVD feature.
8. "In the Director's Chair."
9. Frankel, *From Girl to Goddess*, 176.
10. Estés, *Women Who Run with the Wolves*, 44.
11. Matt Mitovich, "*Smallville*'s Allison Mack Part 2: Here Comes the Bride?" *TV Guide*, October 8, 2008, http://www.tvguide.com/News/Allison-Mack-Smallville-20069.aspx.
12. Estés, *Women Who Run with the Wolves*, 237.
13. Frankel, *From Girl to Goddess*, 82.
14. Mitovich, "*Smallville*'s Allison Mack Part 2."
15. Jung, *Psychology and Religion: West and East*, 1.
16. Natalie Abrams, "*Smallville*'s Allison Mack Excited about Directing Again—and a New Coupling," *TV Guide*, February 11, 2010, http://www.tvguide.com/News/Smallville-Allison-Mack-1014927.aspx.
17. Abrams, "*Smallville*'s Allison Mack Excited About Directing Again—and a New Coupling."
18. Christina Radish, "Erica Durance Interview: Smallville," *Collider*, January 30, 2011, http://collider.com/erica-durance-interview-smallville/73448.
19. "Supergirl: The Last Daughter of Krypton," *Smallville: The Complete Seventh Season*, Warner Home Video, 2008, DVD feature.
20. Valerie Estelle Frankel, *Buffy and the Heroine's Journey* (Jefferson, NC: McFarland, 2012), 12.

21. "Supergirl: The Last Daughter of Krypton."
22. Although the series never explores a romantic relationship between Clark and Tess, her infatuation with him, particularly in season eight, is worth noting.
23. "Bloodline," *Smallville*, The CW (November 6, 2008).

Another Way

Tess Mercer as Ethical Hero

PETER MELVILLE

Filmed in Vancouver and Cloverdale, British Columbia, the science fiction series *Smallville* aired for ten seasons on the WB and CW television networks from 2001 to 2011, making it the longest-running televised adaptation of the Superman story.[1] It has been argued that with the seventh-season departure of the series' original creators Alfred Gough and Miles Millar, *Smallville*'s eighth season marked a new beginning in which "the show was forced to reassess its own creative conception and methodology."[2] One important aspect of this shift in creative direction involved the introduction of the character Tess Mercer, who is described in a pre-season promotional interview with the actress who plays her Cassidy Freeman as *Smallville*'s newest "bad *a*, double *s*."[3] Nominally indebted to two female villains from earlier Superman narratives (Mercedes "Mercy" Graves from *Superman: The Animated Series* [1996–2000] and Eve Teschmacher from *Superman: The Movie* [1978]), Tess replaces Lex Luthor—who mysteriously vanishes at the end of season seven—as the new acting CEO of LuthorCorp, the agriculture and biotech conglomerate that Lex previously used to fund and further his unscrupulous, and quite often illegal, underground research activities. In addition to enjoying "unrestricted" access to the vast resources of LuthorCorp, Tess inherits from Lex an abiding fascination with Clark Kent. She begins to suspect that Clark is "the Traveler" mentioned in the Luthor Veritas journals who arrived on Earth during the first meteor shower that devastated the town of Smallville in 1989, and who is prophesied to one day save the planet from annihilation. Convinced that she is meant to help the Traveler achieve this goal, Tess quickly realizes that her known association with Lex and her meteoric rise to power within LuthorCorp and the *Daily Planet* render her untrustworthy in the eyes of Clark and his friends. This obstacle serves only to strengthen Tess's resolve to "help" Clark using an array of means and methods that cannot but appear as less than straightforward or conscionable within the "highly rigid regulatory frame" of *Smallville*'s "moral universe."[4] Executing her designs with "killer eyes and instincts," Tess has inspired film and media studies critic Michael Duffy to compare her to a certain infamous American vice-presidential candidate: "the evolution of [her] character throughout season eight retains an attitude and demeanor that is undoubtedly Palinesque."[5]

As intriguing and peculiar as this observation may be, Tess has received very little in the way of serious scholarly attention. This essay seeks to remedy this situation by questioning the extent to which Tess, particularly in season eight, can be read as an ethical hero despite being cast as one of *Smallville*'s more ruthless and cunning, albeit not altogether unsympathetic, antagonists. More specifically, I aim to consider Tess in light of French philosopher Alain Badiou's call for a "militant figure" capable of "bring[ing] forth the entirely human connection ... between the general idea of rupture, an overturning, and that of a thought-practice that is the rupture's subjective materiality."[6] For Badiou, the archetype of such a figure is Saint Paul, whom he deems an early poet-thinker and practitioner of the "event." Whereas Paul instigates the break from Judaism to Christianity with the "evental" declaration "Christ is risen," Tess can be seen as the Badiouian agent within *Smallville* who attempts to bring forth the rupture that will transform Clark from small-town hero into the savior of life on Earth—the event, in other words, that declares the birth of Superman. In order to achieve this break and convince Clark of his heroic destiny once and for all, Tess believes she must actively facilitate the conditions for Clark's confrontation with Doomsday, the seemingly indestructible Kryptonian creature that dwells within the body of Clark's adversary Davis Bloome. Taking responsibility for the legacy of violence and destruction that her plan entails (a legacy that extends well into the series' ninth season), Tess effectively sacrifices the integrity of her moral character for the good of her cause. She betrays humanity in the name of delivering to the world its greatest hero, a gesture that associates her not only with Badiou's figure of the militant subject, but also with Judas Iscariot whose betrayal of Christ in the New Testament represents for cultural theorist Slavoj Žižek the principal achievement of "one of the few ethical heroes of the Bible."[7] While my intention is to explore these and other parallels between *Smallville* and the philosophy of Badiou and Žižek, I seek also to consider the ideological ambivalences and commitments of a normative popular text that opens the possibility of the militant ethical hero at the same time that it forcibly forecloses that possibility as a legitimate means of initiating change. Tess is after all a villain who, despite insisting in the season nine episode "Sacrifice" (2010) that she "just wanted to save the world," is eventually made to repent and seek redemption for her actions. Even as viewers are persuaded to reinterpret and question Tess's motives at the end of season eight when it is revealed that she has been taking instructions all along from a Kryptonian Orb that uses her to release a clone of the maniacal Major Zod, her role on the series, I argue, nevertheless retains what Žižek calls a "redemptive moment" that preserves the latent core of her ethical heroism.[8]

The Vanishing Sidekick

Why would someone like Clark need the help of someone like Tess? "Save Me," the *Smallville* theme song, offers a good first clue. Written and performed by Remy Zero, the song was likely chosen by the series' producers for the sense of urgency engendered by its refrain, in which the speaker cries out for someone to rescue him using any means possible. The problem, of course, is that Clark cares a great deal about *how* he goes about saving people, whether it is in the context of a single person requiring rescue or the survival of the entire human race. The best example of Clark's concern over heroic procedure occurs in the season eight episode "Legion" (2009) in which a group of superpowered aliens who call themselves "The Legion" visit Clark from the distant future in order to save him from a time-traveling "human supremacist" known as the Persuader. The head of the Legion, a magnetically charged humanoid named Rokk Krinn, determines that the Persuader's primary objective was to locate and destroy Clark's Phantom Zone crystal, which he manages to do before being forcibly returned to the future. Claiming that the Phantom Zone crystal was "supposed to be used [in the future] to extract Brainiac from whomever he possessed," Rokk and his two Legion companions give Clark the distinct impression that Brainiac's survival will entail some form of human apocalypse. In order to save the future from Brainiac, they tell Clark that he is left with "no other choice" but to take the life of Brainiac's host. That host turns out to be none other than Clark's oldest and closest friend, Chloe Sullivan, whose mind was mysteriously infected by Brainiac in the seventh-season finale "Arctic" (2008). Sacrificing Chloe's life to save humanity's future is entirely unacceptable to Clark. He warns the Legion with fierce determination, "Chloe Sullivan doesn't die—hear me?" Suspecting that Clark might be "more legend than Legion," the disappointed Legion members decide to take matters into their own hands and "pull the plug" on Chloe themselves. When Clark meets up with them in the basement of the *Daily Planet*, where the Legion has temporarily incapacitated the Brainiac-empowered Chloe, Clark halts Rokk's attempt to plunge a dagger into Chloe's chest before chastising the Legion leader: "Does your

Legion have any principles? You speak of a code, but if it had anything to do with me, rule number one would be 'Do not kill, ever!'" Clark convinces the Legion to combine their individual powers to extract Brainiac from Chloe's body, which they accomplish without too much fuss in exactly forty-eight seconds. Clark's determination to find "another way" saves the day: Chloe and the future are free from the threat of Brainiac, and the Legion returns to the thirty-first century having learned not to "take the easy way out." Establishing a major thematic preoccupation of season eight, the "Legion" episode implicitly asks whether Clark will be able, in the challenges that lie ahead, to remain devoted to the task of "preserv[ing] life at all costs." Will he be able to continue saving the world, in other words, and keep his hands clean?

Where does Tess fit in with respect to the questions and lessons of "Legion?" Why might Clark need her in his quest to have his superhero cake and eat it too? *Smallville* is clearly committed, ideologically, to preserving the moral integrity of its hero. As Robert McManus and Grace Waitman point out, Clark is meant not only to be physically superior to the humans that surround him but morally superior as well.[9] In order to maintain this fantasy of superhuman moral certitude, the series necessarily surrounds Clark with a number of sidekicks who, as it were, do his dirty work for him. Of these, Chloe and Oliver Queen (Green Arrow) immediately spring to mind, but Tess's unique contributions to this cause are equally important. Before considering Tess's role in detail, it is useful to take a brief look at Chloe since her actions, particularly in the episode "Identity" (2008), set the pattern that both Oliver and Tess will follow. In the opening scene of "Identity," Jimmy Olsen captures Clark's red-and-blue-blurred image on camera as Clark is in the highly accelerated process of saving Lois Lane from an oncoming SUV. When the *Daily Planet* prints the blurry photograph beneath the headline "*FASTER THAN A SPEEDING BULLET,*" Clark decides that as long as his true identity is in no danger of being revealed he will encourage the public's consumption of the myth that builds around Metropolis's out-of-focus crime-fighting super–Samaritan. To be sure, he realizes by the end of the episode that his destiny may well require "more than just secretly saving people," that it might also involve "giv[ing] people hope, someone to believe in." "Identity" takes a much darker turn in its final scene, however, as Chloe enters the poorly lit hospital room of Sebastian Kane, a mind-reading operative of LuthorCorp whose earlier attempt to murder Lois was foiled by one of Clark's perfectly weighted blows to the chest. When Chloe asks Sebastian (who reads thoughts through physical contact with another person) what knowledge he absorbed from Clark's mind during their brief altercation, he smugly tells her, "Let's just say he shouldn't have touched me." Willing to do whatever it takes to prevent Clark's secret identity from falling into the wrong hands, Chloe grabs Sebastian's arm with her bare hand knowing full well that the inhuman quantities of information that her mind has accumulated since being infected by Brainiac will overwhelm and "crash" Sebastian's brain as he begins downloading her thoughts. Her touch immediately sends a violent surge through Sebastian's body. Bright Kryptonite-green swirls flicker in his eyes before his life finally expires. Hospital staff spring into action with calls of Code Blue as Chloe walks calm and collected from what is, in effect, the site of a premeditated murder. The scene comes as something of a shock to viewers used to seeing Chloe as persistent and protective but never as ruthless or coldhearted. The scene nevertheless highlights, in characteristically melodramatic fashion, the extent to which Clark's friends are forced to betray their own beliefs and values to prevent Clark from having to do the same.[10]

Less surprising to viewers, though equally illustrative of the series' commitment to maintaining Clark's moral high ground at the cost of other characters, is Oliver's assassination of Lex in "Requiem" (2009). This murder takes place only seconds after an enraged Clark decides that Lex must die for having spitefully charged Lana Lang's new Kryptonite-infused "nano" skin so that she and Clark may never again come within a few yards of each other. Lana intercepts Clark on his way to kill Lex and warns him, "If you kill him, you will lose so much more than just us being together—Clark, you'll lose yourself." Before Clark can reflect on Lana's comments and make a proper decision on the matter, the truck trailer from which Lex has been remotely carrying out his plans explodes behind them. Evidence in the wreckage suggests that Oliver (who has his own separate reasons for wanting Lex dead) got to Lex first by planting a bomb on the truck. This climactic convergence of motivations and plotlines is constructed as a happy coincidence, since Oliver seems not to have known that his actions likely saved Clark from "losing" himself, as Lana says. As a narrative convenience, however, the event and manner of Lex's murder imply that without the moral sacrifice of others—whether such sacrifice is made directly or indirectly—Clark could not stand as the super-embodiment of the greater good. If Clark represents a form of justice that seeks to "preserve life at all costs," then Chloe's and Oliver's ignoble actions represent a kind of supplement to the ideal, or what Žižek would call the "vanishing mediator" of Clark's moral integrity.[11] That is to say, their actions mediate between necessity (Clark's identity must be kept a secret, Lex "needs to be stopped") and the ideal itself ("preserve life at all costs").[12] What is more, Chloe's and Oliver's acts of murder remain invisible to Clark—they vanish from the periphery of his superhuman vision. He will never know what Chloe did for him in that darkened hospital room, nor does he know (until much later in the season) what happened to Lex. Their actions likewise vanish from history: in "Legion" we are told that the future has "never heard a thing about any Chloe Sullivan";

while in "Requiem" we learn that Lex's death is misattributed by the police and the press to a deranged former employee of Queen Industries by the name of Winslow Schott. Forfeiting their integrity so that Clark does not have to, Chloe and Oliver are the unsung heroes of Clark's legacy—unknown Judases who betray Clark's cause in the name of the cause itself.

Tess and the Event of Davis Bloome

Tess extends this pattern of the sidekick's moral self-sacrifice even as she aims to break it by getting Clark to do his own dirty work. A string of peculiar facts and strange coincidences all involving Clark leads Tess to suspect the truth about his extraordinary powers and extraterrestrial origins quite early in season eight. In "Turbulence" (2009), she even conspires unsuccessfully to force Clark into revealing his powers while saving her from an explosive device that she herself had implanted on the private jet they both shared on their way to a Los Angeles press conference. It is not until the late episode "Eternal" (2009), however, that Tess completely embraces—indeed, becomes *possessed* by—her faith not only in Clark's identity as the Traveler, but also in her own role in the fulfillment of his destiny. While scouring through Lionel Luthor's Veritas journal, Tess is amazed by what she learns about the meteor shower that brought the Traveler to Earth.[13] The journal explains how, in the aftermath of the shower, soldiers working for Lionel had discovered Davis Bloome as a young boy at the base of a smoldering meteor crater and brought him against his will to the Luthor mansion, where Lionel performed a series of tests to determine whether he was the prophesied Traveler. Disappointed by Davis's normal test results, Lionel admits to having swiftly abandoned the boy after being contacted by Martha Kent, who asks for Lionel's help in expediting the adoption of a second boy that she and her husband found on the day of the meteor shower. "I have the wrong boy," Lionel writes in his journal, "but I believe I have found the true Traveler." Reading this account of the meteor shower in a candle-lit room of the Luthor mansion Tess's eyes appear to widen in a close-up shot as she declares with unqualified certainty, "Lionel was too blind to see the truth—there was another."

Certain though she may be, Tess's declaration has some ambiguity to it. After all, she has just learned that Lionel ruthlessly turned his attention and designs from the boy he found to the one found by the Kents. Tess's allusion to the existence of "another," however, refers not to Clark as the true Traveler, but to Davis himself as a kind of other-to-the-Traveler. Not unlike the famous detective Auguste Dupin from Edgar Allan Poe's "The Purloined Letter," Tess is able to discern from the Luthor journals a truth that appears obvious to no one but herself—namely, that "there were two boys that fell to Earth that day." Lionel's blindness, in other words, pertains not to mistaking Davis initially for the Traveler so much as completely overlooking Davis's significance in the Traveler's destiny. Unaware that an extremely volatile and destructive Kryptonian creature lurks just beneath the surface of Davis's human veneer, Lionel leaves the boy frightened and alone to fend for himself on the streets of Metropolis. Tess, on the other hand, reinterprets the entire theory of the Traveler based on her divination of Davis's role in the Veritas prophecy. Drawing on the ancient Kawatche legend of Naman and Sageeth, she comes to believe that Clark and Davis will each play an integral role in the battle between good and evil, and that Davis must be destroyed to prevent evil from consuming the world.[14]

As if taking her cue from Chloe and Oliver, Tess attempts to murder Davis on her own by detonating a bomb planted in the cab of Davis truck. When the attempt fails to kill Davis (primarily because he is, like Clark, essentially indestructible), Tess begins to recognize that her role in the battle for good and evil is not to fight for one side or the other so much as it is to set the stage for the battle itself. Speaking to herself as much as to Davis (who lies injured but steadily recuperating in a bed at the Luthor mansion), Tess proclaims quite religiously:

> Without Judas, Jesus would never have arisen from the dead to come back and face his greatest challenge: saving humankind. There is a savior among us. You are here to betray him.... I finally realized that until you fulfill your destiny, he won't have his great challenge to overcome. He cannot become the world's savior without triumphing over the world's destroyer.

It is no accident that Tess draws explicitly on a Christian discourse here and at other points in season eight. Clark Kent has long been associated with the figure of Christ.[15] More to the point, Tess's realization that Davis is a mythical "other" sent to defeat Clark and destroy the world represents what I would call her "Damascus" moment. Not unlike Saint Paul's blinding vision of God on the road from Jerusalem to Damascus, the moment wholly redefines Tess's sense of self by giving her a new and powerful purpose.[16] In Badiouian terms, her epiphany about Clark and Davis occurs to her as an *event* or *rupture* that she then works subjectively (in spirit as well as in body) to materialize throughout the final episodes of season eight. According to Badiou, an event entails the emergence of a fully unanticipated and "undecidable" situation or problem that forces the subject (or self) to "think the transformation of life."[17] It arises when the subject's range of experience and understanding cannot adequately account for or resolve the situation or problem. What Badiou calls the "transformation of life" begins when the subject embraces the new terms and conditions of the event and remains faithful to an identity altering "evental statement" or "truth" that "declares that an undecidable has been decided."[18]

In Tess's case, the mystery surrounding Davis presents itself as an "undecidable" problem. Jimmy Olsen first draws Tess's attention to Davis when he leaves a rather untidy dossier on her desk at the *Daily Planet* that implicates the outwardly charming Metropolis General paramedic in a string of unsolved murders committed against some of the city's more criminally depraved citizens. On its own, the dossier is hardly capable of triggering an event in the life of someone with as checkered a past as Tess—though it arguably documents a kind of evental truth that Jimmy himself has experienced with respect to Davis.[19] It is, rather, the coincidence of having received Jimmy's dossier within an episode or two of reading about Davis's childhood encounter with the Luthors in the Veritas journal that catalyzes Tess's evental revelation. For this coincidence yields something quite undecidable about Davis: what does it mean that this man, whose discovery as a child on the day of the 1989 meteor shower is footnoted in Lionel's journal as little more than a curious anomaly or misstep in the history of the Veritas prophecy, has been accused in the present of being a prolific and brutally pernicious serial killer? Lionel's interpretation of the Veritas prophecy is wholly incapable of accounting for this disturbing new information about Davis. To recall a phrase from Badiou, Tess is left with little choice but to return to the journals and "think the transformation" of the prophecy itself. What she achieves in this respect is nothing less than radical; for in *deciding*, as Badiou would say, that "there were two boys that fell to Earth" on the day of the meteor shower, Tess not only revises Lionel's theory of the Traveler, she effectively rewrites the origin myth at the heart of every mainstream Superman narrative.

Tess's evental truth, of course, entails more than a revision of Superman's origin story. Indebted, at least in part, to her reading of the Kawatche legend of Naman and Sageeth (which, presumably, she learns about in the Veritas journal as well), Tess's truth speaks also to Davis's fate as the "bearer of darkness" or the "world's destroyer." If we were to follow Badiou's example and reduce this truth to a single evental statement, it might read as follows: "Clark Kent must defeat and destroy Davis Bloome/Doomsday in order to fulfill his destiny as the earth's savior." Tess commits herself fully to this truth. If her actions in the first half of season eight are defined in large part by a quest to find out what happened to Lex, then her focus and drive shift dramatically toward facilitating the confrontation that will bring Clark and Davis into mortal combat. Thus transformed, she embodies Badiou's idea of the "militant" for truth "who seizes—or is seized by—some such intimation of that which lies beyond their present-best powers of attainment or epistemic grasp yet which none the less exerts an intransigent demand upon their will and capacity to seek it out."[20] It may be beyond Tess's "present-best powers" to destroy Davis on her own, but that does not prevent her from dedicating herself to a "truth procedure," as Badiou would say, that actively pursues—or seeks to materialize—the fulfillment of her reimagined Veritas prophecy. In other words, she turns prophecy into practice.[21]

Tess begins her practice of the truth by telling Clark in "Eternal" what she has learned about Davis and his role in Clark's destiny. Clark's response is predictably guarded: "So, you think that Davis Bloome and I are from a different planet? ...Tess, you're reaching." When he criticizes her for having "bought into this strange obsession that the Luthors have for [him]," Tess calmly objects: "I don't think of it as buying in—I think of it as believing." Apart from Clark's skepticism over the Veritas prophecy, the greatest obstacle to the actualization of Tess's truth procedure is Clark's own commitment to preserving life at all cost—his instinct, that is, "never [to] give up on anyone," which even his mother, Martha, predicts in "Nemesis" (2007) might turn out to be Clark's "greatest weakness." Simply put, he will not kill Davis. He believes that "another way" will once again reveal itself and that he will be able to defeat Doomsday without killing Davis in the process. Tess is convinced that it is her destiny to disabuse Clark of this notion. She advises him in "Injustice" (2009) that "the mark of a true hero is somebody who's willing to sacrifice their own personal morality to help keep the world safe." Forgoing his own moral rigidity appears to be the one sacrifice Clark is unwilling to make, but Tess is not the only one on *Smallville* who insists he ought to. Practically every major character agrees with Tess on this point, which makes Clark the exception to the rule. Supported by fellow crime-fighters Black Canary and Impulse (aka Flash), Oliver reminds Clark in "Beast" (2009) that he *needs* to kill Davis since he is "the only one who can." Chloe, as I have noted, tries to kill Davis herself by enabling his attempt at suicide—an incident that betrays the fact that even Davis believes the world would be a safer place without him.[22] Lois and Jimmy, while they are ignorant of Davis's Kryptonian alter ego, certainly believe his killing spree must come to an end. Even the future seems to grow impatient with Clark's reluctance to deal effectively with the threat of Davis, for as Legion member Garth Ranzz tells us in "Legion," Clark will be known to posterity for having done "whatever it took to save the world." The point to be made is that Tess's fidelity to the Veritas prophecy is essentially "universalizable," as Badiou would say, since everyone (with the sole exception of Clark) either believes or is capable of believing that Clark must accept his responsibility as humanity's protector and destroy the monster inside Davis.[23] More than anything, Tess wants Clark to embrace this cause and to stop relying on others to sacrifice their personal morality for him. Following in the footsteps of Chloe and Oliver, she brings to *Smallville*'s eighth season a new militant form of sidekick heroism. Her uncompromising approach to saving the world may strike some viewers as decidedly inconsistent with the "American way" so often associated with traditional Superman narratives, but Tess's most heroic and morally self-sacrificing gesture, I argue, is precisely to refuse to wait for Clark by deliberately luring him into a decisive and violent confrontation with Doomsday. The longer Clark takes to find "another way" that will enable him to defeat Doomsday without killing Davis, the more human lives he places in jeopardy.

The One Who Refuses to Wait

Near the end of "Eternal," Tess enters the barn on the Kent farm and engages Clark in a conversation about destiny that concludes in the following disingenuous manner:

> **Clark:** I'm not some problem to be solved.
> **Tess:** I get it. It's too early. Just know that I'll wait for you, Clark. I'll wait for you to come to me.
> **Clark:** It's going to be a long wait.
> **Tess (*aside*):** It'll be shorter than you think, Kal-El.

More than illustrating her frustration with Clark's disinclination to accept her help, Tess's prickly aside calls to mind the distinction Žižek makes between the two "incompatible" models of the militant revolutionary subject. On the one hand, there are "those who wait for the ripe teleological moment of the final crisis when revolution will explode 'at its own proper time' according to the necessity of the historical evolution." On the other hand, there are "those who are aware that revolution has no 'proper time,' those who perceive the revolutionary chance as something that emerges and has to be seized in the very detours of 'normal' historical development."[24] It is difficult to speak of "normal" progressions of history in a series like *Smallville* that follows the coming-of-age adventures of an extraterrestrial endowed with superhuman abilities. For Žižek, however, the phrase "'normal' historical development" refers not to a mundane sense of realism defined in contrast to the fantastical elements of speculative fiction; rather, it designates an ideological assumption that history is impelled by (socio-economic) forces that are independent of human influence and that predetermine what is attainable at any given moment. Žižek's first group of revolutionaries abides by this notion, while the second believes that history needs more or less to be forced into existence—that the thrust of socio-economic forces present any number of possibilities for the present, each of which requires human action and intervention to be actualized. This second group takes the risk of proclaiming that the time for revolution is always now, that one cannot passively sit by and wait for the revolution to occur of its own accord. Without this extraordinary "Marxist wager," as

Žižek calls it, the "revolutionary moment" will "never arise, and one will never see it."[25]

Tess falls squarely into this second camp of revolutionaries since, unlike Clark, she refuses to wait for the "proper time" to destroy Doomsday/Davis (between whom she makes no observable distinction). Willing to make the kind of gamble of which Žižek speaks, Tess begins manufacturing the conditions for the moment that will force Clark to revolutionize his heroic code of conduct and kill Davis. After Davis flees Metropolis with Chloe, whose constant presence somehow prevents Davis from transforming into Doomsday, Tess uses her position as head of the *Daily Planet* to publish a series of articles that call attention to and connect Davis's multiple acts of murder. Clark reproaches her in "Injustice" for publishing these articles:

> **Clark:** Do you really think spreading panic is responsible journalism? Making Davis Bloome front-page news every day is reckless.
> **Tess:** Reckless? I think reckless is not doing everything in your power to stop him.
> **Clark:** Starting a massive manhunt isn't helping anyone.
> **Tess:** Clark, if you don't want to reveal your true identity, that's fine. But we both know that Davis Bloome isn't a man. He's a beast.
> **Clark:** If he is this beast, then encouraging the police to go after him is dangerous. People will die.
> **Tess:** And when that happens, you'll know where to find him ... so you can finally slay the proverbial dragon.

Not unlike Oliver, who accuses Clark in "Beast" of "wasting" time in lieu of killing Davis "when [he] had the chance," Tess finds Clark's inaction morally reprehensible. By enticing authorities into hunting a monster they are perilously ill equipped to face, she purposely intends to alarm Clark and draw him out of his developed sense of complacency concerning the threat Davis poses to the world. When Clark points out that Chloe, who remains Davis's "hostage," will be further endangered if the police get involved, Tess wryly responds:

> If you're so worried about her getting hurt, why are you fighting my help? Maybe it's because you're actually afraid to find Davis, because the pure and virtuous Clark Kent can't face what he'll have to do—what you're destined to do—when that moment comes. Clark, I'm just making sure you embrace the inevitable.

Clark's reluctance to embrace this inevitability is arguably narcissistic. As Chloe proclaims in "Beast," the "only reason" he refuses to kill Davis is that he does not "want blood on [his] hands." Obstinately protective of his moral integrity, Clark would rather send Davis to the Phantom Zone, which Chloe maintains would be a fate worse than death as it would amount to condemning Davis to "a life of hell for all of eternity." Playing the role of the vanishing mediator once again, Chloe leaves town with Davis so that Clark will not have to make a decision that she feels would fundamentally compromise his morality.

In Chloe's absence, Tess hires a shapeshifter named Eva Greer to assume Chloe's identity and convince Clark that Davis has finally lost control over his inner beast and needs to be hunted and killed before more innocent lives are lost. When she learns through Eva that Clark's latest plan is to use black Kryptonite to separate Davis's human side from its Kryptonian counterpart and to send the latter to the Phantom Zone, Tess steals the black crystal that opens the Phantom Zone portal and has it destroyed so that Clark is left with "no choice but to kill the beast." "Sending him to some otherworldly prison," she tells him in "Injustice," "is not enough." For as Clark knows only too well, Kryptonians have a history of escaping the Phantom Zone. "I'm doing this all for you," she claims; "I understand that if everyone was more like you the world would be a better place, but the truth is that that's out of your hands now—you can't avoid your fate." Visibly unsettled by the force of Tess's resolve, Clark asks her why she is "so determined to see Davis Bloome die." "That's simple," she says: "an entire civilization's survival depends on it."

As I have mentioned, one of the main differences between Clark's and Tess's approaches to Davis is that while Clark believes in the goodness of Davis's human side, Tess refuses to distinguish between Davis the man and Davis the beast. To put it in more theoretical terms, Clark practices what Jan Jagodzinski characterizes as a Levinasian ethics of "'infinite' responsibility to the other," whereas Tess is more properly Žižekian in refusing to ignore the "inhuman core" or "latent monstrosity" of being-human.[26] As Jagodzinski explains, Clark's relation to the Other (be it to Lex in the first seven seasons or Davis in the eighth) is "asymmetrical and nonreciprocal," meaning that "no matter how much someone has hurt [him] or betrayed [him]," as Clark says in "Salvation" (2010), he remains unconditionally devoted to the idea that "at their core everyone is worth saving."[27] Without any expectation of a return for his efforts, he refuses to pass final judgment on or condemn anyone, even when the deep-seated malevolence of a person's disposition seriously threatens the continued existence of human life on Earth. By contrast, Tess is unafraid to make determinate claims (about people, events, etc.,) and act on them. Recall her categorical assessment of Davis: "Davis Bloome isn't a man. He's a beast." The disparity between Clark's reluctance to judge the Other and Tess's sense of certainty (that is, her undying fidelity to the event) resembles the difference Žižek identifies between "weak thought," which is "opposed to all foundationalism," and "strong thought," which "involves a Leap of Faith" in "the truth about the position from which one speaks."[28] I am not suggesting that Clark is without faith or belief. However, his belief in essential goodness is entirely passive (or *weak*), since it leads only to inaction and engenders a sense of complacency about the inhuman/evil foundation of Davis's being (a foundation that is represented in a flashback from "Eternal" as little more than a sentient stream of yellow-green slime that flows menacingly from an alien pod and slowly morphs into the shape of a human boy).

Unlike Tess's firm sense of conviction, which actively transforms her into an instrument of truth, Clark's complacency about Davis comes at the cost of his duty to protect humankind. As Jagodzinski puts it (in Žižekian terms), "[t]he universal love for humanity that Clark professes is only possible through the brutal hatred of an existing exception who is the enemy of such a possibility."[29] Jagodzinski names Lex as the exception throughout seasons one to seven, but the exception that threatens the possibility of universal love in season eight is undoubtedly Davis. Without the imbalance that would be produced by a hatred of this exception, Clark's "infinite" responsibility to the Other remains ineffectual at best and, given the extreme predictions of the Veritas prophecy, *catastrophic* at worst. According to Jagodzinski, "a choice must be made," for "[l]ove emerges out of the universal indifference, while hatred emerges out of universal love."[30] Clark must choose either to love the exception (Davis) at the expense of humanity or to love humanity and hate the exception. He cannot have it both ways.

Yet, Clark is determined to do just that. Sending Doomsday to the Phantom Zone may be impossible without the black crystal, but Clark stubbornly believes he can still separate and save Davis from the beast with the use of black Kryptonite. Chloe is the one who actually thrusts the black Kryptonite into Davis's chest in the season finale "Doomsday" (2009)—once again saving Clark from having to make another tough decision. "[I did] exactly what you wanted," she tells Clark, "I split him—I split him from the beast." Turning his head to listen for signs of Doomsday's carnage with his superhuman hearing, Clark leaves Chloe to engage Doomsday in a fight to the death. The culmination of a five hundred year old prophecy, their "epic" struggle is over in just under a minute: Clark takes a couple of punches to the stomach and one to the face before he lunges at Doomsday and carries him in a single super leap across the night sky and down into a deep tunnel at a LuthorCorp facility rigged with geothermal explosives. An impressive display of pyrotechnics consumes the pair and kills the beast (viewers are later told that Clark managed, inexplicably, to escape the blast.) For a brief moment, it appears as if Clark has successfully found "another way" to save both Davis and the world; but that fantasy quickly dissolves in the next scene when Davis, jealous of Jimmy's romantic reunion with Chloe, mortally stabs Jimmy from behind with the jagged end of a broken pipe. Before Davis can murder Chloe as well, a dying Jimmy tackles Davis sending him into a table on which lies a crowbar that impales Davis through the chest and kills him. Clark, it seems, was dead wrong about Davis's human side: as Davis tells Chloe in his final fit of murderous rage, without the beast "there is nothing left to save." Wicked to the core, Davis the man and Davis the beast are, as Tess had intuited, one and the same. Without Doomsday, he is a monstrous shell of a human being. The whole encounter between Davis and Jimmy only confirms Oliver's warning to Clark earlier in "Doomsday," "You never wanted to admit it, but there is a darker side to humanity." Clark's inability to see this dark side (first in Lex, then in Davis, and later in Zod) is one of his deepest and most tragic flaws. Until he "fearlessly takes into account the latent monstrosity of being-human," Clark's morally rigid brand of heroism will continue invariably to rely on the moral self-sacrifice of people like Oliver, Chloe, Jimmy, and of course Tess.[31]

Smallville's Redemptive Moment

The obvious objection to my argument about Tess's ethical heroism would be to point out the following three problems with her character: (1) she is the perpetrator of several evil deeds, including, but not limited to, murder; (2) her actions in season eight appear to have been externally guided by instructions given to her by the Kryptonian Orb that releases Zod in the final moments of the season finale; and (3) she actively seeks redemption for her actions in seasons nine and ten. In response to such objections, I would first raise an equally obvious point—that my argument has run willingly against the grain of any "preferred reading" of Tess's character that would be more or less endorsed by *Smallville*'s writers and producers.[32] While some of Tess's actions in season eight are decidedly indefensible (particularly the execution of her own team members Livewire and Eva Greer), her approach to the problem of Davis/Doomsday does raise a challenging alternative to Clark's ethical commitment to preserving life at all costs—an alternative that is neither easily nor convincingly refuted in the season finale. As I have said, Tess is right about Davis being monstrous to the core. It is not until season nine's "Rabid" (2009) that Clark will admit as much (not to Tess, but to Oliver): "I should have gotten rid of Davis instead of believing in him." Furthermore, rather than discrediting her motivations and unwavering faith in the Veritas prophecy, the finale's attempt to rewrite Tess's character as a mere pawn in an elaborate Kryptonian plot to regenerate a clone of Major Zod strikes one as little more than an ill-conceived afterthought chiefly intended to bridge season eight's Doomsday storyline and the otherwise unrelated Kandorian plot arc of season nine. To be sure, this startling and quite radical re-inscription of Tess's true purpose in season eight calls to mind a point about televised serial dramas that Benjamin Lefebvre makes in his article on the hit Canadian series *Degrassi: The Next Generation*: that in such serials the ever-present tension between the architecture of continuing story arcs and the narrative demands of individual episodes or smaller, self-contained plotlines can produce "incongruities" or "gaps" in a character's disposition and behavior.[33] To put it more plainly, season eight's portrayal of Tess Mercer is *in the end* conspicuously inconsistent. I would go so far as to say that the series openly betrays Tess in the closing moments of the season finale by recasting her not as an active militant in pursuit of truth but as the passive subordinate of an alien agenda. This betrayal continues well into seasons nine and ten where Tess is depicted as a disillusioned follower of Zod whose search for redemption consists largely of securing the approval of more dominant male figures like Oliver and Clark. Beneath this betrayal, however, Tess's ethical heroism throughout season eight—which is to say, her militant dedication to the truth of the Veritas prophecy—survives as the kind of "redemptive moment" that so often "gets lost," as Žižek says, in the wholesale rejection of an ideological failure or "lost cause."[34] My purpose in this essay has been to celebrate this moment by calling attention to the dignity of Tess's cause. At the risk of belaboring a crucial point, Tess is right about Davis. Clark's failure to listen to Tess forces yet another person to do his dirty work for him—Jimmy, who sacrifices his life in the act of killing Davis in Clark's stead. If Tess's faith in her lost cause occasionally leads her to take what Žižek calls "the right steps in the wrong direction," then we nevertheless owe it to her character not to disregard the basic integrity of her ethical commitment to "want[ing] to save the world." We likewise owe it to *Smallville* not to let the events and plotlines of seasons nine and ten eclipse the very difficult and compelling questions raised by season eight's rendering of Tess's alternative ethical vision. For in the end, it is precisely the "redemptive moments" made possible by conflicted characters like Tess that make *Smallville* a series worth watching.

Notes

1. Lincoln Geraghty argues that due to its filming locations in British Columbia *Smallville* is, at least in part, "a Canadian TV text" despite being made by Hollywood studios. "[I]ts fictional locations," he observes, "have become real sites of pilgrimage for its many devoted fans—both North American and international" ("'I Have a Feeling We're Not in Kansas Anymore': Examining *Smallville*'s Canadian Cult Geography," in *The Smallville Chronicles: Critical Essays on the Television Series*, ed. Lincoln Geraghty (Lanham, MD: Scarecrow Press, 2011], 129).

2. Michael S. Duffy, "Sacrifice or Salvation? *Smallville*'s Heroic Survival Amid Changing Television Trends," in *The Smallville Chronicles: Critical Essays on the Television Series*, ed. Lincoln Geraghty (Lanham, MD: Scarecrow Press, 2011), 153–171, 153.

3. The CW Source, "Cassidy Freeman Introduces Tess Mercer to the CW Source," *YouTube*, August 14, 2008, http://www.youtube.com/watch?v=OLzMKsZelo0.

4. Robert M. McManus and Grace R. Waitman, "*Smallville* as a Rhetorical Means of Moral Education," in *The Amazing Transforming Superhero! Essays on the Revision of Characters in Comic Books, Film and Television*, ed. Terrence R. Wandtke (Jefferson, NC: McFarland, 2007), 180.

5. Duffy, "Sacrifice," 159.

6. Alain Badiou, *Saint Paul: The Foundation of Universalism*, trans. Ray Brassier (Stanford: Stanford University Press, 2003), 2.

7. Slavoj Žižek, *The Puppet and the Dwarf: The Perverse Core of Christianity* (Cambridge: Massachusetts Institute of Technology, 2003), 143.

8. Slavoj Žižek, *In Defense of Lost Causes* (London: Verso, 2008), 7.

9. McManus and Waitman, "*Smallville* as a Rhetorical Means of Moral Education," 182.

10. This is not the only time Chloe will attempt to end someone's life for Clark. In "Eternal" (2009), she pulls a lever in a LuthorCorp lab that releases a liquid Kryptonite shower over Davis Bloome even after Clark tries to stop her. The attempt ultimately fails to kill Davis, but when Clark berates Chloe for trying ("there's always another way," he says), she responds: "I wouldn't change what I did ... he could have killed you, Clark. I won't risk the safety of the world because of your code of ethics, because you refuse to stop the things that threaten you."

11. Slavoj Žižek, *For They Know Not What They Do: Enjoyment as a Political Factor* (London: Verso, 2002), 182.

12. Chloe verbally confirms this strategy of mediation in the episode "Persuasion" (2010) from season nine. When Clark asks her why she prevented him from killing Tess while he was under the Kryptonite spell of tainted pixie dust, Chloe tells him: "Because sometimes protecting you means protecting you from yourself. You're someone we all have to believe in. Nothing can compromise that."

13. "Veritas" is the name of the secret society founded by Dr. Virgil Swann (played by actor Christopher Reeve). Consisting of members of various wealthy families, including the Luthors and the parents of Oliver Queen, Veritas believed that it was their vocation not only to identify the Traveler when he came to Earth, but also to shepherd him in his destiny to save the planet from destruction.

14. The Kawatche are a fictional Native American tribe whose ancestry purportedly began with a Kryptonian male who visited Earth over five centuries ago and fell in love with the "mother" of the Kawatche people. Naman and Sageeth are represented pictorially in Kawatche cave drawings as opposing halves of a two-headed monster. According to their legend, Naman will fight to protect the world from Sageeth's attempt to enshroud the world in darkness.

15. As Karin Beeler points out, *Smallville* pays tribute to the Clark-as-Christ-figure tradition in the pilot episode when a high school prank results in Clark being "tied to a cross in a cornfield" ("Televisual Transformations: Myth and Social Issues in *Smallville*, in *The Smallville Chronicles: Critical Essays on the Television Series*, ed. Lincoln Geraghty [Lanham, MD: Scarecrow Press, 2011], 29). Also, after sacrificing himself to save Earth from Zod in the ninth-season finale "Salvation" (2010), Clark falls from the top of a tall building as his body assumes the iconic pose of the crucified Christ.

16. As described in the Book of Acts, Paul (originally Saul of Tarsus) was a Pharisee in Jerusalem who persecuted members of the early Christian church. On the road to Damascus, where he was sent to arrest followers of Christ, he claims to have been struck by a blinding light and to have heard the voice of Jesus, who tells him to change his ways. With a newfound faith in Christ's divinity, Saul is subsequently baptized, rechristened Paul, and dedicates his life to preaching and spreading the story of Christ's life and resurrection.

17. Alain Badiou, "Thinking the Event," in *Philosophy in the Present*, eds. Peter Engelmann, trans. Peter Thomas and Alberto Toscano (Cambridge: Polity Press, 2009), 12.

18. Ibid., 38.

19. After witnessing Davis kill a man in "Turbulence" (2009), Jimmy becomes obsessed with proving that Davis has been murdering people across the city. Insisting that his "mind has never been so clear" about anything, Jimmy makes a series of incriminating discoveries supported by photographic evidence; but his allegations against Davis are casually dismissed by Chloe and others as having originated in the paranoid fantasy of a drug-induced hallucination.

20. Christopher Norris, *Badiou's Being and Event: A Reader's Guide* (London, England: Continuum, 2009), 10.

21. For Badiou, the truth of an event never precedes the subject, but is generated and sustained by the subject's commitment to a "procedure" or "process" through which the truth can be articulated and pursued. As he says in *Saint Paul*, an event's "only 'proof' lies precisely in its having been declared by a subject" (5). It is worth noting at this point that *veritas* is the Latin word for "truth." Thus, to recast my own formulation, Tess turns the *truth* prophecy into a *truth* practice.

22. Before Chloe pulls the lever that will spray him with Kryptonite, Davis pleads with Clark: "I want this to end. I can't live with myself.... You know that you should let me die.... I was sent here to destroy you."

23. Although an eventual truth always "erupts as singular," Badiou insists that its singularity is "universalizable" rather than "identitarian" (*Saint Paul*, 11). It may not be held automatically or universally true by everyone, but neither does it restrict itself to a specific subset or group of people. Structurally democratic, the eventual declaration makes itself immediately available for all to embrace.

24. Slavoj Žižek, "Introduction: Between the Two Revolutions," in *Revolution at the Gates: Žižek on Lenin: The 1917 Writings*, ed. Slavoj Žižek (London: Verso, 2004), 10.

25. Slavob Žižek, "Badiou: Notes from an Ongoing Debate," *International Journal of Žižek Studies* 1.2 (2007): 28–43, 35. Much like the Badiouian event, Žižek's revolutionary moment is "intrinsically subject-involving insofar as [its] discovery, development and promulgation are the business of certain (no matter how few or how many) committed individuals" (Norris, Badiou's Being and Event, 18).

26. Jan Jagodzinski, *Television and Youth Culture: Televised Paranoia* (New York: Palgrave Macmillan, 2008), 192; Žižek, *In Defense of Lost Causes*, 166.

27. Jagodzinski, *Television and Youth Culture*, 192; "Salvation," *Smallville*, The CW (May 14, 2010).

28. Žižek, *In Defense of Lost Causes*, 1, 2.

29. Jagodzinski, *Television and Youth Culture*, 192.

30. Jagodzinski, *Television and Youth Culture*, 192; Slavoj Žižek, "Neighbors and Other Monsters: A Plea for Ethical Violence," in *The Neighbor: Three Inquiries in Political Theology* (Chicago: University of Chicago Press, 2005), 183.

31. Žižek, *In Defense of Lost Causes*, 166.

32. In this respect, my own Badiouian-Žižekian argument is similar in spirit to Jess Batas' provocative, and quite compelling, queer reading of *Smallville*: "The Kryptonite Closet: Silence and Queer Secrecy in *Smallville*," in *The Smallville Chronicles: Critical Essays on the Television Series*, ed. Lincoln Geraghty (Lanham, MD: Scarecrow Press, 2011), 45–63.

33. Benjamin Lefebvre, "Adolescence Through the Looking-Glass: Ideology and the Represented Child in *Degrassi: The Next Generation*," *Canadian Children's Literature* 33.1 (2007): 102–103.

34. Žižek, *In Defense of Lost Causes*, 7.

Girl Friday Power

Chloe Sullivan and the Hacker Sidekicks of Twenty-First Century Teen Television

TARA K. PARMITER

> "Sometimes heroes can't do it all on their own, Chloe—that's why they need sidekicks."—Lois Lane, "Metallo" (2009)

"Ladies, get out your boxing gloves and bustiers," Jennifer Steinhauer proclaims in "Pow! Slam! Thank You, Ma'am," a *New York Times* piece on the proliferation of tough female action stars in the popular media of the early twenty-first century.[1] With Buffy, Xena, and Dark Angel, among others, "slapping, immolating and kickboxing their way through life," Steinhauer sees women and girls charging into a "formerly male-dominated arena: sheer physical prowess." Since the turn of the century, these new heroines have rallied under the banner of girl power and deftly stomped on old stereotypes that relegated women to romantic interests and damsels-in-distress. As Sherrie Inness notes in *Action Chicks: New Images of Tough Women in Popular Culture*, not only have "these tough women heroes" taken on heroic roles formerly reserved for men, but they "do not require men to help them, a shift that removes women from their stereotypical role as men's helpers."[2] These superwomen embrace their roles as leaders in a brave new world, refusing to be the second sex any longer.

Whereas the "action chick" rules with brute force, the "hacker diva" rules with her intellect, her high-tech gadgets, and her incredibly fast typing skills. Perhaps as prominent a pop cultural phenomenon as the physically empowered heroines, female hackers of the turn-of-the-twenty-first century run the gamut from the sexy Acid Burn of *Hackers* (1995) and Trinity of *The Matrix* (1999), to the cute and geeky Willow of *Buffy the Vampire Slayer* (1997–2003) and Mac of *Veronica Mars* (2004–2007), to the Goth and reclusive Lisbeth Salander of Stieg Larsson's *Millennium* novels and films. These hackers provide an alternative view of women's empowerment, focusing less on their ability to whale on their opponents than on their ability to break into computer systems to gather top-secret information.[3] Like the action chicks before them, the hacker divas have also charged into a formerly male-dominated arena, challenging the "almost exclusively white, masculine, and middle-class" stereotype of the hacker that Andrew Ross describes as the "maverick though nerdy cowboy."[4] However, while the action heroines charge once more into the breach, the hacker divas may still be said to hold that "stereotypical role as men's helpers"—in teen television in particular, the hacker is initially more of a helpmate than part of the offensive line, more of a sidekick than a headliner. In terms of roles for young women, then, the hacker occupies a complicated position: she may not be as physically tough as the hero or heroine she serves, but her intellectual capacities remind us that physical prowess is not the only source of power. What does it say about our ideas of gender and heroism, then, that these young women with such advanced intellectual powers are continually relegated to a support staff position in the hero hierarchy?

Smallville (2001–2011) presents one of the best examples of this tension, for while the obvious hero of the series is Clark Kent, the future Superman, his best friend Chloe Sullivan is arguably just as important to Clark's crime-fighting success as his X-ray vision and super speed. What the young Clark provides in brawn, Chloe provides in brains, conducting the online sleuthing that allows her hero to save the day. Clark turns to her for help in episode after episode; indeed, whenever Clark assures someone "We'll figure out who did this," he seems to be using shorthand for "we'll go ask Chloe."[5] In her role first as the editor of the high school newspaper, the *Smallville Torch*, then later as a reporter for the *Daily Planet*, Chloe proves herself an intrepid investigator, always eager to get to the bottom of a mystery and quick to surf the web for data. Later in the series, Chloe provides the technical support for the entire Justice League, joining Clark in virtual battle from her computer terminal. Part Nellie Bly, part Nancy Drew, Chloe has the technological savvy to mark her as a truly twenty-first century heroine, confident and powerful enough to wrestle the keyboard away from the male hackers of the previous generation. Yet, although she seems to be celebrated for her wits and skills, Chloe, like her fellow hacker sidekicks, also represents a twenty-first century return to the Girl Friday of mid-twentieth-century pulp fiction and films, those dependable and proficient assistants to newspapermen and private eyes who supported their heroes from the shadows. By examining Chloe's role as hacker sidekick, I will consider what it might mean to combine the retrograde role of the Girl

Friday with progressive girl power to celebrate a heroine who is not simply an action chick but who exemplifies what I call legitimate Girl Friday Power.

The History of Girl Fridays

Commonly a good girl in contrast to the femme fatale, the Girl Friday of early Hollywood films could be depended on to take care of the boss's problems with efficiency and tact, taking phone calls, setting up appointments, and, very frequently, pining for him from afar. For example, Sam Spade of *The Maltese Falcon* (1941) knows he can rely on his secretary Effie Perrine not only to run the office but to use her "women's intuition" to offer her insights on the case at hand. Compared to the sexy Iva Archer or the seductive Brigid O'Shaughnessy, Effie stands out as smart, efficient, and a little dowdy. When Spade offers her the ambiguous compliment, "You're a good man, sister," we can see that he admires her as part of his office staff, but does not look at her as a woman, or even as an adult.[6] By calling her "sister," Spade suggests that he considers Effie to be like a sibling or, worse, a child, and his compliment thus becomes more patronizing than flattering. Such infantilizing treatment from the boss is common with Girl Friday characters, though that is not surprising considering the use of the word "girl" in their job title. As Mary DiBattista reminds us, the word "girl" used in this context, similar to Spade's use of the word "sister," is an "endearment that suggests both the dream of easy companionableness—a girl is a pal—and a reticence in admitting adult sexual feeling."[7] Girl Fridays, thus, may be framed as loyal and trustworthy companions but they are rarely the romantic leads or the leads in general. Indeed, the Girl Friday is placed in a doubly subservient position, for the name "Friday" comes from Robinson Crusoe's faithful native servant. Not only is she infantilized, then, but like the original Friday, she is there to serve her supposed superior. Not surprisingly, then, Girl Fridays infrequently enter the discussion of empowered female characters, and the femme fatale has garnered far more critical attention.

However, the Girl Friday has long been a more complicated figure than her reputation might suggest, and though at times she is subservient, at other times she can be gleefully subversive. Perhaps the most famous Girl Friday, Hildy Johnson of the 1930s screwball comedy *His Girl Friday*, is not even a true Girl Friday at all, for she works side by side with her ex-husband and newspaper editor, Walter Burns, to land the hot stories of the day. Hildy is an indomitable force in the film and can surpass Walter in snappy banter and hunting down a lead. And yet, even though they are placed on surprisingly equal footing, we still see Hildy working to support Walter, perhaps most notably when the two crack a breaking story and she volunteers to type because she can do it faster. As the typist taking down Walter's dictation, she may help get the story out there for the evening edition, but she cedes some of her power as the independent newspaperwoman, becoming in this moment "his" Girl Friday. Nevertheless, Hildy Johnson provides a hopeful model for the Girl Fridays of today, particularly a fellow female journalist like Chloe. She contributes her information-gathering strengths and her quick wit to the service of the paper, even foregoing marriage and a conventional life in the suburbs to remain in the city and broadcast the news. Though she does report to her editor, we also see that her contributions to the newspaper fulfill her desire to seek out the truth and have her voice heard. Hildy offers the possibility that the Girl Friday can work for her boss and yet still be a heroine.

Chloe as Girl Friday

When considering Chloe as a Girl Friday, we first have to acknowledge that her character develops tremendously over the ten years of the series, so she at times reveals both the strengths and the limitations of this character type.[8] In the early years, despite her seemingly self-confident exterior and her pit bull-like tenacity when it comes to chasing a news story, Chloe fits the traditional Girl Friday stereotype of pining for the man she works for, suggesting that her identity may depend more on her romantic aspirations than her own self-actualization. As Robert M. McManus and Grace R. Waitman note in their examination of the gender roles in *Smallville*, Chloe's "motivation seems to stem only from her feelings for Clark, instead of factors which would allow her to maintain a more independent identity, such as that of an assertive reporter."[9] In particular, her high school years highlight Chloe's unrequited love for Clark, leading sometimes to comic results, as when she drinks Kryptonite-spiked sports drink and becomes Clark's overly-devoted cheerleader in season four's "Devoted" (2004) or when she spies Clark and Lana Lang kissing and in her anger makes a devil's bargain with Lionel Luthor to investigate her best friend in season two's "Exodus" (2003). Whether as the slavish lap dog or the woman scorned, such perspectives on Chloe seem at odds with her otherwise confident demeanor, highlighting the least empowering aspects of the Girl Friday character.

Even when Chloe finds romance with Jimmy Olsen and Oliver Queen in the second half of *Smallville*'s run, the series' writers still relentlessly hold on to the possibility that Chloe still has not left her feelings for Clark behind, thus perpetuating the view that Chloe is driven more by her love for Clark than by her personal aspirations. When Brainiac lets loose a computer virus that almost brings the world to its knees in the season five finale "Vessel" (2006), Chloe gives Clark an impetuous goodbye kiss. Later, in season six's "Crimson" (2007), when Clark crashes Lex Luthor and Lana's engagement party under the influence of red Kryptonite, Jimmy cannot understand why Chloe would excuse his erratic behavior unless she still loved him. Finally, in season nine's "Escape" (2010) when Silver Banshee possesses Chloe at a remote bed and breakfast, Chloe ambushes Clark in the shower, taking the opportunity to "stare at that farmer's tan in all its glory." Since the Superman mythology tells us that Lana is Clark's high school sweetheart and Lois Lane is his eventual soul mate, Chloe's continued crush on Clark could not lead to romantic involvement without serious revision to the canon. Indeed, some of Chloe's ardent fans did hope to rewrite that history: so in love with Chloe, they created the "Chlois Theory," which proposed that Chloe Sullivan would eventually change her name to Lois Lane and claim her rightful place as Clark's true love.[10] Season ten's high school reunion episode "Homecoming" (2010) nods at those adoring fans when an ex-classmate tactlessly gushes to Lois, "I always thought [Clark] and Chloe were meant for each other—they had that whole best-friend-with-the-hope-of-more thing." Despite Chloe and her fans' wishes, however, Clark's feelings for her are rarely more than platonic, and the lasting focus on her unrequited love suggests that even though the *Smallville* writers let Chloe mature over the course of the series, they, too, have a hard time giving up that lovelorn storyline.

Besides having an ongoing crush on Clark, Chloe literally fits the role of Girl Friday by helping him solve the mysteries he faces each week, and in this arena she has more opportunity to shine. From the pilot episode (2001) when she first introduces Clark to the "Wall of Weird," a bulletin board plastered with articles about *Smallville*'s own X-Files, Chloe is presented as Clark's most valuable resource as he researches various meteor-infected foes. She has a surprising access to information for a high school student, not only from the Internet and newspaper archives but also from a lengthy network of contacts, including her "guy" at the coroner's office and her "bio-chem buddy" at Metropolis University. Even Lois, who eventually rises to the role as the superior investigative reporter in the series, cannot compare with Chloe when it comes to online research; as Chloe says to Lois with a grin in "Arrow" (2006), "watching you bumble through our database is like watching Clark try and dance." Lois is more of a hybrid between the action chick and the intrepid reporter: She goes on assignment into the field and seeks her information in person, often having to kickbox her way to safety once she finds her lead. Chloe, by contrast, does her research from the computer terminal; indeed, one of the most frequently recurrent images from the early seasons reveals Clark standing behind Chloe, looking over her shoulder at the data she has called up on the screen.

Though she is clearly researching the information to help Clark solve the mystery of the week, that repeated image of Clark standing behind her suggests that in the cybersphere, Clark is actually the sidekick.

Chloe as Super-Hacker

As she says in "Fanatic" (2005), Chloe may be proficient at letting her "fingers do the walking" when she searches for general information online, but it is her hacking skills that make her an unparalleled asset to Clark's clandestine crime fighting. Though the term "hacker" often contains negative connotations, particularly with images of nefarious individuals using their techno-savvy to release computer viruses or steal our identities, the term originally referred to computer aficionados whose main goal was not to destroy but to learn. As Steven Levy explains, the "hacker ethic" honors curiosity and free access to information; according to Levy, hackers believe that "anything which might teach you something about the way the world works—should be unlimited and total."[11] Chloe embraces this quest for knowledge, using her hacking talents to support Clark in what he calls in "Drone" (2002) his fight for "truth, justice ... and some other stuff." In contrast to the Girl Friday, a hacker is usually seen as a more rebellious, independent figure. So important is her computer prowess that the *Smallville* directors regularly represent Chloe with a close-up of her hands, composed like a frame from a comic book. Whether she is typing at lightning speed or pausing with her finger on the mouse, trying to decide whether to save or delete a piece of the Clark Kent puzzle, these close-ups are a synecdoche for Chloe herself. In a series that obsesses over superhuman strength and augmented bodies, the repeated images of Chloe's hands remind us that although she is Clark's Girl Friday, she too has extraordinary abilities.

Even as the hacker sidekick, though, Chloe still has moments when she feels Clark does not fully appreciate what she offers as his Girl Friday. For example, when Clark is without his powers in season five's "Mortal" (2005), Chloe navigates him through a high-stakes break-in at a LuthorCorp lab using her laptop and an arsenal of supplies obtained, naturally, through eBay. Clark is so impressed by her accomplishments that he muses, "Who needs superpowers with you around?" What he overlooks here is that Chloe's hacking skills *are* a superpower: as she playfully scolds him in season six's "Sneeze" (2006), "I'm a decent hacker, but I'm not a miracle worker. You know, you really don't give me credit for all this stuff—it's not easy." Earlier in the series, Chloe would not have been so patient. Though she relishes the investigations, she does not learn until part way through the fourth season that she is the sidekick to a *super*-hero, so at times she resents his reliance on her computing skills. In a particularly angry moment in season two's "Rush" (2003), Chloe yells at Clark, "You don't have any real feelings for me, do you Clark? Every time we hang out it's just to get answers. Chloe, why don't you research this, or Chloe, why don't you look up that? I'm nothing more to you than your own personal search engine, and I'm sick of it." Chloe raises an important issue for Clark here: what is more important to him, the information needed to solve the case, or the person who procures that information? Just like Sam Spade, whose back-handed compliment "You're a good man, sister" simultaneously strips his Girl Friday of her womanhood and adulthood, Clark too often treats Chloe as an information aggregator rather than as a friend.

In her occasional dissatisfaction with her sidekick status, Chloe is closely aligned with Willow of *Buffy the Vampire Slayer*, who similarly fills a Girl Friday–like position in the Buffyverse. Although Willow brings her incredible intelligence and technical prowess to Buffy's aid, her computer skills are not the privileged power on the series—Buffy's mystical powers are. Willow may be uncommonly smart and may always have the privileged seat at the computer terminal, but when compared to Buffy, Faith, Oz, Angel, and others with supernatural powers, Willow's skills seem more clerical. Perhaps Willow turns to witchcraft, then, to become more of a superheroine herself and to escape her sidekick status. As much as she longs to help, Willow chafes at being valued for her computer skills alone: for example, when Buffy advises Willow not to use her magical powers in season four's "Fear, Itself" (1999), Willow snaps back at her, "I'm not your sidekick," challenging Buffy's insistence on always telling the others what to do. Later, when Willow transforms into Dark Willow in season six, she unleashes her rage at Buffy for all those years of being relegated to the support staff. As Willow and Buffy square off to fight to the death in "Two to Go" (2002), Willow sneers, "This is a huge deal for me! Six years as a side man, and now I get to be the Slayer." In her desire to be the "slayer" rather than the hacker or the sidekick, Willow seems to be turning her back on her former, brainy self. The intellectual curiosity that spurred her hacking still defines her identity as a witch, but her taunt suggests that Willow sees "slaying" as a superior role.

By transforming Willow into a superheroine—in the series finale "Chosen" (2003) she is even referred to as a "goddess"—*Buffy* suggests that hacking is merely a mortal power, secondary to the mystical and physical powers of slayers, witches, werewolves, and vampires. *Smallville* similarly equates superpowers with super *physical* powers, and even attempts a Willow-like transformation for Chloe in season six. The former meteor freak hunter discovers that she too has been infected by a concentration of Kryptonite in her heart. Unlike other denizens of Smallville whose meteor powers make them a threat to others, Chloe discovers that her meteor power allows her to heal others, even from the brink of death. Not only is her power an extension of her Girl Friday caring and loyalty, but with its overtones of resurrecting the dead it also suggests a Christ-like ability. As Sarah R. Kozloff argues, the Man of Steel has long been associated with the Son of God.[12] The pilot episode of *Smallville* even makes this link explicit with its imagery of Clark tied up as a school prank in the classic crucifixion pose. By granting Chloe this particular meteor power, then, the *Smallville* writers implicitly connect Chloe with Clark as a superhero. Nevertheless, while this power seems to elevate Chloe to Clark's level, it only does so by privileging physical powers over mental capabilities. Empowered by her meteor-enhanced heart, Chloe loses her true agency. Granted, she can decide whom she wants to heal, but she now relies on her body simply as a mechanism for giving life, in effect casting her as a maternal surrogate to those she resurrects. Thankfully for Chloe's intellect, the meteor power story line is short lived, perhaps because Chloe's more interesting powers have always been the powers of her mind.

Chloe as Superheroine

Indeed, one reason why Chloe does not need to become a meteor-infected Lady Lazarus to be considered a heroine is that *Smallville* presents her as uncommonly smart and talented from the beginning of the series. Despite the limitations of her Girl Friday position—the lovelorn moping, the lonely nights at the computer terminal—we could make a strong argument for seeing Chloe as a heroine of equal importance to the series as Clark. The official narrative recognizes Clark as the hero and Chloe as the sidekick, and while a sidekick is inherently not the hero, what makes Chloe a superheroine in her own rights is her unparalleled access to knowledge.[13] Even though the series centers on Clark Kent's journey to becoming Superman and thus would seemingly be about the development of his powers, thematically the series is much more interested in intelligence gathering. All the characters are obsessed with concealing secrets, trusting others with those secrets, or discovering the secrets from those trying to hide them. Martha and Jonathan Kent strive to hide Clark's extraordinary powers from a world that would either exploit or fear them; Lionel and Lex Luthor and Tess Mercer strive to learn Clark's secret identity to capitalize on his unearthly powers; Lana Lang strives to learn Clark's secret to feel closer to the man she loves; Lois Lane and Jimmy Olsen as investigative reporters strive to solve the mystery of Metropolis's Red-Blue Blur; and Clark of course carries the largest burden of all, concealing not only his alien ancestry but his nagging guilt that the meteor shower that brought him to Earth also caused the environmental contamination that spawned the series' meteor freaks. Chloe, too, holds secrets—about her love for Clark, about her investigations into her friends and foes, about her fears of becoming a meteor freak or winding up in an asylum as her mother did; however, more than the other characters Chloe has the greatest capacity for uncovering secrets. Sometimes the scoop lands in her lap, most notably when Clark's ex-girlfriend Alicia Baker outs him in "Pariah" (2005), staging an accident so Chloe can witness his super strength and speed. However, even though Chloe cannot "catch a car like it was a beach ball" as Clark can, her proficiency at the computer keyboard arguably grants her powers of equal importance.[14]

Much of Chloe's incredible power derives from the hacker ethic with its celebration of curiosity and open access to information. From the pilot episode, Chloe is characterized by her hunger for the truth, a trait portrayed as both a character flaw and strength. "Since when is curiosity a crime?" she asks innocently in "Extinction" (2003), among other times, insisting that curiosity is the healthy inspiration of all new knowledge. At other points, like in "Suspect" (2003), she openly admits that "usually when I do this people get really mad at me," acknowledging that in her eagerness to search for the truth, she has the tendency to trample into other people's personal space. As Lex chides her in season three's "Velocity" (2004), "Privacy laws don't seem to faze you much, do they?" Whether defying laws or compromising friendships or even risking her life, Chloe lets nothing stand in her way when seeking information. Lois goes so far as to equate Chloe with the search for truth, telling her in "Pariah," "Chloe, you're a reporter. You investigate and expose. *That's who you are*" (emphasis mine). But Chloe does not strictly expose; as the series progresses and the secrets she uncovers get bigger and bigger, she often conceals what she learns, recognizing that sometimes you have more leverage when you hold on to your information. As Tess puts it in season nine's "Escape," "Information is also power," and that truism may be both one of the most prominent themes of *Smallville* and one of the most compelling reasons for seeing Chloe as a heroine on par with Clark.

Chloe's curiosity drives *The Chloe Chronicles*, a series of short webisodes posted first on AOL and later distributed as DVD extras for seasons two and three. Filmed using a handheld camera in the style of amateur investigative reports, each *Chronicle* features Chloe delving deeper into the back-stories of a *Smallville* episode. Rayna Denison sees these supplementary stories as more than just ancillary material, suggesting that they fill an important gap in the larger *Smallville* narrative. Alfred Gough, one of the creators of *Smallville*, described the series as focusing on the four pillars of "Heart. Hero. Mystery. Family." and Denison argues that "whereas the plots of *Smallville* usually revolve around the romance, melodrama, and action genres," *The Chloe Chronicles* emphasize "the mystery part of the equation."[15] Besides highlighting the mystery element, *The Chloe Chronicles* gives Chloe the opportunity to flex her investigative muscles at a time in the series when her *Smallville* plotlines focus more on her unrequited love. Actress Allison Mack relished this side project, finding it a relief for Chloe to be "[d]igging into stuff that didn't belong and being her intelligent, snarky self. ...It was cool to do that again," Mack explained, "because that was sort of lost [in the second season]. Chloe was crying all the time. I was just always in tears and that got old. My whole storyline was all about Chloe being pathetic and I was like 'C'mon guys, she's stronger than this.'"[16] Rejecting Chloe's Girl Friday pining, Mack celebrates Chloe's stronger Girl Friday qualities, those that emphasize her "intelligent, snarky self." Although *The Chloe Chronicles* can be overlooked as DVD extras, despite Denison's claims to the contrary, they are notable not only for giving Chloe top-billing but also for highlighting how valuable Chloe's information gathering is to the solving of *Smallville*'s mysteries.

More importantly, *The Chloe Chronicles* reveal one of the ways that the *Smallville* creators implicitly connect Chloe with Clark throughout the series, not just as the Girl Friday and her hero but also as two characters with similarly extraordinary powers. Stan Beeler notes that early in *Smallville* Chloe is "the mirror image of Clark in the emotional sense: she desires a man who does not seem to care for her, and her unrequited love causes a host of personal problems."[17] However, we see far more parallels between Chloe and Clark than their troubled love lives. In the introductory episode of *The Chloe Chronicles* (2003), for example, we hear Chloe not only making the case for herself as a heroine, but also taking on that mantle in the assumed absence of any other competing hero. Breaking the fourth wall and speaking directly to her audience, Chloe informs us that "the one thing the meteor shower did not grace upon our humble burg was a superhero, so in his absence you're left with me, one girl, on a mission, who refuses to leave any rock, especially if it's from outer space, unturned. I'm Chloe Sullivan, and I'm here to tell you the truth."[18] The coy reference to the lack of a superhero could be seen as dramatic irony, a joke that the audience recognizes but Chloe does not because she has yet to learn Clark's secret. What it also suggests, however, is that "telling the truth" itself is worthy of superhero status, even if the truth teller is merely "one girl."

These parallels occur frequently in the series, linking Chloe in crucial ways to *Smallville*'s official hero. Like Clark, for example, Chloe has a secret identity to conceal. Early in the series, that secret identity is tied to her role as the lovelorn Girl Friday. As she confesses to Clark in season two's "Fever" (2003) as he lies uncharacteristically unconscious, "I'm not who you think I am. In fact, my disguise is so thin I'm surprised you haven't seen right through me. I'm the girl of your dreams masquerading as your best friend." Although Chloe's words spring from years of unrequited longing, the language of this confession suggests that Chloe is more than a lovesick teen; the emphasis on disguises and masquerading, on living a double life, could easily have been spoken by Clark. *Smallville* writers regularly play such word games, giving a knowing wink to the viewers who know the Superman mythology. In a classic example from the pilot episode, for instance, Lana sees Clark reading Nietzsche and asks if "he's man or Superman." Later in season nine's "Kandor" (2009) when Clark confesses that he had kissed Lois, Chloe quips, "I'm not surprised, Clark—you've had feelings for Lois since, like, the 1930s." But these examples refer to specifics of the mythology: Clark *is* Superman, and he *has* loved Lois since the comic first appeared in the 1930s. As one of the few primary characters specifically created for *Smallville*, Chloe does not have an extensive back history for the writers to refer to, so it is telling that they chose to borrow Clark's back history for Chloe's allusions.

Even as Chloe's secret identity evolves from lovelorn teen to phenomenal super hacker, we still see crossovers in the language used to describe her and Clark. In the season seven episode "Sleeper" (2008), for example, a comic exchange between Jimmy and Clark suggests just how much Chloe has in common with the series' hero. When the government asks Jimmy to spy on Chloe, believing her to be part of a terrorist organization (their misinterpretation of the Justice League), Jimmy turns to Clark for advice. The government agents had informed Jimmy about some of Chloe's illicit activities, such as "compromis[ing] government-run power grids, cellular towers, DMV records"—in that very episode she was attempting to hack into a NASA satellite to search for signs of Kara/Supergirl and Brainiac in outer space—and Jimmy was clearly nervous about the extent of his girlfriend's powers. The humor in his exchange with Clark, though, comes from Clark's assumption that Jimmy is talking about Clark and Clark's powers. When Jimmy mentions a friend keeping a "really, really big secret," a friend with "crazy skills," Clark immediately worries that he will have a lot of explaining to do. Only when Jimmy utters the feminine pronoun—"The person that I thought I knew isn't who she says she is"—can Clark regain his composure. The joke works because of the audience's privileged position; *we* know that Jimmy could be describing either Chloe or Clark, but Jimmy does not. However, it is a telling moment for Clark, for when he repeats "She?" part in relief and part in surprise, we see that he is remembering he is not the only one with a tremendous secret or tremendous powers. Without the word "she" Jimmy's comments would easily be mistaken as meaning Clark, and in this subtle emphasis on the gendered pronoun Clark is reminded to consider Chloe a superheroine as well.

Chloe's superheroine status becomes explicit in the final seasons of the series, particularly as she first embraces and then walks away from her role as "Watchtower," her code name as the computer guru and surveillance expert of the Justice League. The name Watchtower, first used in season six's "Justice" (2007), has a distinctly Orwellian tone, suggesting Chloe's "Big Sister"-like abilities to survey the world around her through her vast array of computer monitors. Becoming Watchtower is depicted as a major personal development for Chloe, who floundered in seasons seven and eight, getting fired from the *Daily Planet* and trying to cover Lana's position at the Isis Foundation, a support center for the meteor infected. By returning to her seat at the computer terminal, Chloe separates herself from the jobs held by Clark's two love interests, forging an identity that is neither the Lois-type she filled in high school, a role that became redundant once Lois actually joined the cast, nor the Lana wannabe. As Watchtower, Chloe takes her role as Clark's Girl Friday to new heights: not only does she gather information from any source imaginable, but she also guides Clark's day-to-day hero work, hacking into the police call center to send Clark directly to the scenes of crime. Like the operators of *The Matrix*—expert hackers who stay on the ship and monitor the avatars who have entered the computer world—Chloe both serves her hero and directs him, using her knowledge to ensure the success of their missions.

As Watchtower, then, she gains a new level of control. While she still uses her computers and her hacking skills in the service of Clark and the Justice League, she is also recognized as one of their members. This promotion is highlighted in season nine's "Checkmate" (2010) when the titular covert government organization captures Green Arrow and then pursues Clark. The surprise, however, is that the superheroes are not the true target—Chloe is, or Chloe as Watchtower, for Checkmate desperately wants the information Chloe has amassed in Watchtower's database. Checkmate's leader, the White Queen Amanda Waller, clearly recognizes Chloe's worth; as she scolds Clark, "The Blur, he patrols the streets of Metropolis protecting every citizen he can but he lets the most valuable ally fend for herself.... You left your greatest asset vulnerable." Though Waller suggests that Chloe needs protecting, potentially demoting her to a damsel-in-distress, more important is that she acknowledges the centrality of Chloe's information gathering skills to Clark and company's heroic feats.

Exhilarating as her role as Watchtower may be, Chloe also recognizes the limitations of constantly monitoring her computer screens. Catching herself referring to her computer as her "life" in "Leech" (2002), she has to confess, "OK, how pathetic did that just sound?" When she upgrades to dozens of screens and terminals, she is at an even greater risk of confusing the computers for her life. In season nine, "Watchtower" comes to refer not merely to Chloe but to her high-tech lair in downtown Metropolis, and at this point Watchtower becomes both her refuge and her prison, trapping her in the world of machines and distancing her from the world outside. We see this tension revealed in the very design of Watchtower: the exterior shot shows the building rising like a Panoptical tower above the rest of the city, its circular windows peering like giant eyes in the four cardinal directions. Not only do the windows of Watchtower peer out at the people of Metropolis, but also the interior space is filled with a second layer of "windows," a circle of computer screens that allows Chloe to search her massive database, the Internet, or any computer or security camera she chooses to hack into. As the perpetual watcher, though, she rarely gets the chance to act outside of her privileged domain. In typical Chloe-speak, she admits to Clark in season nine's "Hostage" (2010), "I got tangled in my own little World Wide Web and I just lost track of what was important... [I]t's easy to think that having all the information is the same as having all the answers. But I can't be the eye in the sky any more... I want to plug into the real world. Virtual reality bites." It is because of this difference between "information" and "answers" that Chloe steps down from Watchtower. Although she leaves her position as Clark's Girl Friday in leaving Watchtower, Chloe stays true to her hacker ethic in this final career change, insisting that her curiosity cannot be satisfied unless she seeks not simply raw data but answers to the mysteries around her.

The series finale (2011) opens and closes with Chloe at an undetermined point in the future, reading a *Smallville* comic book to a tow-headed tyke with a set of toy bow and arrows, presumably her son with Oliver/Green Arrow. Some might quibble that Chloe seems to have been domesticated, switching from Girl Friday to mom while Clark and Lois remain in the thick of the action. Nevertheless, I see this ending as a logical continuation of Chloe's development: not only is she the one in charge of the narrative, showing again that she is the holder of all the knowledge, but her glance at the toy arrows suggests that she is already nurturing a new generation of superheroes. When Chloe retires from Watchtower, she professes that she wants to pursue her true calling: "finding heroes and helping them reach their true potential." As she explains to Clark in "Fortune" (2011), "in every epic tale, there's always one person who believes in the hero first. Someone who helps inspire them to greatness." The message here is not the clichéd "behind every super hero is a super hacker," but that epic tales need more than just warriors. And this is the essential point, for while it is exciting to see the action chicks punching and kicking their way to equality for women, the hacker divas have just as much a claim to our admiration, particularly because their strength is concentrated in their minds rather than their biceps. While it may be tempting to see the proliferation of tough female heroines as a sign of progress, we do our heroines, and our heroes, a disservice when we favor physical toughness over mental toughness. As Clark is finally forced to confess in "Checkmate," "You may not be saving people from train wrecks or shoot outs, but you are just as much a hero as the rest of us." With this recognition, *Smallville* conflates Girl Friday and girl power, acknowledging what we have known all along: Chloe is a remarkable heroine in her own right.

Conclusion

Chloe's elevation from the lovelorn Girl Friday to the high-tech "information goddess" reveals just how much the *Smallville* writers allowed all their characters to mature and evolve over the course of the series, not just their Kryptonian protagonist.[19] It also reveals how complicated the character of the Girl Friday can be when given a boost of girl power. She may not be the leader of the pack, like a Buffy or a Xena, but she is, as Clark puts it in "Checkmate," no longer on the "sidelines" but "in the middle of the game." As Chloe shows us, Girl Friday Power, with its celebration of knowledge and problem solving, is more collaborative than the physical prowess of the action chicks. Chloe may still work for her hero, but she does so as a valued team member. More important, her powers derive not from a meteor infection or alien ancestry or a mystic birthright but from her own devoted search for answers. In the DVD commentary to the season ten opener "Lazarus" (2010), Mack reflects on what makes Chloe and Oliver such extraordinary figures in a series about extraordinary figures: "I love the fact that we're both, well, we're superheroes but we're superheroes without any special powers, so we're just super, super smart and super, super cunning, and I love that.... We're super humans."[20] Perhaps that is the most important reason for valuing Girl Friday Power: it suggests that "super humans" are not only the ones in "boxing gloves and bustiers" but also those bringing their intelligence to the aid of a team, those who will leave no stone, nor computer keyboard, unturned in their mission to tell us the truth.

Notes

1. Jennifer Steinhauer, "Pow! Slam! Thank You, Ma'am," *New York Times*, November 5, 2000, http://www.nytimes.com/2000/11/05/weekinreview/ideas-trends-pow-slam-thank-you-ma-am.html.

2. Sherrie A. Inness, ed., *Action Chicks: New Images of Tough Women in Popular Culture* (New York: Palgrave Macmillan, 2004), 14.

3. This is not to say, of course, that these female hackers cannot also be action chicks—Trinity of *The Matrix*, for example, probably spends more screen time acrobatically thrashing her opponents than typing at a keyboard. What I will argue, however, is that the hacker divas are primarily recognized for their high tech savvy and thus are celebrated more for their intellects than their physical prowess.

4. Andrew Ross, "Hacking Away at the Counterculture," *Postmodern Culture* 1.1 (1990), paragraph 16.

5. "Crisis," *Smallville*, The WB (March 3, 2004).

6. *The Maltese Falcon*, dir. John Huston, Warner Bros., 1941.

7. Maria DiBattista, *Fast-Talking Dames* (New Haven: Yale University Press, 2001), 277.

8. Interestingly, a Google search for the phrase "Girl Friday" promptly turns up an old fan site devoted to Allison Mack, the actress who portrayed Chloe. This fan saw "Girl Friday" as a positive description for her favorite *Smallville* character, again suggesting that the Girl Friday is a more complicated figure than she's usually given credit for being. See "Girl Friday: A Chloe Sullivan/Allison Mack Worship Site," August 18, 2004, http://www.loony-archivist.com/girlfriday/.

9. Robert M. McManus and Grace R. Waitman, "*Smallville* as a Rhetorical Means of Moral Value Education," in *The Amazing Transforming Superhero! Essays on the Revision of Characters in Comic Books, Film and Television*, ed. Terrence R. Wandtke (Jefferson, NC: McFarland, 2007), Kindle location 2740.

10. "Chlois Theory," *Fanlore*, accessed January 2, 2014, http://fanlore.org/wiki/Chlois_theory.

11. Steven Levy, *Hackers: Heroes of the Computer Revolution* (Garden City, NY: Anchor Press, 1984), 27.

12. Sarah R Kozloff, "Superman as Saviour: Christian Allegory in the *Superman* Movies," *Journal of Popular Film and Television* 9.2 (1981): 78.

13. Chloe is a very popular sidekick: the viewing public loved actress Allison Mack's performance so much that they nominated her for the Teen Choice Award's "Best Sidekick in a TV Series" seven out of ten years of the series. Mack won twice, in 2006 and 2007, corresponding with the years when Chloe first works side by side with Clark in full knowledge of his secret identity.

14. "Arrival," *Smallville*, The WB (September 29, 2005).

15. Rayna Denison, "It's a Bird! It's a Plane! No, It's DVD! *Superman*, *Smallville*, and the Production (of) Melodrama," in *Film and Comic Books*, eds. Ian Gordon, Mark Jancovich, and Matthew P. McAllister (Jackson: University Press of Mississippi, 2007), 172.

16. Tara O'Shea, "The Allison Chronicles," Allison-Mackwww, July 29, 2003, http://allison-mack.com/exclusive2.htm.

17. Stan Beeler, "From Comic Book to *Bildungsroman*: *Smallville*, Narrative, and the Education of a Young Hero," in *The* Smallville *Chronicles: Critical Essays on the Television Series*, ed. Lincoln Geraghty (Lanham, MD: Scarecrow Press, 2011), 19.

18. "Video One," *The Chloe Chronicles, Smallville: The Complete Second Season*, Warner Home Video, 2003, DVD feature.

19. As Stan Beeler suggests, *Smallville* can be seen as a *bildungsroman* for all its primary characters: "*Smallville*, like most contemporary television, is an ensemble production, and it would have been impossible to present Clark Kent's progress to adulthood without paralleling the process with his companions" (Beeler, "From Comic Book to *Bildungsroman*," 22).

20. Commentary on "Lazarus," *Smallville: The Complete Tenth Season*, Warner Home Video, 2011, DVD feature.

PART THREE:
Bodies, Identities and Politics

Rummaging Through the Closet

(Un)Masking the Signified Other in Smallville's First Four Seasons

JONATHAN A. AUSTAD

This essay examines *Smallville*'s intersection between the science fiction and teen drama genres through two primary story arcs: "Meteor Freaks" and "Clark Kent's Journey to Self-Discovery." Both arcs celebrate diversity with their depiction of the signified other. Clark battles both alienation and social acceptance due to his otherness. His differences compound his teen angst, as he struggles to develop and understand his complex identity. Like other teen dramas, Clark labors between social acceptance and rejection, and on his journey to self-discovery, he encounters other people who struggle with similar issues because they too are different. Clark finds people confronting familiar problems such as bullying, sibling rivalry, athletic competition, eating disorders, recreational drugs, steroids, racism, running away, moving to a new school, teen crushes, obsession, sex, teen pregnancy, abuse, mental illness, divorce, death, and suicide. *Smallville* handles these issues with science fiction twists. Like in other sci-fi series, Clark's alien abilities provide him heroic means, but they also distinguish and alienate him from his friends. Clark continually struggles with his desire to reveal and conceal his true identity. Part of his apprehension exists in his uncertainty of who he is and whether his abilities benefit or harm society. Clark's journey to self-understanding allows him to meet several others who also deviate from the established norm and are narrowly defined as "meteor freaks" (those are affected by fragments of Kryptonian meteor rock, or Kryptonite). This essay will illustrate that the journeys of Clark and his fellow Smallville High classmates to cope with their differences serve as a thinly veiled code for social otherness. This exploration will also assert that *Smallville* urges for a more complicated understanding of diversity.

Normality and Abnormality in *Smallville*'s Early Years

Seasons one and two of *Smallville* suggest that the meteor freaks are harmful, placing social stability in jeopardy. Meteor freaks during these two seasons generally end up in an asylum, prison, or dead. Seasons three and four complicate the myopic distinctions of otherness presented in the first two years, whereby meteor freaks do not always harm people. Although most of the inhabitants of Smallville still reject meteor infectees because of their differences, the series reveals that labels such as "normal" or "freak" are too simplistic. Binary distinctions between normal and abnormal, same and other, and mainstream and different are limited, and require a more complex treatment of diversity: one of acceptance, appreciation, and celebration. This directly correlates with Clark's journey to self-discovery. His interactions with meteor freaks allow him to appreciate his abilities and embrace his (and others') differences. *Smallville* cleverly constructs then deconstructs simplistic definitions of otherness to promote diversity. This essay highlights that the story arc "Clark's Journey to Self-Discovery" compliments that of "Meteor Freaks" because Clark's contact with meteor infectees helps him to value diversity.

Throughout *Smallville*'s first four seasons, meteor rocks cast an ominous shadow over the town, and threaten the lives of its inhabitants. Careful analysis of the pilot episode (2001) demonstrates the series' initial coding of meteors as dangerous and destructive to the town's homogeny. Smallville is a utopian town in Middle America. Red and yellow colors unify the town as Jonathan and Martha Kent enter the local flower shop to buy "uncomplicated" tulips. This representation of Smallville evokes nostalgia for the halcyon, simple days of yesteryear. However, this sequence also presents very little racial, ethnic, or economic diversity. White, middle-class, and seemingly heterosexual individuals and families dominate the location. The incoming meteor shower and Clark's arrival therefore destroy *Smallville*'s harmony and hegemony. The pilot, which debuted on October 11, 2001, offers a meteor shower wreaking havoc on the town in what is eerily reminiscent of the 9/11 attacks. The meteors first destroy the cornfield, signifying the destruction of the quintessential source of Midwestern American income. They then hit the town, decimating shops and cars as people helplessly run for cover in the streets. A close-up of young Lana Lang's parents waving to her across the street before a meteor kills them represents the dissolution of the traditional family and, with it, the town's harmony and simplicity. The third strike hits the town's sign, destroying the symbolic essence of Smallville. The sequence culminates with a low-angle crane shot of Jonathan and Martha standing in a cornfield, signaling their newfound powerlessness to foreign invaders. Smallville lies in shambles after the meteors have purged the town of its congenial ways.

Twelve years have passed in the next scene. The town's sign now ironically celebrates what caused the change: "Meteor capital of the world!" High school student Chloe Sullivan is the first to address the town's dystopian state: "Strange things happen in this leafy little hamlet." Her "Wall of Weird" is a shrine for all the curious behaviors and activity attributed to the meteor shower. She tells Clark about the Wall, "It started out as a scrapbook, and it just sort of mutated.... I call it the Wall of Weird. It's every strange, bizarre, and unexplained event that has happened in Smallville since the meteor shower. That's when it all began. The town went schizo." Although Smallville rebuilt and reestablished harmony after the incident, the meteor freaks intermittently disrupt that harmony with chaos and danger. The question presented throughout the first four seasons is whether Smallville will return to its utopian past or move to a dystopian future.

Season four's "Pariah" (2005) further stresses the delicate balance between utopia and dystopia created by the meteor shower with Tim Westcott's attempted ethnic cleansing of meteor freaks. He tells Lois Lane that the meteors caused *Smallville*'s decline: "Smallville circa 1988. Before the meteor shower. After that, things changed. My father used to say that the meteor shower affected Smallville somehow. It brought an evil upon our town. ... No one cares about right and wrong or morality." To Tim, the meteor shower is the moment Smallville became corrupted. In a sense, the series asserts that diversity has made the town immoral, changing it from a simplistic homogeny to heterogeneous complexity and moral decay. Diversity affects, infects, and irrevocably alters the town.

Adilifu Nama asserts that aliens in science fiction films are allegories for racial otherness. Nama specifically looks at the codes for blackness, which range from structured absence to viewing racial blood as contaminated. *Smallville* represents socially marginalized groups.[1] Lynn Weber's seminal work explores social ideologies through her examination of how dominant groups impose definitions onto subordinate groups to preserve power over them. Weber defines the dominant group as white, middle-class, male, and heterosexual. Smallville, prior to the meteor shower, is comprised of this dominant group. However, the meteor shower introduces diversity and the town struggles to adapt. Weber asserts that dominant groups further impose rigid definitions of normal and abnormal behaviors to legitimize their superiority and paint subordinate groups as deviations from the norm. These dominant groups also define minority groups as their polar opposites—i.e. racial minorities are defined as nonwhite, females are defined as non-males, and homosexual are defined as non-heterosexuals.[2] Omi and Winant give the example of Susie Guillary Phipps, who was defined as black based on 1/32 of African American blood.[3] Nama furthers this point: "[T]his racial convention is an integral part of the cultural politics of race in American society in which 'black blood' is viewed as not only a potent pollutant but also a fundamental element in assembling an essential racial identification for both whites and blacks."[4] Weber asserts that racial identity is not biological but social, and dominant groups try to mask this by attributing biological justifications for inferiority.[5]

Smallville borrows these binary distinctions by imposing notions of normality and abnormality and pure and contaminated based on whether someone is infected by meteor rocks. Groups deemed normal behave in a socially acceptable manner, and, as Lincoln Geraghty asserts, they balance individual needs with the needs of society.[6] "Normal" people in *Smallville* are locals who are not infected by meteors; they obey laws and are gregarious. Meteor freaks in the series are coded as abnormal; they often are reclusive outsiders who behave selfishly. They also adhere to a specific set values and feel immune to laws and social restrictions. The first season in particular emphasizes the mutations caused by contact with meteor rocks. Such signifiers illustrate the classification of diversity. Even more interesting are the behavioral cues of those deemed either normal or abnormal. Meteor rocks give those infected strange powers, yet this empowerment also causes them to become deviant, bizarre, unpredictable, and harmful.

"Pilot," "Metamorphosis," and "Hothead" (all 2001) establish conventions for how meteors infect and change people. The first presented victim of the meteor shower is Jeremy Creek. Placed in a cornfield as a scarecrow in a ritualistic hazing of freshmen students, he witnesses the first meteor strike. Years later, no longer a victim, the meteors empower Jeremy with electricity-based abilities. However, the powers alter his appearance and behavior. He arrives at Frank's Auto Garage in complete darkness with an intense stare, disheveled hair, darkened eyes, and grubby clothes. He aggressively resorts to violence to enact his vendettas. Jeremy's transformation marks the effects of the meteor rocks on humans, turning once docile people into deranged psychopaths. Clark tries to stop Jeremy when he appears at the homecoming dance to eliminate others, but Jeremy asserts the nobility of his actions: "I'm not doing this for me. I'm doing this for you and all others like you."[7] Jeremy's response has interesting implications. He was initially oppressed by jocks because he was not athletic and did not fit into their classifications of the norm. However, prior to his meteor infection Jeremy was docile. He did not seek to harm anyone. After contact with meteors, he again deviates from the mainstream, and becomes psychotic. Jeremy suggests that he is trying to eliminate discrimination, as he felt marginalized and now wants to resist the oppression of dominant groups. However, *Smallville* deems this empowerment as dangerous if (and when) abused or misused. In line with Weber's arguments, the series asserts that if minority groups obtain power, they could abuse it, obscuring and damaging social morality.

Greg Arkin ("Metamorphosis" [2001]), like Jeremy, already possesses some abnormal characteristics: dirty clothes, glasses, acne, and an interest in entomology. He records Lana without her knowledge, but is generally harmless. However, this changes after a large group of meteor-infected bugs swarm him. He turns from geek to rebel, exchanging his dingy attire for hip jeans, a black t-shirt, and leather jacket. The largest deviation from the norm comes from appropriating new moral behaviors: "I've been freed.... I have no rules, Clark. I eat what I want, I go where I want, and I take what I want." Greg's transformation is typical for those infected by meteors. The infected gain superhuman characteristics but lose their morality. Greg views people as a means to his end. Those whom he has no use for are eliminated: he kills his mother when she intervenes in his life; he tries to kill Lana's boyfriend Whitney when he warns Greg to stay away from her; and he kidnaps Lana when she refuses his romantic advances. Meteors similarly warp Coach Walt's judgment in "Hothead" (2001). Although an intense coach before his contact with meteor rocks, Walt turns deranged as the infection takes hold. His legacy is his only concern, as he burns the arm of a referee and tries to murder the school's principal for trying to expose the coach's secret. Walt's journey to the abyss climaxes with a bout of rage that consumes him. Comparable to Greg, meteor rocks alters Coach Walt's moral perception and enhances his more base desires.

Such conventions shown in these first episodes establish the influence of meteors. The abilities that meteor infectees gain vary from person to person and powers typically depend on what the person was doing when infected. However, what links them generally is their loss of mainstream moral values. Rather than focusing on the common good, infectees become self-centered and amoral. Their values are based on self-preservation or -gratification. The true problem for meteor infectees is that social restrictions no longer limit their behavior and they embrace their base impulses. These notions assert that diversity destroys the community with individual desires.

Later episodes merely allude to a person's infection. For example, in "Hourglass" (2001), Cassandra Carver only has to refer to being blinded by the meteor shower for the audience to understand that her trauma gives her visions of the future. Earl Jenkins mentions his contact with meteors in "Jitters" (2001) to establish that a meteor infection is the cause of his tremors. Tina Greer's bone morphing ability in "X-Ray" (2001), Bob Rickman's and Kyle Tippet's power to persuade people in "Hug" (2001), Ryan James's telepathy in "Stray"

(2002), Sasha Woodman's ability to manipulate bees in "Drone" (2002), Desirée Adkins's ability to lure men in "Heat" (2002), Byron Moore's deformation and incredible strength in "Nocturne" (2002), Ian Randall's duality in "Dichotic" (2002), Emily Dinsmore's speed in "Accelerate" (2003), Alicia Baker's teleportation in "Obsession" (2004), and Geoff Johns's ability to temporally paralyze people in "Recruit" (2005) are either just briefly described or mentioned in passing. Yet, the conventions established in the early episodes create precedence for their infections and signals that meteor rocks contaminate people's bodies and alter their behavior. Their main danger, though, lies in their exaggerated sense of self-worth, lack of remorse, apathy, and failure to take responsibility for their actions. In "Obsession," Alicia makes this point by telling Clark that their otherness makes them immune to social restrictions of 'normal' people: "We're special. People like us don't have boundaries and limitations."

Interestingly, meteors infect some people due to an accident, and some willingly infect themselves to gain some benefit from them. Most individuals who willingly infect themselves are outsiders who want to use the rocks to gain popularity and acceptance. In "Craving" (2001) for instance, Jodi Melville's classmates tease her about her weight, calling her a "whale" and "chubby," so she uses meteor-influenced vegetables in a shake to help her lose weight. The nutrients from the meteor rocks cause rapid weight loss, and students at school take notice that she is "thinner" and "looks great." Her sudden weight loss has severe repercussions. She begins to have massive hunger pains and must binge on whatever she finds. In turn, Jodi becomes monstrous. Her innocent intentions to lose weight lead to dire consequences, and she then takes to consuming a student. In "Witness" (2003) Eric Marsh inhales meteor rocks to enhance his physical abilities. A former straight-A student interested in chemistry, the meteor rock allows him to turn to a record-setting baseball career. Like Jodi, Eric's desperate encounters with meteor rock cause him to behave abnormally and do things beyond the socially accepted boundaries, robbing LuthorCorp trucks to increase his supply of refined meteor rock and unsuccessfully trying to kill Clark. Early on, the series asserts that whether someone is accidentally or purposely infected by meteors, the result is the same—infectees are socially detrimental. *Smallville* indicates that people become dangerous once meteors enter the bloodstream, and such distinctions harken back to racial classifications. As Nama indicates,

> Race is the ultimate science fiction, and America has a lengthy history of promulgating how biological features such as skin pigmentation, hair texture, eye color, and facial features are used not just to classify people into different racial groups but also, unfortunately, to justify preconceived notions of each race's behavioral characteristics and mental abilities. The culmination of these biological differ-

ences is the idea of and belief in superior and inferior races. At its most strident, the social constructions of race express the concept of racial purity and, through a mishmash of scientific jargon and rudimentary elements of Darwinism, legitimizes and justifies social and sexual boundaries and compels races to maintain and enforce them. Nowhere is this concept clearer in practice than in the colloquially defined "one drop rule," which asserts that "one drop" of "black blood" compromises white racial purity.[8]

Like other media of its genre, *Smallville* adheres to these conventions. Meteor rock is a metaphor of the "one drop rule." Once it enters one's bloodstream, it compromises that person's purity and alters his or her genetic composition. More importantly however is that meteor rocks ascribe behavioral characteristics to those infected, like how they corrupt Jodi and Eric. Jodi was once kind, but after her meteor rock veggie shakes, her primal hunger drives her. After his ingestion of meteor rock, Eric is also no longer a good upstanding citizen; his only concern is playing professional baseball.

Foreign objects, coming from a distant galaxy, present xenophobic fears of integration. The threat of contamination casts a menacing shadow over Smallville. Episodes such as "Nicodemus" (2002), "Fever" (2003), and "Scare" (2005) reveal the dangers of meteors infecting the entire town. In "Nicodemus," Dr. Steven Hamilton uses meteor rocks to resurrect an extinct and deadly flower that previously jeopardized the area in 1871 by removing infectees' inhibitions and threatening their lives. Jonathan neglects his farm chores, makes out with Martha during the day, berates Lex, and threatens a bank officer when denied a loan. Lana likewise alters her behavior after exposer to the flower. She dresses more seductively, skips school, flirts with Clark, closes the Talon early, and finally steals Lex's car. Lana declares that she has a new "self-confidence" and is "free." She no longer feels hampered by restrictions. The flower shares meteor rock's effect on people's loss of inhibitions. However, her newfound liberation has dire consequences. Not only does she do whatever she wants without consideration of others, the infection causes a toxic reaction in her body that threatens her life. "Fever" introduces a ground toxin that plagues Martha and Clark. As several men in Hazmat suits comb the Kent farm, the episode asserts that foreignness is impure and dangerous. "Scare" furthers this concept as LuthorCorp unleashes a deadly meteor toxin into the air. Those infected fall unconscious and experience their worst fears in a nightmare. Each of these episodes argues that meteor contamination poses a threat to *Smallville*'s inhabitants.

Throughout the first four seasons, those infected by meteors become bizarre, unnatural, deviant, and dangerous. Such classifications shape the social language, and subordinate groups are defined through their structured representations. *Smallville* furthers this with its representation of Clark Kent by asserting that he is a foreign invader responsible for the town's decomposition. He brought with him the meteor shower that initially destroyed Smallville, and these meteors now cause infections that continually threaten the town's inhabitants. In "Extinction" (2003), Lana indirectly blames Clark for the town's demise: "Life would have been so better for everyone if the meteor shower never happened." And when he sees the Wall of Weird for the first time in the pilot, Clark poignantly indicates his responsibility, saying, "My fault. It's all my fault." As episodes like "Lineage" (2002) illustrate, *Smallville* also ascribes guilt to Clark for the Luthors entering the town and bringing with them their corrupt politics and chemical pollutants. Lionel Luthor helps Jonathan with Clark's adoption, and he then demands Jonathan to persuade the Ross family to sell their creamed corn factory, which "helped the Luthors get a footing in Smallville." Clark learns that he is responsible for much of the town's diversity, but also its contamination.

Smallville establishes otherness as corrupt through its representation of meteor freaks, but challenges this representation through its portrayal of non-lethal meteor freaks, dangerous people who are not infected by meteors, and Clark. Such complexity undercuts these simplistic codes and urges for a deeper appreciation of diversity. For instance, in "Hourglass" Cassandra Carver is innocuous. She can see people's destinies by touching their hand to provide guidance in their lives. In "Hug," Kyle Tippet, initially reclusive, desires to keep Bob Rickman from polluting Smallville and eventually aims to use his gift to help people. Additionally, the series illustrates that a few individuals who are not infected by meteors can be harmful. Chrissy Parker ("Redux" [2002]) and Kyla Willowbrook ("Skinwalker" [2002]) have special abilities, but they do not gain them from meteors. Chrissy drains the adrenal glands of young students to remain young and Kyla is a shape shifter who stalks both Lionel and the foreman of a LuthorCorp construction site. These rare interludes reveal that not all meteor infectees are harmful and people who are not infected by meteor rocks also can be deadly. This complicates simplistic categorizations of meteor freak activity. *Smallville* proposes stereotypes regarding meteor freaks and then complicates them by suggesting that they are pejorative and superficial.

Clark Kent's Journey of Self-Discovery

Clark poses an interesting dynamic that further complicates the series' simplistic notions of diversity because he simultaneously embodies normalcy and otherness. Meteor freaks are at least partially human and have mutated due to their contact with meteor rocks. Clark, on the other hand, is entirely alien. The series delicately balances between Clark's otherness and his ability to assimilate into small town. His flannel shirts and folksy demeanor easily associate him with other people in the town, yet the series stresses his differences just as much, if not more so. In a manner comparable to Nama's discussion of blood distinguishing racial boundaries, *Smallville* underscores how Clark's blood makes him different. In "Fever," Jonathan tells Dr. Helen Bryce before she draws Clark's blood to examine it "Clark isn't exactly what you would call a normal boy." The series bases Clark's diversity on his genetic differences. However, *Smallville* then questions these conventions by asserting that his diversity may be beneficial. In season three, Clark discovers that his blood, rather than being a pollutant, is highly valued. Morgan Edge calls it "liquid gold" and hires Clark to break into Lionel's vault to steal it in "Phoenix" (2003). Lionel uses Clark's blood to resurrect patients with a rare liver disease, hoping to find a cure for his terminal illness, and upon learning about this in "Resurrection" (2004), Clark wonders whether he should reveal his secret to cure others: "I think that Lionel Luthor has found a way to use my blood to bring people back to life. If my blood can save lives, maybe I should come forward." Although Clark brings with him meteors that wreak havoc on the town, he also improves the world with his genetic material, and with his abilities.

The first four seasons of *Smallville* exhibit Clark's journey to appreciate diversity, and, in the process, he goes through Matthew Meuleners's three stages of diversity: recognition, tolerance, and celebration. Meuleners defines people in the state of recognition: "'Racist,' 'bigot,' and 'ignorant' are some of the words which are aimed at those who are locked in the stage of recognition. These are the people who respond negatively when they come in contact with someone they don't understand or who is different from them. The problem here is lack of information."[9] Meuleners argues that the recognition stage causes people to view otherness in simplistic terms of normal or abnormal, and oftentimes, people are motivated by fear in this stage. *Smallville*'s townspeople represent this well: they view those with differences with apprehension, mistrust, and fear. Clark initially is part of this atmosphere, but the series emphasizes his evolution, moving from recognition to celebration. Season one displays Clark's recognition of diversity. He learns that he is responsible for the meteor shower and that infectees mainly behave negatively. His experiences cause him to conclude that all individuals infected by meteors are devious and menacing, and he even wonders this about himself.

As Clark learns more about his Kryptonian heritage in season two, he enters the stage of tolerance. Meuleners notes, "For people in the tolerance stage, the different people are accepted, but they are not welcomed. A good way to describe it might be respectful distance. They respect the other person's right to exist as long as they keep their distance."[10] The more Clark learns about his Kryptonian father Jor-El, the more he becomes convinced that he is inherently evil and must distance himself from the town. In "Calling" (2003), Jor-El tells Clark that his son will soon begin "his quest to rule the planet," "will be a god among men," and will "rule [humans] with strength." Clark tries to prevent this by destroying his spaceship to eliminate Jor-El's influence, but these efforts cause further harm and place a pregnant Martha in the hospital. Soon after in "Exodus" (2003), Clark leaves for Metropolis to maintain a "respectful distance" and spare Smallville further destruction. Limited experiences and lack of knowledge create Clark's negative response to otherness.

Season three reveals subtle changes to Clark's understanding of diversity. The season premiere "Exile" (2003) begins with Clark in Metropolis. Known as Kal (short for Kal-El) and heavily influenced by the red meteor rock that alters his inhibitions, Clark assumes aspects of his Kryptonian identity and embraces his powers. Yet, because he still views them as corrupt, he mimics the moral behavior of meteor infectees that he has previously encountered. He robs ATM machines and banks to purchase expensive cars; ignores the emotional toll of his absence on Lana; and neglects that Jonathan and Martha are losing their farm because he is no longer there to help. Chloe finds Clark in Metropolis and observes his new erratic behavior. Clark responds, "Maybe this is the real me." True, Clark does embrace his name and powers in Metropolis, but the series asserts that Clark's amoral behavior is an abnormality. When Clark temporarily removes his red Kryptonite ring, he becomes calmer and less self-centered. He calls Martha and appears in his loft, revealing his desire to be home. Although Clark believes that his Kryptonian nature places him in diametric opposition to his life in Smallville, the series argues that Clark must learn that his diversity is not a curse.

Metropolis offers Clark an ability to appreciate diversity on a completely new level. He is no longer surrounded by small-mindedness, and he does not have to hide his secret from his friends. When Clark returns to Smallville in "Phoenix," he stresses to his parents his apprehension to returning to his old life. Metropolis allowed him the opportunity to "do whatever he wanted," and he felt that that there was a "huge weight" lifted from him. Living away from Smallville provides relief because he does not have to live in the proverbial closet. Clark knows that to be socially accepted in Smallville, he must repress his otherness. For these reasons, Clark struggles with his desire to reveal and conceal his secret. Even Pete initially rejects Clark after discovering his secret in "Duplicity" (2002), to which Clark explains that part of the reason for his secrecy is that people would look at him differently and that he must conform to normalcy to be accepted: "Pete, another reason that I didn't tell anybody is because people would look at me the exact same way that you are right now.... Like a freak. ...I've tried my whole life just to blend in—to try and be more normal than anyone else." In "Scare," Clark faces his worst nightmare as Lana discovers that he not only is "different" but also the source of *Smallville*'s disintegration. Lana looks at him with disgust, blaming him for both the meteor shower and death of her parents. As Clark states, "I wanted to tell you, but I thought that you wouldn't accept me." However, the series reveals that the more Clark learns about his Kryptonian ancestry, the more he understands that it is not monstrous. Education is the key to appreciation and acceptance.

Clark returns to Smallville in season three with a better perception and understanding of the challenges faced by those who are different. In "Extinction," Lana asserts her disgust for meteor freaks following Van McNulty's assassination of Jake Pollen. While Clark defends them, Lana justifies her prejudice.

> **Clark:** Personally, I find a gaping wound more disturbing.
> **Lana:** If the shooter didn't show up when he did, I'd be dead. So, excuse me for not having more sympathy for Gill Boy.
> **Clark:** Jake was exposed to meteor rocks. He didn't ask for [his powers].
> **Lana:** Just like Greg Arkin didn't ask to be bug boy, or Tina Greer didn't ask to become a bone morpher. The fact is that once they got their powers, they became psycho and tried to kill me.

Lana's statement embodies the state of recognition, expressing her ignorance by stereotyping all meteor infectees as villainous. Clark's challenge to Lana's narrow-mindedness shows his growth from season two. He no longer accepts the idea that meteor rocks inevitably or absolutely cause people to behave negatively and ultimately offers support to those who are different: "I just think that shot in the head is a little more extreme." He accurately points out that Van McNulty, though a "normal" human, is much more dangerous with his hit list of meteor infected. Clark realizes that meteor infectees are not always responsible for their differences and he becomes more sympathetic to their struggles.

Clark's contact with meteor infectees in season three confirms his newfound appreciation of diversity. In "Magnetic" (2003), Seth Nelson becomes infected by meteors and gains the ability to move metal objects. He uses his powers to persuade Lana to date him, but he never becomes monstrous or psychotic. Jordan Cross's ability to see the moment of a person's death helps Clark to save Megan Calder and Lana in "Hereafter" (2004). Alicia Baker ("Obsession") offers Clark a glimmer of normalcy, as he able to share his secret with someone who also is different. She understands Clark's loneliness and isolation and further helps to humanize meteor infectees for Clark. Alicia goes too far in her obsession with Clark by killing her father, using meteor rocks to stop Clark, and trying to kill Lana. However, the episode treats her not just as purely evil or crazy, but more misunderstood. Her fixation with Clark derives from the fact that Clark is the only one who truly understands her differences, not that she is simply insane.

Smallville also reveals that the mainstream closed-mindedness perhaps is to blame for meteor infectees' behavior. Specifically, the series poses the possibility that society's rejection of meteor infectees causes them to behave poorly. We see this subtle argument in the humans who have an opportunity to possess Clark's powers. In the first four seasons, three individuals assume Clark's abilities but in each instance, they dangerously abuse Clark's powers. During a lightning strike in "Leech" (2002), Eric Summers obtains Clark's powers. However, rather than using them to help others, Eric grows selfish, conceited, and dangerous. He launches to fame by stopping a thief from stealing Chloe's purse. The local newspaper initially applauds Eric's heroism, but his parents' fear of his powers undercuts his notoriety. His father tries to send Eric to Metropolis to be examined by a doctor, but Eric protests, "I'm not sick. I'm special." Part of Eric's difficulty is that he uses his powers to reach popularity. Once Eric has been branded a hero, his dress and demeanor change. He trades his glasses and trench coat for an attitude and leather jacket. He aggressively flirts with a female student in front of her boyfriend and then throws the boyfriend across the parking lot. Eric finds that his "coming out party" is not as widely celebrated as he initially thought. People view him differently. The female student who Eric tries to impress exclaims, "Get away from us, you freak." Eric is rejected for his otherness in part because he is different and in part because he abuses his powers. Like many meteor freaks, Eric feels above social restrictions. He believes that his powers entitle him to special privileges and that laws no longer restrain him. He declares to his parents, "I can do whatever I want ... and no one can stop me."

In season three's "Talisman" (2004), Jeremiah Holdsclaw gains powers similar to Clark through an ancient Kawatche knife, and the power quickly becomes intoxicating. Clark warns Jeremiah, "It's the blade; it's corrupting you." However, Jeremiah ignores Clark's counsel and unsurprisingly uses his superhuman abilities for selfish, nefarious ends. He blows up Professor Willowbrook's car, tries to kill Clark, and places Lionel on an altar to sacrifice him. Lionel too experiences Clark's abilities in season four. In "Transference" (2004), Lionel switches bodies with Clark and gets to "see the world through a whole new pair of eyes." However, rather than protecting people, Lionel (via Clark's body) teases Chloe with intimacy, flirts with Lana, manipulates Jason Teague, and threatens his son Lex. Clark accurately tells Lionel, "No matter how hard you try, you will never be me." True, Lionel, Jeremiah, and Eric can never be Clark because they are human; they are corruptible.

Smallville asserts that humans are impure and as such, when a human gains a superhuman ability, he or she typically uses it to their own advantage. After Jonathan observes Eric's meltdown in "Leech," tells Clark, "Seeing how crazy Eric got, reminds me of how special you really are." In season three,

Jonathan temporarily holds Clark's powers and later tells him in "Talisman," "I've had your power only for a short while and having all that power was very intoxicating." Thus, the series argues that human fallibility, not meteor rocks, leads to corruption and suggests that humans, coded as normal, are also to blame for *Smallville*'s demise. Clark, in opposition to humans, aptly balances his powers with his humanity and rarely abuses them for personal gain. Clark's difference is that he is alien, and this makes him less corruptible than those around him. Clark's excursion in Lionel's body in "Transference" heals not only Lionel's illness but also his disposition to evil. Afterwards, Lionel admits, "Something inside me has changed, profoundly. I'm not the same man."

Similarly, in "Perry" (2003), Perry White tells Clark, "You really are a freak.... You help people, even fools like me, without anything in return." Despite Perry's poor behavior, Clark comes to his aid as Perry falls over the Saunders Gorge to prevent a suicide attempt. Perry exasperatedly states, "I don't get you kid. I blackmailed your parents, ticked off your girlfriend, and offended your lady editor, and yet here you are still trying to play the editor (i.e. hero)." The arrival of Clark's Kryptonian cousin Kara, or at least a girl posing as her, in season three's "Covenant" (2004), further emphasizes human corruptibility. Kara tells Clark that she can sense his sadness from feeling like an outsider, and she asserts that part of this is because humans are flawed. She stresses that Clark cannot trust anyone, and, even those closest to him, will "lie, betray, or leave" him. Clark then discovers that Lex has been investigating him for three years, that Pete is moving to Wichita with his mother, and that Chloe is presumed dead after an explosion. He laments, "Maybe Kara was right. She warned me that all my friends would betray me. Maybe I don't belong here. Maybe there's a better place for me." This episode emphasizes the corrupt nature of humans more than any preceding episode, and Clark learns that part of the reason that he does not fit into Smallville is that he is not human. He does not have human fallibilities, and thus decides to accompany Kara to the Jor-El's portal in the Kawatche cave to leave human corruption. Season three concludes with Clark still in the tolerance stage of diversity. He again leaves Smallville because of his diversity. He stands between two worlds: the corruption of humanity and uncertainty of Krypton. He learns the difficulty of living between these two worlds and feels as though they cannot coexist.

Season four begins with a metaphoric rebirth of Clark. In "Crusade" (2004), Lois Lane finds him naked in the fetal position after a lightning strike and brings him back to Smallville. Having temporarily forgotten his past, Clark feels less burdened by not having to live in between the two worlds because he completely embraces his Kryptonian destiny. Martha disrupts this by exposing Clark to black Kryptonite, segmenting Clark and Kal-El and forcing a battle between his human and Kryptonian sides. Although Kal-El declares that Clark's humanity has made him "weak," Clark defeats him. Season four complicates representation by undercutting the simplistic definitions of all Kryptonian elements as corrupt and all human elements as weak. This relates to Judith Andre's call to eliminate pejorative stereotypes. Andre states that complexity is the key to removing derogatory representations by challenging the stereotype and "calling attention" to its limitations.[11] She continues: "Responsible portrayals encourage us to see in one another both our individuality and our roles in a social system. Stereotypes blind us to the first, and keep us from being enlightened about the second."[12] By calling attention to the limitations of its constructed stereotypes, *Smallville* confronts simplistic representations.

Momentarily freed from Jor-El, Clark resumes his normal life as an "outsider" at Smallville High in "Façade" (2004). Yet, he returns with even greater sympathy for meteor freaks and moves toward achieving what Meuleners describes as celebration of diversity. Meuleners states that "Celebrating diversity is the equation for true synergy.... By acknowledging that every member of your community, organization, or family has something to contribute and recognizing that his or her contributions add value to your life, you are moving toward the stage of celebration."[13] By the end of season four, Clark learns that his diversity makes him an important member of his community, and he ascertains that each individual holds complexities within himself/herself. Episodes throughout season four illustrate Clark's newfound understanding of and appreciation for diversity, asserting that meteors do not predispose one to be harmful or destructive. In "Façade," Dr. Elise Fine uses meteor rock to enhance the appearance of her daughter Abigail, but Abigail's contact with meteors does not corrupt her disposition. She forgives jock Brett for teasing her in the past, and the two share a special moment in the locker room. Although meteor rocks affect the way in which Brett sees himself in a mirror and he eventually runs in front of a car, but this is not Abigail's design. Later cheerleaders use meteor rocks to spike the football players' cooler in "Devoted" (2004), but the players do not turn selfish or dangerous. In fact, they become selflessly devoted to the cheerleaders. Hence, season four argues that meteor rocks do not automatically cause infectees to become harmful. Similarly, the season also asserts that not all humans are corrupt or weak. Dr. Fine and the cheerleaders represent only a small aspect of human behavior. Lois arrives in Smallville frantically looking for information on Chloe's disappearance, and she meticulously and lovingly monitors her sister Lucy. Lionel reforms his previous dubious image and devotes his life to his new charity. Lionel's amelioration is a direct attack on stereotypes. Andre asserts that simplicity is an aspect of stereotypes, which "ignore, or falsify, or oversimplify the causes of behavior."[14] *Smallville* further removes stereotypes through complex representation in "Onyx" (2005), as

Lex reveals his duality after being exposed to black Kryptonite. "Good Lex" reaches out to help others, while "Evil Lex" is more selfish and sees people as a means to an end. The episode pushes for a more complex understanding of human behavior through its multiple dimensions of Lex's character.

Bart Allen also is part of this, as his character falls between the series' codes of otherness. He is not from Smallville, not infected by meteor rocks, and not quite human. Bart also occupies obscure behavioral boundaries, as his actions in "Run" (2004) reflect neither a full hero nor full villain. He saves Jonathan from a runaway truck, but in the process steals his wallet. Bart's moral code is strikingly similar to that adopted by meteor freaks in earlier seasons. When Clark tells Bart that stealing MP3 players is wrong because there are laws, he responds, "For normal people." Bart feels that his "gifts" permit him the freedom to do whatever he wants. However, Bart is not entirely selfish or corrupt. He steals Lex's ancient manuscript but then has a change of heart and returns it. The episode argues that people with power can use their power for good or evil, sometimes both. Having power does not predispose a person to any particular behavior. Furthermore, Clark wishes that he could be more like Bart by embracing his abilities. Clark tells his father that he feels like two separate people because he must occupy two different worlds. Ultimately, Clark learns from Bart that his abilities are not a curse and embracing them will enable him to be a more valuable member of society.

Although season four displays Clark beginning to appreciate his diverse identity, he still must live in secrecy to be accepted. Alicia Baker returns to convince Clark to come out of his closet and reveal his secret in "Pariah" (2005). She believes that Clark divulging his secret will cause people in Smallville to be less judgmental, but their prejudice of Alicia only provides Clark more evidence why he cannot trust others with his secret. When classmate Tim Westcott attacks Lana in a locked room, Lana, Jason (Lana's new boyfriend), Chloe, and Lois immediately suspect Alicia is responsible. Clark confronts Alicia about the attack on Jason. He explains that people think that Alicia did it, and Alicia reveals the town's prejudice against people who are different: "Why, because of my powers? Because I'm a freak? You know what, Clark, maybe if everyone knew your secret you would be a suspect too." This episode reveals the harm of prejudice. Jason, Lana, Chloe, and Lois assume Alicia's guilt because of her known differences, eventually damaging in her relationship with Clark. "Pariah" places an interesting twist on the series' conventions. Although Clark's secret typically places people (Pete, his family, etc.,) in jeopardy, "Pariah" emphasizes that his inability to reveal his secret to people causes harm. Yet, at the same time, "Pariah" correlates with other episodes in its representation of *Smallville*'s closed-mindedness. Tim's extreme actions to frame and then kill Alicia are outward manifestations of the town's inward intolerance. To Clark, this encounter confirms the necessity to conceal his secret.

Season four concludes with "Commencement" (2005), echoing the opening scenes of the pilot with a second meteor shower. However, the responsibility for this meteor shower does not lie just with Clark. His failure to assume his Kryptonian heritage and unify three Kryptonian stones allows the stones to fall into human hands. Lionel, Lex, Lana, Jason, and Genevieve Teague (Jason's mother) compete for possession of the stones to gain their power. The threat that now enters Smallville is more complex than xenophobic fears of foreign invasions because, unlike the first meteor shower, humans share the blame for this second wave of destruction. Human blood stains one of the stones and unleashed a force that now threatens the town. This encourages a new more complex understanding of diversity. Closed-mindedness, avarice, and malice are to blame, but these are no longer attributed to just one particular group.

Appropriately titled, "Commencement" demonstrates Clark's graduation to Meuleners's final stage of diversity—celebration. Clark awakens to Jor-El's warning voice: "It's coming." Jor-El's assertion hints at the impending meteor shower, but it also looks to Clark's acceptance of his Kryptonian heritage and value of diversity. When Clark hears Jor-El, he immediately responds. He no longer hesitates partly because of the approaching meteor shower and partly because he no longer fears his otherness. With more information about Jor-El, Krypton, and who he is, Clark is not concerned about his heritage. Jor-El tells Clark to acquire all the elements before they fall into the wrong hands, and, this time, Clark willingly unifies the stones. Jonathan tells Clark, "All the years that your mother and I spent raising you from a wide-eyed toddler running around on this farm to the man who is standing in front of me right now was for this moment."[15] The episode stresses Clark's value: as the meteors fall, he continuously and anonymously saves people from harm. He must still live in secrecy, but he embraces his identity because he now understands the benefits he brings to society. Although Smallville, Kansas, lags behind in its acceptance of otherness, Clark forges ahead to embody new ideas and experiences. And with the unified stones, Clark possesses all the knowledge and history of Krypton. Season four concludes with Clark once again separated from Smallville, but his arrival in the Arctic demonstrates his desire to embrace his otherness and progress toward fully understanding his identity and the value of diversity. In its first four seasons, *Smallville* asserts that the first meteor shower irreparably changed Smallville, but Clark's embrace of his abilities and his otherness by the end of "Commencement" illustrate that he and the town are headed toward a brighter future.

Other series similar to *Smallville* tend to mask the fact that definitions of subordinate groups are socially constructed and this maintains the power and privilege of the hegemony. Weber indicates, "By masking the true nature of race, class, gender, and sexuality oppression, the image helps to preserve the status quo."[16] *Smallville*, on the other hand, is exceptional because it reveals the limitations of all social constructs. Seasons one and two present simplistic definitions of marginalized groups to demonstrate their parochiality, and seasons three and four introduce complexity to constructed images to push for a more complete and diverse representation of the human experience.

NOTES

1. Adilifu Nama, *Black Space: Imagining Race in Science Fiction Film* (Austin: University of Texas Press, 2008).
2. Lynn Weber, "A Conceptual Framework for Understanding Race, Class, Gender, and Sexuality," *Psychology of Women Quarterly* 22.1 (1998): 18.
3. Michael Omni and Howard Winant, "Racial Formation," in *Racial Formation in the United States: From the 1960s to the 1990s*, 2d ed. (New York: Routledge, 1994), 53.
4. Nama, *Black Space*, 43.
5. Weber, "A Conceptual Framework for Understanding Race, Class, Gender, and Sexuality," 19.
6. Lincoln Geraghty, *American Science Fiction Film and Television* (New York: Berg, 2009), 4.
7. Ibid.
8. Nama, *Black Space*, 43.
9. Matthew Meuleners, "Treat Students Right by Valuing Their Diversity," *Education Digest* 67.4 (2001): 47.
10. Ibid., 48.
11. Judith Andre, "Stereotypes: Conceptual and Normative Considerations," in *Racism and Sexism: An Integrated Study*, ed. Paula Rothenberg (New York: St. Martin's Press, 1988), 262.
12. Ibid.
13. Meuleners, "Treat Students Right by Valuing Their Diversity," 50.
14. Andre, "Stereotypes: Conceptual and Normative Considerations," 259.
15. Ibid.
16. Weber, "A Conceptual Framework for Understanding Race, Class, Gender, and Sexuality," 24.

Kryptonian Encounters

Model Immigration and Superman's Impossible Dream

Roger Almendarez

In "Hereafter" (2003), an episode of the *Justice League* (2001–2004) animated series, Superman has died, thus bringing sadness and worry to both the city of Metropolis and the series' cast of superheroes. To express their mourning, a variety of characters from across the DC Comics universe gather to remember their fallen comrade. Chosen to speak on behalf of the Justice League, Martian Manhunter leads the ceremony with the Man of Steel's eulogy.[1] Although the majority of his speech deals with the Metropolis Marvel's participation in the group, Martian Manhunter nonetheless draws attention to the fallen hero's history by concluding, "Kal-El from Krypton: immigrant from the stars who taught us all to be heroes." As the series progresses, Superman's absence leaves the League in shambles. As they struggle to defeat a pack of unruly evildoers, the team scrambles to fill the Man of Steel's role and "[adhere to] his example." When placed alongside the superhero's canon, "Hereafter" adds to a discourse that iterates the many ways that the Last Son of Krypton is an outsider, who by virtue of his peripherality, is liminal to any terrestrial, national, and/or American culture or law. With an interest in this marginalization, this essay focuses on how *Smallville*, and the Superman canon more broadly, constructs and delimits the Kryptonian Kal-El for the benefit of the American Clark Kent.

I contend that embedded within the *Smallville* universe is an underlying premise that constricts acceptable models of assimilation into American life. I argue that the series suggests that the act of assimilation requires the formation of alternative communities, which serve to better American society, but only through the concealment of any foreign cultural elements. The series' representations of such communities and their ways of life, which can be otherwise stated as *Smallville*'s depictions of ethnicity, are also related to its framing of diverse bodies.

Readily seen in its display of alien and/or extraordinary human physiques, *Smallville* deploys tactics of racialization, which result in a denunciation of non-human and/or non-citizen behavior as alien. With regard to the Man of Steel, *Smallville* racializes Kal-El's superhero identity so as to "other" this aspect of his character, which constructs him as an extraordinary non–American. Charles Ramirez Berg argues that the alien figure in American science fiction has come to represent an apprehension of undocumented immigrants.[2] Similarly deploying this alien trope, *Smallville* subverts this apprehension by allowing its protagonist to pass for a typical American human, but only if he hides his superhero abilities from mainstream society. The effect of this suppression is that Clark's labor, his work in protecting the human race, becomes invisible. In doing so, *Smallville* creates what Mae Ngai terms an "impossible subject," a laborer whose illegal status prevents them from fully enmeshing themselves into mainstream American society.[3] Because of this relationship between identity and labor, studying *Smallville*'s depictions of immigration and assimilation gives insight into early twenty-first century American society.

In line with Rachel Rubin and Jeffrey Melnick's arguments, I conceive of *Smallville* as a major cultural production that is not only expressive of its socio-historical moment but also constructive of what Karin Beeler refers to as "myths," which inform both culture and society.[4] By examining how *Smallville* represents Superman as the ideal immigrant, we can see how early twenty-first century American popular culture positions immigrants and other marginalized identities. Furthermore, we can come to understand how the series constructs its representations of idealized American citizenship. Though this essay prioritizes *Smallville* in its reading of the Superman mythos, the Man of Tomorrow's other canonical works undoubtedly affect our understanding of the character prior to, during, and after the series. In order to contextualize my reading of *Smallville*, it is imperative to first highlight key moments in the Man of Steel's textual history.

Truth and Justice ... and the American Way?

While the Metropolis Marvel is an alien in many senses of the word, both not of Earth or the United States, Superman's otherness in *Justice League*'s "Hereafter" stands in stark contrast to popular representations of the Man of Steel as dutifully patriotic. Popularly associated with the slogan "Truth, justice, and the American way," the red-caped hero's earlier texts do not invoke this exact phrasing. According to the stories in Action Comics, the 1940s Mutual Broadcasting Network radio serials, and Fleischer Studios's *Superman* cartoons prior to World War II, the Metropolis Marvel's primary catchphrase indicated that he stood for "truth and justice." However, as *New York Times* columnist Erik Lundegaard notes, his slogan changed during World War II when the United States was struggling to defeat its opponents. As Lundegaard questions, if the U.S. military was at war, "Why shouldn't Superman" also fight?[5] The Mutual Broadcasting Network also saw the opportunity to uplift national morale, which resulted in their enlisting him on August 31, 1942, for the revival of its radio serial that now promoted "Truth, justice, *and* the American way."[6] Although the serial later omitted "the American Way" from its opening, it was not the end of the slogan's tenure with the character. It became synonymous with the superhero on September 19, 1952, when announcer William "Bill" Kennedy introduced the phrase into the syndicated television program, *Adventures of Superman* (1952–1958), forever wedding it to the first live-action television version of the Man of Steel.[7]

Having become the official fictional protector of the United States throughout the second half of the twentieth century, Superman grew to represent a popular version of an ideal American. However, this representation shifted during the early twenty-first century when some of the comic's creators questioned his Americanness, which some went so far as to deny completely. The 2011 nine-hundredth issue of Action Comics is the most pronounced example of this transformation. In this anthology, "The Incident" describes a scenario where the Man of Steel has become upset by the United States government's use of force against Iranian protesters. Discouraged by this violence, he purposely renounces his citizenship in order to prevent his "actions [being] construed as instruments of U.S. policy," which highlights the superhero's sense of alienation from the United States and Earth.[8] Seeing this change in interpretations of Superman as key, I argue that *Smallville* negotiates its development of Clark Kent in light of this juncture and situates the superhero in limbo between alien and American.

The Reconstruction of Kal-El, the Kryptonian

Smallville, unlike other iterations of the Superman mythos, is exceptional in its in-depth approach to depicting Clark Kent as an average teenager who becomes, rather than is inherently, a superhero. Compared to the majority of Superman derivations that focus on the Man of Steel's adult years, the series adopts a "no flights, no tights" policy that prioritizes Clark's maturation through adolescence and downplays his destiny as Earth's savior. Though Clark eventually accepts his position as a hero, the series splits into what I see as three transitional periods: (1) Clark and the fall of the All-American Midwestern boy, (2) the emergence of Kal-El as the Blur, and (3) the assimilation of Kal-El into mainstream American society. Within each era, the series depicts Clark as wholly insecure about who he is and what he represents. By beginning with Clark's discovery of his alien origins, *Smallville* displays an evolving character who undergoes a process of assimilation that leads him to develop the marginal, yet sanctioned, identity of the Blur, the series' interpretation of Superman.

Smallville's contribution to the Superman mythos is that it develops the story of Clark as the ideal, albeit insecure, Midwestern boy. While the Man of Tomorrow traditionally appears as an adult, no other iterations before *Smallville* so carefully crafted a background story that demonstrated Clark Kent *in media res* prior to his becoming Superman. Unlike his characterizations in *The Adventures of Superman* as interpreted by George Reeves, Tom Welling's version of Clark is that of a displaced being who is not the weak and insecure "critique on the whole human race" that filmmaker Quentin Tarantino once described.[9] As Rayna Denison similarly notes, "*Smallville*'s initial difference to previous incarnations of Superman in film and television is presented through seemingly negative understandings of the franchise's iconography."[10] It is precisely this inversion of the superhero into a timid pariah that sets the parameters for *Smallville*'s version of Clark.

One such limitation that Clark finds in the series is that his appearance as a typical American boy does not prevent him from still being inexplicably—unutterably—different from other humans. In *Smallville*, Clark's inability to fit within the school's community, an opinion expressed by Clark when he refers to himself as a "loser" in the pilot episode (2001), suggests that assimilation into a foreign culture requires an awareness of one's own ethnic differences, which for Clark is located in the body and manifests as his superhuman strength. In the pilot, for example, Clark asks his parents for permission to try out for the football team. Jonathan Kent, his adopted father, rejects the request on the basis that Clark could potentially hurt the other students. This in effect restricts him from participating in a typical cultural activity because of physical differences due to him being an immigrant alien. By emphasizing his inability to assimilate into his high school, *Smallville* displays Clark as not only feeling the frustrations of being socially awkward and excluded from the mainstream but also depicts the limitations of inhabiting an alien and othered body. Although this is an instance of Clark's marginalization, he is not visibly alien until he enacts his superhuman abilities, which allow him to pass for a normal Anglo American.[11] However, as he bemoans in the pilot, he would "give anything to be normal," suggesting that even his ability to pass will not prevent him from always being othered. The significance of the series' inaugural episode is that it sets the stage for Clark to exist outside of society, although he continually struggles to confront his status as an undocumented, immigrant alien. This alienation ruptures any sense of potential normal Americanness, thus allowing the series to transcend mediating the Midwestern Clark and focus instead on revealing the alien Kal-El.

In one of the series' most groundbreaking episodes, season two's "Rosetta" (2003) features the star of the Warner Bros. film *Superman: The Movie* (1978) and its subsequent sequels, Christopher Reeve, as the scientist Virgil Swann. In this episode, *Smallville* demonstrates how Clark's cultural lineage to Krypton demands a marginalization of his body within American society. The episode begins with Swann, a famous astronomer, confirming the existence of Clark's home planet Krypton. Throughout season two, Clark had begun piecing together facts about his origins from Kryptonian artifacts. Due to his Kryptonian biology, Clark could intuitively analyze those artifacts, which subtly suggests a relationship between cultural knowledge and genealogy. However, though Clark could glean some information from his lost history, he still needs Swann's expertise to decipher their meaning. Ultimately, Clark learns from his time with Swann that his identity as Kal-El is not inseparable from his own as Clark Kent. As the series later demonstrates, Clark learns to embrace his Kryptonian identity as Kal-El, which in turn allows him to interact with the simulation of his biological father Jor-El in the Fortress of Solitude, an ice palace in the arctic that houses Kryptonian knowledge about the universe. However, Kal-El's introduction into Clark Kent's identity, though necessary, causes dramatic changes to Clark's life.

As the series illustrates, difficulties arise from Clark's embrace of Kal-El when he tries to merge his two distinct ethnicities. His adoptive parents, most prominently his adoptive father Jonathan, help foster his sense of identity. However, as the series progresses, Jor-El and Jonathan develop an heightened level of animosity as they each struggle to indoctrinate Kal-El and/or Clark into their belief systems and cultures, revealing the incompatibilities between Midwestern American and Kryptonian identities. Ultimately, *Smallville* breaks this tension in season five's "Reckoning" (2006) when Jonathan dies as a result of Clark asking Jor-El to travel back in time to save his love interest Lana Lang after her death in a car accident. In choosing to work with Jor-El, Clark (unintentionally) sacrifices his adoptive father by not being able to save him from a heart attack. Although Jonathan was a major influence in Clark's early life, his death marks a turning point for Clark as he transitions away from Midwestern boy to Kal-El and the Blur.

Assimilation and Cultural Citizenship

Though Krypton was destroyed, other Kryptonians, the culture's language, and its knowledge all still linger in the *Smallville* universe. Clark selectively melds aspects of his Kryptonianness into his identity, but the series nonetheless complicates Kryptonian identity by representing some aspects as positive and constructing others as incompatible with Americanness. In doing so, *Smallville* creates a mold for a benign Kryptonian ethnicity capable of assimilating into American culture while simultaneously excising any cultural incompatibilities. This selection process guides the narrative, resulting in Clark remaining earthbound yet still connected to his alien roots. One of the places where this dialectic between acceptable and detestable Kryptonianness is most visible is in "Red" (2002) where Clark is exposed to red Kryptonite and, in turn, deviates from many of his previous cultural norms.

The story begins with Clark buying a high school class ring that contains a piece of red Kryptonite. Though he knows that green Kryptonite causes him to feel intense physical pain, Clark is unaware of red Kryptonite and its influences. From the moment he puts his ring on, his inhibitions slither away, and he becomes an increasingly narcissistic version of himself who spends money on a wealth of needless material possessions, leading to a credit card company contacting his parents about excessive spending. Although this flamboyant characterization of Clark stands opposite to the humble working-class farm boy, Jonathan notes at the end of the episode that this shift in attitude is a result of his Kryptonian identity. In response, Clark, while wearing the ring, declares that his parents are limiting his desires and pressuring him to adhere to their assigned cultural norms, which "[forces] him to hide who" he really is. As he further exclaims, "It's like [he] has these two identities and [he does not] know which one is the real [him]." While Clark ultimately breaks free from the ring's influence after Jonathan takes a sledgehammer to it, the series nevertheless suggests that it is harmful to over-identify with Kryptonian identity. I argue that this narrative conclusion conveys the idea that assimilation requires absorption of new cultural ethics and morals at the sacrifice of some residual cultural beliefs and behaviors. Although this episode highlights Clark's internal conflicts over his identity, *Smallville*'s sixth season goes even further in explicitly demonstrating the need for the United States to purge Krypton from its dominant culture.

In perhaps one of the most pivotal episodes of the series, season six's "Fallout" (2006) contains the moment when Clark decides to no longer reject his Kryptonianness in favor of his Americanness. Throughout the sixth season, *Smallville* introduces a cast of antagonistic Kryptonian prisoners who wreak havoc throughout the town. Like Kal-El, they make their way to Earth via extraterrestrial means. However, unlike him, they are not immediately embraced as Americans and given a path toward assimilation. Rather, these prisoners adhere to Kryptonian cultural/behavioral norms that directly conflict with that of the rest of Smallville. In creating these characters and pitting them against Clark, the series produces an ambiguous message about immigration where some can be accepted into society and others cannot. This acceptance, then, rests entirely upon the immigrant's ability to assimilate. Though resonant with current discourse about the inassimilable nature of some marginalized immigrant groups—particularly Latina/os and Asians—*Smallville* goes even further in its ambiguity by having Clark decide at the end of the episode that he must embrace his Kryptonianness and train at the Fortress of Solitude. The question of assimilation, then, becomes central to determining not only the rest of the series' trajectory but also in understanding Superman's mythos in his various iterations throughout American history.

As Aldo Regalado notes, Jerry Siegel and Joe Shuster, the Man of Steel's original creators, were "the children of immigrant Jews," and as such their understanding of America from an immigrant's perspective perhaps colored their imaginations and helped create the comic in a way that broadened "American standards of whiteness ... to include foreign-born immigrants ... as long as they [made] an effort to assimilate into American mainstream culture and [used] their talents to contribute to society."[12] For Regalado, assimilation is a two-part process where the immigrant both acquires a new "mainstream culture" as well as uses "their talents to contribute to society."[13] With this understanding of assimilation, one can see why Clark must necessarily help humanity through the use of his Kryptonian strength. However, Regalado's interpretation of immigration neglects what Raymond Williams terms "residual culture," whereby the immigrant's previous culture inflects their understanding of their emerging culture, which allows for the hybridization of culture.[14] Recalling Martian Manhunter's observation that the Man of Tomorrow taught the world to be heroes, this hybridity comes to define Clark in *Smallville*. However, the hybridity does not always result in a complete balance of cultures. The greatest example of this shifting balance appears in the sixth season episode "Subterranean" (2006).

"Subterranean" opens with a long shot of an amber field with Latina/o laborers tilling soil. A setting sun fills the screen with a flare as a silhouetted man walks into the frame. A switch in light levels reveals a grimace on an Anglo male's face, which depicts a figure akin to an overseer (the person in charge of monitoring slaves in pre-emancipation America). Immediately after this shot, the camera cuts to two teenagers speaking English with an American accent oddly devoid of any Spanish inflection. At this point, the series introduces Javier, the co-star of the episode who becomes a source of identification for Clark as he goes on to help the young undocumented immigrant.

Javier, a recent immigrant brought over by "coyotes," migrant smugglers, comes to the United States to reunite with his mother, also an undocumented worker. Unfortunately for Javier, instead of going to see her, the farm's owners transport him to this prison-like location. Unwilling to accept his predicament, Javier escapes his captors by hiding in the Kent barn. Eventually, Javier meets Clark, and seeing that the boy had been injured during the escape, Clark immediately tries to take him to the hospital. However, because of his undocumented status, Javier refuses. At this moment, the episode pits Clark's personal sense of morality against a patriotic adherence to American laws and customs.

Understanding that he cannot reveal the boy to the authorities because they would prevent Javier from reuniting with his mother, Clark decides against seeking help. A few scenes after this meeting, Clark enters the kitchen to speak with his mother, Martha. However, he refuses to tell her about Javier. Clark's omission implies that he believes that Martha, a U.S. senator, would vehemently uphold American law and want to evict Javier. During Clark and Martha's conversation, a Latino police officer arrives at the Kent home, informing Clark that a young Latino boy had been seen running down the road and (without acknowledging the problematic assumption that being Latina/o meant participation in illegal activity) is presumed to be an undocumented alien. In order to avoid appearing suspicious, Clark allows the man to search his barn. As he voices the opinion that undocumented immigrants should "stand in line and wait their turn like everyone else" for legal entry because that is what *his* parents did, the officer fails to find Javier hiding in a locker in the barn. Javier exits the cabinet post-inspection but Martha sees him, leading to an argument between her and Clark. As Martha states, her status as a senator demands that she report Javier. To counter her argument, Clark states that he is also an "illegal alien," and that the Kents falsified documents in order to adopt him.

Though Clark's identity has primarily been that of a Midwestern American, he explicitly claims his otherness in this episode by identifying as an "illegal alien." In doing so, he gains justification for both aiding a fellow migrant and maintaining moral standards that exceed any national laws. Though an overtly political storyline that is unusual for *Smallville*, so much so that this episode received many negative reviews for its "leftist propaganda," "Subterranean" reveals the struggle at the fore for *Smallville*: the negotiation between Clark and Kal-El.[15] Ultimately, Martha uses her political connections to gain residency for Javier and his mother, but only after Clark explicitly chooses to side with Javier based on their common link as undocumented aliens. While Clark, prior to his father's death, struggled to identify with American culture vis-à-vis his extraordinary Kryptonian features, after the sixth season *Smallville* changes course. Rather than chide Kal-El for his incompatible ethnic traits, the series demonstrates Clark forming alternative communities where he freely expresses his identities as both Clark *and* Kal-El.

In "Justice" (2007) Clark and fellow superheroes join forces to destroy Lex Luthor's mysterious Level 33.1. At this point in the series, Lex has been collecting and running experiments on "meteor freaks," a "pejorative term used to refer to humans who have acquired superpowers through exposure to meteor rock" and who have threatened *Smallville*'s residents since the meteor shower that brought the young Kal-El to Earth.[16] As made evident in the fourth season episode "Jinx" (2004), Lex, unbeknownst to Clark, rounds up meteor freaks so as to acquire as much information as he can about the meteor shower. "Justice" is particularly important for the later part of the series because it marks the introduction of the Justice League, a faction of superheroes headed up in this iteration by Oliver Queen/Green Arrow and also featuring Arthur Curry/Aquaman, Bart Allen/the Flash, and Victor Stone/Cyborg. Though no one else on the team hails from Krypton, mainstream society has still exiled their secret identities. It is this status as superhuman outcasts that binds the group together and will aid in their dismantling of Luthor's Level 33.1.

Although Level 33.1 is a prison for meteor freaks, it is most importantly a space densely populated by Kryptonian-influenced peoples. By working to destroy Level 33.1, the Justice League forms its community around the act of eradicating unwanted Kryptonian elements. Furthermore, inclusion in the League requires that its members keep their identities hidden from the public and perform invisible labor. Unifying the League through this behavior serves as the basis for a superhuman "cultural citizenship" with which Clark discovers as a means of not only existing as a Kryptonian, but also using it against itself so as to properly assimilate into a marginal, American society.[17] Although it is a community linked through physical otherness, the Justice League nevertheless contains earthlings. However, despite their earthly origins, the series still promotes the idea that through the formation of alternative cultural communities a group can enmesh itself into society, use its diverse talents to improve that society, and thrive as a diverse collective.[18] Though it seemingly embraces this marginal enclave, *Smallville* necessitates that the League's labor remain invisible in the face of the society that it purports to protect, which further conveys an ambiguous attitude toward immigrant assimilation.

Invisible Labor and the Need for Anonymous Citizenship

As he does throughout the entire series, Clark attempts to keep his Kryptonian history secret. Although he slowly reveals his otherness to his close friends, for the majority of the time Clark navigates through *Smallville* as a seemingly normal, human American. However, his best friend/reporter Chloe Sullivan, fellow Justice League member Oliver Queen, and his father Jor-El constantly challenge his decision to do so. They try to entice Clark with notions of fame and prosperity if he were to identify primarily as Kal-El, but Clark continuously refuses to thoroughly embrace his superhero nature, choosing to instead keep his work anonymous. In representing Clark as explicitly denying an uninhibited Kryptonian identity, the series suggests that it is Clark and *not* society itself who imposes concealment; it appears that Clark does not *necessarily* have to be a secret hero in order to assimilate into mainstream American culture. Season eight, in turn, continuously returns to this issue to tease out why Clark refuses to fully identify as Kal-El.

Season eight marks a major turning point in the series' production because *Smallville*'s creators Alfred Gough and Miles Millar decided to no longer continue with the series. As Michael S. Duffy notes, "Seasons five, six, and seven began to struggle with stretching the internal complexities of the show's own premise and legacy."[19] The subsequent seasons, in contrast, demonstrate an increased divergence from the series' typical format. One such deviation is the creation of Clark's superhero alter ego, which becomes solidified and named in the episode "Identity" (2008) after Jimmy Olsen manages to take a picture of Clark amidst his superhero activities.

Naming the figure in the picture the "Red-Blue Blur," which will eventually shorten to just the Blur, the episode focuses on various characters attempting to convince Jimmy to not print the picture, even though he suspects that Clark is the Blur. Ultimately, Oliver steps in as a double for the Blur so as to prove to Jimmy that Clark is not the famed hero (repaying the favor from when Clark posed as Green Arrow to protect Oliver's identity in "Hydro" [2007]). By so adamantly striving to keep Clark's superpower secret, the episode highlights the question of why Clark chooses to remain anonymous, something the series fully explores later in season eight with the episode "Infamous" (2009).

In "Infamous," the antagonist Linda Lake (played by Tori Spelling) aims to coerce Clark into revealing his Kryptonian identity. Rather than continue to fight what appears to be a hopeless battle against her, Clark decides to disclose the truth to Lois Lane so as to have some control over how society will receive the news. Though at first his proclamation appears to be well-received, federal agents, a media blitz, and fans quickly demand that he put his powers to the test (e.g., some fans start jumping off of a building with the expectation that he will rush to save them), which makes Clark regret his decision to admit his secret identity. As the episode progresses, Clark sees that his announcement not only threatens his legal status, as federal agents attempt to take him into custody, but it also summarily destroys his public persona, which he discovers by no longer being able to navigate the world under the guise of an average

Midwestern American. The episode concludes with Kal-El using the Legion Ring to alter time and keep his secret safe.[20]

"Infamous" is particularly significant for the series, and this essay, because it wrestles with the consequences of attempting to publicly fuse Clark and Kal-El within an already-existing American culture devoid of Kryptonian influences. Though I argue that the series constantly seeks to hybridize Clark and Kal-El, it does so through the formation of an alternative community that can then graft itself onto mainstream culture. A prerequisite of that melding, though, is a level of anonymity where Kal-El's exceptionalism is relegated to secrecy so as to preserve the existence of the average Midwestern American Clark. By making his otherness evident and disallowing him from passing as average, Clark loses the ability and/or right to exist within the country as an autonomous and legal subject. Although Kal-El, the immigrant, uses his talents to aid society, he must do so invisibly or otherwise become subject to policing. It is through this required sense of censure and fear that Clark most fully represents the series' understanding of illegal immigrant phenomenology, which gives insight into a popularly shared American conception of immigration and the immigrants who perform it.

Conclusion

Smallville ran for ten years and proved to be one of the WB's and later the CW's most successful series. Throughout its run, the series underwent numerous cast and crew changes that helped bring diversity and creativity to the production and maintained a sense of innovation to its already novel objective of recreating the Superman mythos for the twenty-first century. However, *Smallville* manages to both retain a sense of logical consistency within itself while also speaking to a major element within the Superman mythos that has, until recently, been completely taken for granted: Superman, the immigrant from the stars, did not originally, and continues to not exclusively, represent American culture. As evident through the comparison of the Man of Steel to an undocumented immigrant in a Mexican corrido by Los Hermanos Ortiz, the Last Son of Krypton transcends national borders and serves as a point of identification for a variety of people outside mainstream America, including immigrants and people in other countries. While the series balances the relationship between Clark and his Kal-El counterpart, it nonetheless does so with an air of ambiguity that keeps it from fully committing to a pro-immigration stance. However, the mere exposure and emphasis of this aspect of one of the United States' most enduring and beloved fictional characters represents a momentous shift from traditional understandings of both America and its popular culture. Ultimately, it remains to be seen to what extent Superman's depiction as an undocumented immigrant alters perceptions of current American immigrants, but it is clear that a change has definitely occurred, which most recently has allowed for this deviation to not only occur but also sustain itself amongst a diverse, popular, American, *and* international audience.

NOTES

1. In this essay I use the monikers Superman, The Man of Steel, The Metropolis Marvel, The Last Son of Krypton, The Man of Tomorrow, The Blur, and Kal-El, Clark Kent, and Clark. However, I do not use them interchangeably. The Man of Steel, The Metropolis Marvel, The Man of Tomorrow, and The Last Son of Krypton describe the character as the traditional Superman. Kal-El emphasizes a Kryptonian lineage. Clark Kent and Clark denote an American/Smallville origin. The Blur refers to Clark Kent's secret identity in *Smallville*.
2. Charles Ramirez Berg, "Immigrant, Aliens, and Extraterrestrials: Science Fiction's Alien 'Other' as (among Other Things) New Hispanic Imagery," in *Latino Images in Film: Stereotypes, Subversion, and Resistance* (Austin: University of Texas Press, 2002).
3. Mae Ngai, *Impossible Subjects: Illegal Aliens and the Making of Modern American* (Princeton: Princeton University Press, 2004).
4. Rachel Rubin and Jeffrey Melnick, *Immigration and American Popular Culture* (New York: New York University Press, 2007); Karin Beeler, "Televisual Transformations: Myth and Social Issues in *Smallville*," in *The Smallville Chronicles: Critical Essays on the Television Series*, ed. Lincoln Geraghty (Lanham, MD: Scarecrow Press, 2011), 25.
5. Erik Lundegaard, "Trust, Justice and (Fill in the Blank)," *The Chicago Tribune*, June 30, 2006, A23(L).
6. "Superman Comes to Earth as Clark Kent," *The Adventures of Superman*, Mutual Broadcasting Company (August 31, 1942).
7. "Superman on Earth," *The Adventures of Superman*, Mutual Broadcasting Company (September 19, 1952).
8. David S. Goyer (w), Miguel Sepulveda, (p), and Paul Mounts (i), "The Incident," Action Comics #900 (June 2011), Little, Brown [DC Comics]: 75.
9. *Kill Bill: Vol. 2*, directed by Quentin Tarantino (USA, Miramax Films, 2004).
10. Rayna Denison, "No Flights, No Tights: *Smallville* and the Roles of Special Effects in Television," in *The Smallville Chronicles: Critical Essays on the Television Series*, ed. by Lincoln Geraghty (Lanham, MD: Scarecrow Press, 2011), 65.
11. I use the word Anglo to refer to white, non–Latina/o Americans of European descent.
12. Aldo Regalado, "Modernity, Race, and the American Superhero," in *Comics as Philosophy*, ed. by Jeff McLaughlin (Jackson: University Press of Mississippi, 2005), 92.
13. Ibid.
14. Raymond Williams, *Culture and Society: 1780–1950* (New York: Columbia University Press, 1983).
15. "Fan Episode Reviews," TV.com, last modified June 21, 2012, http://www.tv.com/shows/smallville/subterranean–864005/reviews.
16. "Meteor Freak," *Smallville Wikia*, accessed January 31, 2014, http://smallville.wikia.com/wiki/Meteor_freak.
17. William Flores and Rina Benmayor, *Latino Cultural Citizenship* (Boston: Beacon Press, 1997). I use the term cultural citizenship in the same way that William Flores and Rina Benmayor do in *Latino Cultural Citizenship* to refer to the ways in which Latina/os (a marginalized American group) form communities that transcend citizenship status so as to allow

for the distribution of resources to other Latina/os whom are relegated to the status of illegal immigrant/impossible subject.

18. Only some are entirely human; Martian Manhunter (J'onn J'onzz) is not American or human, Victor Stone is a cyborg, and Chloe Sullivan is a meteor freak who was also infected with a Kryptonian virus.

19. Michael S. Duffy, "Sacrifice or Salvation? *Smallville*'s Heroic Survival and Changing Television Trends," in *The Smallville Chronicles: Critical Essays on the Television Series*, ed. by Lincoln Geraghty (Lanham, MD: Scarecrow Press, 2011), 153.

20. The Legion Ring is from the thirty-first century and belongs to the Legion of Super-Heroes (LSH). The LSH is comprised of aliens who were inspired by Clark. The ring gives its wearer the ability to fly as well as time travel.

Bodies as Unreliable Signifiers

The Inconsistency of Smallville's *Character Construction*

Daniel Kulle

It is "Ring Day" in high school in the *Smallville*'s season two episode "Red" (2002). When Clark Kent buys a ring against his parents' wishes, the ring puts him under the influence of red Kryptonite (which up to this point in the series is an unknown substance). In accordance with the Superman mythology, the red meteor rock causes a complete character change in Clark, lowering all his inhibitions. He experiences improved self-esteem, increased sexual desire, and a hedonistic need to buy material things with his parents' stolen credit card. Clark wants to party, to smooch any girl, to listen to heavy metal music, and to drive his new motorcycle. In short, Clark exhibits typical signs of machismo teenage rebellion parsed down to iconic media clichés. Of course, toward the end of the episode, Clark is saved by his father Jonathan Kent and buddy Pete Ross and freed from the influence of red Kryptonite. Back in tune with his good character, he repents and apologizes to friends and family. Yet, some uncertainty remains; this well-behaved Clark Kent is not as stable a character as he had appeared to be. Change can happen fast in the world of *Smallville*.

Smallville tells the story of young Clark Kent, a brooding teenager who, though gifted with alien superpowers, has still a long way to go before he will become the true Superman. The series covers a string of contemporary topoi, such as the construction of the contemporary conservative American family, sexual ethics, the image of a small rural town, and the role of industrial and economic development in an idyllic mythological space. Yet, it is foremost a series about bodies, and the possible—and impossible—changes they can undergo. Thus, *Smallville* is also a story of self-knowledge and of (re)gaining self-control over one's own body and its dangerous potential.

In *Smallville*, bodily change is a threat. Therefore, a number of containment strategies are exercised to bind bodies back to their original form and function. Change must be punished, the metamorphosis must be reversed—or at least regulated—or the character will soon be banned from the fictional universe. However, at the same time, the series introduces a subversive imbalance: bodies are constructed as unreliable signifiers, signifiers that can deceive, change, or even redouble. As this essay will illustrate, the conservative containment strategies often fail to sufficiently counterbalance the character inconsistency that comes along with the instability of the semiotic process, thus offering viewers a variety of reading approaches to the series.

The Body and the Character

Since the normative poetics of Aristotle and Theophrastus, character construction has been a main focus of narratology.[1] The character (as opposed to a real-life person) is the origin of any willful story action and a fundamental entry point for the viewer's empathy and engagement with the story.[2] Fictional personae are formed by the text through attribution (when the text ascribes several traits to a character) and through differentiation (when the text establishes several characters in a contrasting or functional relation to each other).[3] In the story, a character fulfills a structural function, be it such a basic one such as described by Algirdas Julien Greimas's actants or a more differentiated one like fulfilling a narrative role.[4] Moreover, fictional characters always interact with social roles and stereotypes found in other media and in everyday life.[5]

The differences between literary and audiovisual characters are centered around the body and its visibility. Unlike characters in literature that can be described in changing degree of detail thereby leaving much to fantasy, the iconic sign of a cinematic body is a "full sign" defining the body in greatest visual detail and leaving next to nothing to the imagination.[6] This visibility of the body opens up the discussion to such concepts as that of aura, presence, eroticism, fetishism, or general ideas of photogénie that film theorists have discussed since the 1920s.[7] It also introduces a basic semiotic instability of the iconic sign, since the depicted body is a double signifier, referring to the fictional character as well as to the real-life actor playing that character.[8] On the other hand, a filmic body is rarely shown in full. Often, we see only parts of it, the head, the torso, or a hand. This divisibility and its counterpart, the montage of images, demonstrate the constructive quality of the character.

Jens Eder has proposed a model consisting of four levels of character analysis in fictional film and television. Firstly, a character can be analyzed as an aesthetic or medial construct, focusing on the visual and audible body, its performance or its language, as well as the function of montage, mise-en-scène, lighting, or sound. Secondly, an analysis can treat the character as a real-life persona, applying biological, anthropological or psychological models of persons onto this fictional entity. Thirdly, a character can be interpreted as a signifier in itself, as a symbol or allegory, thus introducing a second tier of signification. And fourthly, the character can be analyzed not only as part of a media text but also as an element of a larger dispositive or communicative network.[9] We can ask, for example, what the producers intended when making a character act this or that way. What were the economic relationships between media industries and the intended target audience that shaped a character? What do viewers do with their own special characters in their everyday media practice? Or, in what way might a character resonate with larger discourses of religion, politics, and geography?

A Model of Character Instability

Loosely following Eder's levels of analysis, we can distinguish several layers of semiotic relations in the construction of characters: firstly, a visible body has to be constructed through images and sounds by the means provided by the medium in question; secondly, the body itself becomes a signifier in the sense that it is a visual representative of the individual character (although character construction can be influenced by the surrounding space or by auditory atmosphere as well); finally, we can treat the whole character as a sign itself, interpreting it as a symbol or allegory. In all three processes of signification, a moment of semiotic instability can be introduced.

In *Smallville*, the coherence of the body as constructed by the media text is rarely undermined on an aesthetic level. The series deploys classical, non-experimental film aesthetics that hide their artificiality and focus on the continuity of space and its inhabiting objects. Yet, *Smallville* uses at least two different devices to destabilize the body itself without leaving the continuity system: special effects and doppelgangers. The use of CGI special effects can depict the change some bodies undergo in the series, thus constructing a body whose coherence is questioned over time. And with doppelgangers, in which one pre-filmic actor-body plays two different but similar character-bodies, we can see that the signification process between the visual representation of a body and the (constructed) body itself can be destabilized on an ontological level.

Semiotic processes between the body and the character, on the other hand, are regularly undermined in *Smallville*. Since a body is considered a visual representation of a character, we, as viewers, sketch the character schema from the bottom-up on what we see the body do and how it looks like while doing it (of course, the text can also offer us other framing devices in mise-en-scène or lighting that can shape our interpretation of a character). Yet, we also apply the character schemata that we have constructed so far, top-down onto the perceived body, to build up expectations about the character/body, or to use it as a frame of interpretation for the body's action. It is on this level that characters in *Smallville* most often turn into unstable entities: characters act "out of character," they no longer live up to the expected behavior, or they experience sudden unforeseen desires. Bodies can change their appearance. Characters can split, double, or transform. Different characters can share the same body; while, at other times, different bodies can be so similar that they are mistaken for each other. In other words, *Smallville* shows a general tendency to separate the body as signifier and the character as signified, turning the body into an unreliable, unstable, or even subversive signifier.

I would like to bring order into the diversity of forms of this unsteady

	Change	Control	Confusion
Semiotic Instability	C ↙ ↘ B B'	C C' ↘ ↙ B	C C' | | B ----- B'
Description	Two distinguishable bodies refer to one and the same character	One body refers to different characters (one original and one controlling)	Bodies are so alike that they can be confused
Subtypes	Metamorphosis Shapeshifting Alter Ego Chimera	Intoxication Possession Body Swap	Twin Clone Impersonation

relationship with a model for character instability. The model is based on the work of Hans-Jürgen Wulff and Alexandra Fried who have written on doppelgangers, clones, twins, and other types of body instability.[10] My model distinguishes between three basic narrative devices: change, control, and confusion. These three devices should not be taken as separate categories of character instability, but rather as aspects or as narrative strategies of character construction that can as easily mix and combine, and interact in the creation of one instable character.

In the first main device, change, two visually different bodies refer to the same character. In most cases, the two bodies do not exist simultaneously but rather morph into each other over the course of time. At the core of this type is the question of integrity, of being one (or more than one) and the question of stability. What is in danger here is the coherence of the body itself.

In a first variant of the change device, called metamorphosis, a body mutates permanently and (unless cured) irreversibly. Such a transformation often occurs as a starting point of a given plot. In a second variant, called shapeshifting, the change can be reversed. Examples of the former would be Grimm's Froschkönig, Kafka's Gregor Samsa, or the beast in *La belle et la bête*. Examples of the latter would be the Greek god Zeus, the robot T-1000 in *Terminator 2: Judgment Day* (1991) or Odo in *Star Trek: Deep Space Nine* (1993–1999).

While in these first two variants the disintegration is contained to the level of the body, sometimes the material mutation can also introduce a (partial) disintegration of the personality of the character. In the case of the alter ego, for example, the character splits into two partial identities (although these are still part of the same fictional person). Such a split can be regular and reversible similar to the shape-shifter, as in *Dr. Jekyll and Mr. Hyde*, or a one-time transformation, as in *Fight Club* (1999). The transformation can be uncontrolled, as in Robert Louis Stevenson's novel, or conscious, as in the secret identity of superheroes or secret agents. And the alter ego often opens up to allegorical interpretations of the partial identity as a representation of the character's subconscious on the one hand, or its superego on the other. Chimeras and hybrids form another and rather unusual variant of change that goes beyond the level of the body as for example in *The Fly* (1958) or in the 1920s transplantation movies such as in *Orlacs Hände* (*The Hands of Orlac*) (1924).[11] Here, the two bodies do indeed coexist simultaneously, amalgamated into one body. The chimera thus can be interpreted as the opposite to the alter ego; while the alter ego is characterized by a split of one personality into two, the chimera fusions two personalities and bodies into one.

In the second main device, control, the same body refers to two different characters or agencies. Unlike with the first type, here, the body itself often does not change substantially. The fictional persona rather acts "out of character," thus questioning the role expectations put onto the body-character construct. Even if the body does change, the transformation is ascribed to an agency outside the character. At the core of this type, we thus find the topos of self-control and self-discipline, of having agency over one's own body and the ability—or failure—to integrate character and body into a coherent whole.

In a first variant of this device, possession, a character is controlled or manipulated by another one, leaving the first character next to no influence over his or her own(ed) body. The second character can take over the body, as happens for example in *The Exorcist* (1973) or in *Being John Malkovich* (1999). In a second variant, intoxication, the manipulating agency is a non-personal entity; it is for example a substance or a drug. This variant is similar to the alter ego. However, while in the case of the alter ego the split between body and personality is caused by the character itself, in the case of intoxication the responsibility for the transformation is attributed to an entity outside the character. Finally, a third variant of the control device can be found when two characters swap their bodies, forming a relationship that can be analyzed as a mutual possession in which two persons control a body that does not belong to them.

However both devices, change and control, nevertheless presuppose the identity of any depicted body, no matter how much modification the body undergoes and no matter how much the body's integrity has been undermined. If a body looks alike when we see it in the next scene, we can assume that it is still the same body. This is not the case in the third device, confusion or mistaken identity. In this case, two bodies and two characters are actually clearly distinguished narrative entities. Yet, their bodies are visually so similar that they are confused. Here, the semiotic disintegration does not take place between depicted body and character but on the level of images and sounds constructing one—or in this case two visually indistinguishable—bodies.

The first variant of this device, the twin or the doppelganger, creates two characters that look so much alike that they are confused with each other. This variant is a common genre element in, for example, the comedy of errors or the thriller. The twin, especially in the form of the evil twin, is also closely connected to the variant of alter ego. In fact, the distinction between alter ego and twin is only a matter of degrees centering on the question of how far the split in character has produced two distinct entities (evil twin), or one double-sided entity (alter ego).

The next variant, the clone, builds on the twin but draws in discourses of genetics, robotics, or biological determinism. The clone is always accompanied by a discourse of "techné," as cloning implies a technical process and dispositive behind it.[12] Furthermore, clones do not only share a similarity on the level of the body but also on the level of character, thereby presupposing an algorithmic determinism in the nature of the self. Clones thus neither count as one character, nor are they two separate characters, hence questioning the individuality of the self.

In a last variant of mistaken identity, called impersonation or imitation, the topos of confusing two similar bodies is combined with a superficial form of shapeshifting. Here, the two character-bodies do not look alike, originally. Rather, the first character changes her or his appearance to imitate the body of a second character (by changing the body in case she/he is a shape-shifter, or by just simulating a change with clothing and make-up) to imitate the body of a second character. This variant is probably the most common device from the trickster in mythology to modern-day comedy of errors.

Character Instability and Bodily Change in Smallville

In *Smallville*, the three devices of change, control, and confusion and all of their variants occur in some episode or other, often in combination with each other. Tina Greer, appearing in season one's "X-Ray" (2001) and season two's "Visage" (2003), is a shape-shifter (and an obsessive homosexual lover, thus implicitly reflecting the homophobic attitude of the series). Season six's "Hydro" (2007) introduces Linda Lake, a shapeshifter who can morph into water-based forms. Additionally, Brainiac, a consistent antagonist for Clark in the series, is a supervillain and impersonating shapeshifter. Byron, a teenager in love, changes into a werewolf every full moon, thus presenting a rather common narrative of the alter ego variant in "Nocturne" (2002). In "Dichotic" (2002), Ian, the boy who can duplicate himself, is a special case of the alter ego variant, because here the two bodies can exist simultaneously, thus reaching in to the twin variant. Lex and Alexander Luthor and Clark and Bizarro form two pairs of good/evil twins in season four's "Onyx" (2005) and portions of season seven, respectively. There are clones, such as Emily Dinsmore ("Accelerate" [2003]) or Lex's brother Julian (season seven). In addition, cases of body swap occur, as in season four's "Transference" (2004) where Lionel Luthor and Clark swap bodies, or in season eight's "Hex" (2009) where the swapping pair is Chloe and Lois. Finally, there are cases of partial body swap, in which superpowers are exchanged between characters, for example, when Clark's powers are transferred to Eric Summers in season one's "Leech" (2002) or to Lana in season seven's "Wrath" (2007). Finally, the cyborg characters Victor Stone (Cyborg) and John Corben (Metallo), allow cases of body chimerae find their way into the series.

In this diversity of body and character instabilities, two main clusters stand out as rather prominent: the "meteor freaks" and characters out of control. In the character type of the meteor freak, a teenager comes into contact with the alien meteorite that accompanied Clark's crash-landing to Earth. After the contact, the teen body then gains fantastical powers that are considered alien to humans. In the pilot episode (2001), Jeremy Creek controls electricity; in season one's "Kinetic" (2002) three thieves can move through solid objects; Eric Marsh and his friends have increased strength in season two's "Witness" (2003); and Kevin Grady's abilities can cause amnesia in season four's "Blank" (2005).

Often, these changes in ability are accompanied by slight modifications in form or habit as well, reflecting the changed actant position or the new morality of the character in question. Because, unlike Clark, who tries to learn how to use his gifts to help others, meteor freaks regularly draw on their new superpowers for selfish goals. Most often, the meteor freak can even be read allegorically as a manifestation of bad traits or sins such as vengeance, jealousy, greed, or vanity. Elise Fine enhances her daughter Abigail's beauty in season four's "Façade" (2004); football player Geoff Johns and Coach Walt Arnold use their powers to cheat in sports in "Recruit" (2005) and "Hothead" (2001) respectively; Justin Gaines takes revenge on someone who wronged him in season one's "Crush" (2002); and the "weather girls" manipulate wind and temperature to pursue their thieving career in season seven's "Fierce" (2007). Especially throughout the first seasons of the series, meteor freaks serve as the main adversary on a weekly basis, the "villain of the week"—or "Freak of the Week" as they grew to be called—that Clark and his friends can uncover and overcome.

The meteor freaks are thus characterized by an infringement of a bodily order, an order that prescribes what a body can do and what it should look like. That material infringement is then closely connected to a violation of a moral order that must be punished accordingly, often by death or exclusion from the diegesis. Therefore, the meteor freaks are an example of the first device, change, in which two bodies relate to one character. The first body is the one a Western audience would expect from a teenage boy or girl, and it is the body that he/she had before contacting meteor rocks. The second version is the one with superpowers used to selfish ends.

One could argue that elements of alter ego and even of control play into this character type as well. The meteor infected, once transformed, exhibit a changed behavior, possessing now the power to do as they wish. As in the case of many an alter ego, they are manifestations of previously subconscious desires. However, unlike in the case of the alter ego, with the meteor freaks, the two personalities are not played against each other, nor are they dialectically resolved. The transformed body is considered a violation of a material and moral order, and is not treated as a metaphorical conflict of the soul.

The same holds true for the aspect of control. One might argue that the meteor freaks are just under the influence of the meteor rock. Yet, here, meteor rock serves as a narrative trigger, not as a permanent external influence that can be taken away again as with Clark's ring. The change itself is often located in the backstory of a single episode, the super body of the meteor freak serving as a reminder of the infringement. Accordingly, there is no cure for the meteor freaks. Sometimes, the episodes end with the death of the antagonist. Most commonly, however, the meteor freaks are excluded from the "normal" fictional universe and deported into the mental institution/prison Belle Reve, or the research facility known as the Summerholt Institute, where they cannot harm the outside world anymore—and where they can wait for a possible cure that will never come.

The characters out of control, on the other hand, focus on the topos of self-discipline and self-control, using the subtypes of intoxication and possession. In many episodes, characters become intoxicated by some impersonal exterior agent that changes the expected behavior tremendously: a truth serum in "Truth" (2004) and "Lara" (2007); a love potion in "Devoted" (2004) and "Crimson" (2007); magical champagne in "Fortune" (2011); a flower that strips people of their inhibitions in "Nicodemus" (2002); or a parasite that inspires people to engage in risky behavior in "Rush" (2003). Another important plot device—in the adult Superman universe as well as in *Smallville*—is the Kryptonite (or meteor rock) that influences only Clark: green Kryptonite regularly incapacitates Clark; red Kryptonite lowers his inhibitions in "Red," "Exile" (2003), "Unsafe" (2005), and "Crimson" (2007); blue Kryptonite strips him of his abilities in "Blue" (2007); silver Kryptonite makes him extremely paranoid in "Splinter" (2005); black Kryptonite separates him from his fully Kryptonian side, Kal-El, in "Crusade" (2004); and a possessed Oliver Queen tries to use gold Kryptonite to remove Clark's powers in "Finale" (2011).

In other cases, the control of a character is ascribed to a personalized exterior agent: salesman Bob Rickman imposes his will onto others in "Hug" (2002); Desirée Adkins controls men with pheromones in "Heat" (2002); Lana's short-term boyfriend Seth Nelson controls her emotions in season three's "Magnetic" (2003); the hacker Molly Griggs sends out emails to Clark and his friends that hypnotizes them to kill Chloe in "Delete" (2004); and Maxima's kiss controls men to do her bidding in "Instinct" (2008). Furthermore, there are even more extreme and extended cases of control that take the form of possession: the witch Isobel possesses Lana throughout season four; Jor-El takes over Lionel's body in season five; a Phantom Zone escapee attempts to take over Clark's body in "Labyrinth" (2007); the Egyptian goddess Isis possesses Lois in "Isis" (2010); and in the first half of season ten, Oliver is influenced by the power of Darkseid.

In all these examples of control, the change is reversible. Once the external influence is eliminated, the characters return to normal. Yet, unlike in the case of the meteor freaks, there is usually no material manifestation of change, no superpowers, and no modification in the appearance of the body. In fact, it is the visual identity of the body controlled by the character and the one controlled by the external influences that lies at the core of this narrative device. We, as the viewers, ascribe role expectations to a body that can then be disappointed by the character acting "out of character." We perceive one body that might refer to two different controlling agencies or characters.

Thus, it comes to no surprise, that the characters possessed and controlled are not villainous antagonists, but rather Clark or his friends. The possessed characters are therefore not excluded from the universe by the story. Unlike the cases of the meteor freaks, where a violation of a material and moral order takes place and must be punished, the cases of control (or loss of control) pose questions of integrity between body and personality, questions of self-discipline and self-control. The affected characters can be healed by excluding the external agent and by proposing a higher degree of restraint in the character.

Bodies in *Smallville*, to formulate an intermediate conclusion, are thus a generally subversive matter that pose a constant threat to the material and moral order: bodies change or do not behave in the ways we expect them to. They elude control and they question the identity between body and mind. Therefore, bodies in *Smallville*, as they are constructed by images and sounds in the series, fail to fulfill their semiotic function as a stable signifier for a character. Role expectations are constantly irritated, our cognitive schemata frequently put into question. "Why is she that way?" "And is that really him?" are questions to be asked repeatedly throughout the series, as bodies do not necessarily play into our character or personality expectations.

Smallville exhibits a series of conservative containment strategies to counter this material and semiotic subversion of the body—containment strategies that go alongside a general conservative alignment of the series and its high praise of heteronormativity, family norms, state, and authority. Meteor freaks and other perpetrators are punished by death or deportation into a mental institution. Contaminated bodies that lose control only for a limited time are healed and saved. However, the containment strategies deployed by the series are never impenetrable. Bodies serve as a constant source of subversion and instability. The transformed bodies of meteor freaks and other villains can always come back from the mental institution. Even the main characters have to impose a constant degree of self-discipline and self-awareness not to lose control over their own bodies and abilities.

This becomes even clearer in the second half of the series when other superheroes—characters who serve as the "good" version of meteor freaks—are introduced. In these instances, *Smallville* postulates that people with superpowers can learn to master their abilities to use them for the "greater good" instead of just for their own hedonistic goals. Nevertheless, many of the new superheroes presented in the series have to undergo a learning process that stresses the need for self-discipline and order. While Bart Allen starts out as a willful teenager with superpowers that he uses to steal from people in season four's "Run" (2004), he subsequently learns how to submit to the moral order imposed by Clark, and eventually accompanies him and the other superheroes in their battle against evil in "Justice" (2007) and beyond. And Jaime Reyes, who transforms into the Blue Beetle when he in contact with an alien robotic suit, initially hurts people until he is mentored by Booster Gold in "Booster" (2011).

The topos of need for constant self-control for all superheroes is most clearly visible in the conflict between Clark and his cousin Kara, whose superpowers are more developed than Clark's but who has no wish to control or hide them at all. In "Fierce" Clark admonishes Kara for her rash and open behavior, telling her, "you just have to fit in" and "it's all about control—which you don't have." Of course, despite the conflict, Kara eventually learns from her overprotective cousin how and why to control and hide her abilities. Yet, the tension between Kara and Clark also suggests that the central character of *Smallville* might be a valuable source of character instabilities and inconsistencies that he is desperately trying to hide.

The Inconsistency of Clark Kent

Smallville sketches its main character as a deeply inconsistent construct. Clark is not only a character of a self-contained television series, but is also deeply intertwined in the intertextual story universe of Superman, thus opening the character to questions of discrepancy or continuity to the rest of the fictional universe. Although *Smallville* distances itself from the DC universe that forms the fictional diegesis of all other Superman stories, the series is still firmly embedded in the Superman legend. The story of the superhero has been told, expanded, and told again for more than seventy years across several media, thus forming a complex transmedial narrative with often diverging or contradictory storylines, relaunches, or multiverses.[13] *Smallville* not only builds on the basic story line of Superman, it also adopts several side stories from comics, films, or other series that existed before. The series includes additional superheroes such as the Flash, Green Arrow, Aquaman, Cyborg, and many more. Finally, yet importantly, this Clark inherits one important inconsistency from this intertextual background: the superhero's secret double identity.

The secret identity is a basic feature in most if not all superhero stories, contrasting the character's everyday "normal" life with his/her superhero responsibilities. These dueling identities often result in binary character traits like shy versus bold, or well adjusted versus rebellious. The superhero thus can take the form of an alter ego character in which the alternative personality manifests not in the subconscious but the superego. Alternatively, it can be read as some kind of self-empowerment in which the character breaks loose of society's tight constrictions to serve a higher moral goal. However, this double identity is not implemented fully in the *Smallville* story. Superhero powers are rarely depicted as self-empowering, but rather as dangerous traits that necessitate self-control and discipline. Even more, at the source of Clark's powers and his attitude toward them lay a deeply rooted guilt, as his arrival on Earth accompanied a deadly and destructive meteor shower. Clark's split identity between normal schoolboy and superhero—and between human and alien—is neither a stable one, nor even a visually distinguishable one. The superhero Clark does not wear a costume and cannot be told apart from its teenage counterpart, both personalities intertwining in the same scene.

Often enough, the superhero in Clark is not that easily recognized at all. Clark is repeatedly seen feeling helpless, unable to make sense of situations, and in need of his female friends—especially when it comes to the social problems a teenage series needs to present. His strong body, his display of superpowers, and his claim to be a moral paragon is often clearly opposed to his inability to master even the most basic social situations. The superhero thus becomes not an alternative personality of Clark Kent but rather a mirror stage image or future role that the young teenager and Superman-to-be tries and repeatedly fails to fulfill.

These inconsistencies of character are continuously visible in the performance of the body. Tom Welling's purposeful underplaying as Clark supports his shy, insecure teenage outsider act. However, when it comes to the identity of the superhero, this acting style quickly seems awkward in its lack of motion and expression. Both—lack of expression and lack of movement—are aided by the use of special effects. Most of Clark's superpowers do not involve any motion on his side. He rather stands and stares into the void while the CGI effects do their work. Welling's acting style plays into the character prototype of the brooding young man prominent in such similar series like *Roswell* (1999–2002) or *Buffy the Vampire Slayer* (1997–2003). It may also be read as an allusion to the comic representation of Superman with his strong jaw and minimal expression or as a reference to the comic medium in general with its montage of single expressive poses.

The inconsistency of a body with superpowers that does not move and is incapable of expressing itself is complemented by an obvious difference in age and body shape. When shooting began in 2001, Welling was almost 24 years old, his hyper-athletic body thus quite different from the insecure and clumsy teenager he portrayed on the series. The body of the superhero-to-be that does not move and that is frequently incapacitated by Kryptonite or by social problems thus becomes an inactive fetishized object or erotic display; this introduces another discrepancy in view of the puritan body and sexual norms that pervade the series.

Clark is not only an inconsistent character because of his role as a Superman-to-be or his status as an immobile object of desire. The moral geography of the series that separates "freak" bodies from "normal" ones positions the series' main character in an unstable place at the center of these opposite poles. Clark's body is constantly changing, threatening his personal identity and integrity. Similar to the meteor infected, Clark's transformation often stands for an unconscious, allegedly sinful development; his superpowers are like some kind of sexual desire he has to get under control. In "X-Ray," his new vision is just too good *not* to invade girls' privacy in the locker room—until he learns that this is wrong. The heat vision he develops in "Heat" at first behaves like an unwanted classroom erection—until he learns how to control it and use it as a weapon. However, whereas the meteor freaks succumb to the temptation of their superpowers and have to be punished or excluded from the story world, Clark resists such impulses over time and learns to exercise self-discipline.

The characterization of Clark as a freak contrasts with his strong longing to be normal, to belong. This desire of his is presented from the very first season which—equating popularity and normality—uses prototypical American highschool tenants such as starring on the football team as important goals for Clark to reach. However, even when Clark does become a football team member, Clark remains the immigrant and illegal alien who must hide his identity in front of even his closest friends. His desire to be normal is accompanied by a strong fear of being recognized as his true self. Exposure is considered a threat and living in the closet is regularly embraced as the ultimate goal.

Coherent, consistent reasons for this secrecy are never fully explained in *Smallville*. Some episodes suggest that the threat of experimentation from mad scientists and rogue government agencies necessitates secrecy, while others point to the fear of being turned into a public pariah or being stripped of all human rights. Moreover, many episodes stress Clark's strong desire for normalcy and belonging, things that would be eliminated were his secret exposed to the world—or even his small group of friends. In "Rogue" (2002), the corrupt cop Sam Phelan who tries to blackmail Clark and the Kents, sums it up nicely, "Of course, if you don't agree, I will tell the world what I know. Best case, Clark's under a microscope, worst case, he's a freak in a jar. Either way, his normal life is over." Blackmail thus poses another threat that forces superheroes into secrecy, even with their closest friends.

Within the strict morality of the series, being different carries with it the threat of exclusion, or deportation into a mental institution. In the series' final season, this threat is augmented beyond the previously benign characterization of government authorities when the U.S. Department of Domestic Security introduces the Vigilante Registration Act and establishes a prison not only for meteor freaks and other dissenters, but for superheroes as well. The urge to keep the secret and to stay in the closet is a goal that exceeds all other moral obligations. Clark even imposes double standards when it comes to his closest friends. In the early seasons when Clark and Lex share an uneasy friendship that will eventually crumble, Clark constantly accuses Lex of dishonesty, mistrust, and of hiding his true intentions. Clark's own strategy of lying to his friend and of hiding his identity, on the other hand, is questioned much less often. This is yet another inconsistency in Clark's character—especially when the series uses Lex's dishonesty and mistrust to paint him as the primary villain of later seasons.

Conclusion

It is "Ring Day" in at Smallville High School. Clark will eventually be saved from the influence of the red Kryptonite—saved by his friends and family who will work together as an improbable united force. Yet, the threat of the Kryptonite will return again and again, unexpectedly (or perhaps entirely expectedly), in later episodes. Clark's body will never be secure from his own desires and urges, or from his superpowers. Change can happen fast in the world of *Smallville*. Bodies in *Smallville*, to formulate my final conclusion, are profoundly unstable. They can transform and morph, double or split, be possessed or intoxicated. Bodies fail to be reliable signifiers for the characters in question. The relationships between body and character are constantly unbalanced, thereby irritating our character schemata and role expectations. The two main narrative devices employed in *Smallville*—the meteor freaks and characters out of control—show that these instabilities are used as an ideological lesson, to illustrate the importance of not only a moral order, but also a material order of the body on the one hand, the significance of self-control and self-discipline to maintain that order on the other.

However, the constant threat to and by the bodies to subvert that order, added by the inconsistencies of the main character work as a counterbalance to these conservative containment strategies. Clark is a superhero capable of lifting great weights but lacking social skills, a teenager in the body of an adult, a motionless superhero, an illegal immigrant, an American farm boy, and a freak intolerant of freaks. These inconsistencies let conservative containment strategies and subversive body strategies clash onto each other without offering a final resolve, opening *Smallville* up to different reading approaches for very different ideological viewer (and consumer) identities.

NOTES

1. For an overview on the narratology of characters see Fotis Jannidis, "Character," in *The Living Handbook of Narratology*, eds. Peter Hühn et al. (Hamburg, Germany: Interdisciplinary Center for Narratology, n.d.); Jens Eder et al., "Characters in Fictional Worlds: An Introduction," in *Characters in Fictional Worlds: Understanding Imaginary Beings in Literature, Film, and Other Media*, eds. Fotis Jannidis, Ralf Schneider, and Jans Eder (Berlin: Walter de Gruyter, 2010), 3–66; Henriette Heidbrink, "Fictional Characters in Literary Media Studies: A Survey of Research," in *Characters in Fictional Worlds: Understanding Imaginary Beings in Literature, Film, and Other Media*, eds. Fotis Jannidis, Ralf Schneider, and Jans Eder (Berlin: Walter de Gruyter, 2010), 67–110; Uri Margolin, "Character," in *Routledge Encyclopedia of Narrative Theory* (London: Routledge, 2005), 52–57; Henry Taylor and Margrit Tröhler, "Zu ein paar Facetten der menschlichen Figur im Spielfilm," in *Der Körper im Bild. Schauspielen, Darstellen, Erscheinen*, eds. Heinz-B. Heller, Karl Prümm, and Birgit Peulings (Marburg, Germany: Schüren, 1999), 137–151; Marc Vernet, "Le personage de film," *Iris* 7 (1986): 81–110. The different structuralist and semiopragmatic positions important to this discussion are covered in Monika Fludernik, "Histories of Narrative Theory (II): From Structuralism to the Present," in *A Companion to Narrative Theory*, eds. James Phelan and Peter J. Rabinowitz (Malden, MA: Blackwell, 2005, 36-59; Markus Kuhn, *Filmnarratologie. Ein erzähltheoretisches Analysemodell* (Berlin: Walter de Gruyter, 2011); Angela Keppler, "Zur Wahrnehmung medialer Akteure im Fernsehen," in *Fernsehen als "Beziehungskiste." Parasoziale Beziehungen und Interaktionen mit TV-Personen*, ed. Peter Vorderer (Opladen, Germany: Westdeutscher Verlag, 1996), 11–24; and Hans Jürgen Wulff, "Die entmachtete Sexualität. Politik, Klonieren und Replikation im neueren Kino," in *Unheimlich anders: Doppelgänger, Monster, Schattenwesen im Kino*, ed. Christine Rüffert (Berlin, Germany: Bertz and Fischer, 2005), 141–152.
2. Murray Smith, *Engaging Characters: Fiction, Emotion, and the Cinema* (Oxford, England: Clarendon Press/Oxford University Press, 1995).
3. André Gardies, "L'acteur dans le système textuel du film," *Etudes Littéraires* 13.1 (1980): 71–108.
4. Algirdas Julien Greimas, "Actants, Actors, and Figures," in *On Meaning: Selected Writings on Semiotic Theory* (Minneapolis: University of Minnesota Press, 1987), 106–120; Taylor and Tröhler, "Zu ein paar Facetten der menschlichen Figur im Spielfilm."
5. Jörg Schweinitz, "Stereotypes and the Narratological Analysis of Film Characters," in *Characters in Fictional Worlds: Understanding Imaginary Beings in Literature, Film and Other Media*, eds. Fotis Jannidis, Ralf Schneider, and Jens Elder (Berlin, Germany: Walter de Gruyter, 2010), 276–289.
6. Gardies, "L'acteur dans le système textuel du film."
7. Taylor and Tröhler, ""Zu ein paar Facetten der menschlichen Figur im Spielfilm."
8. Gardies, "L'acteur dans le système textuel du film."

9. Jens Elder, *Die Figur im Film: Grundlagen der Figurenanalyse* (Marburg, Germany: Schüren, 2008).

10. Wulff, "Die entmachtete Sexualität. Politik, Klonieren und Replikation im neueren Kino"; Alexandra Fried, *Transformation von Charakteren. Das Alter Ego als narratives Element im Animationsfilm*, Thesis (University of Applied Sciences Upper Austria, Hagenberg, 2010).

11. Ursula von Keitz, "Orlacs Hände und die Körperfragment-Topik nach dem Ersten Weltkrieg," in *Unheimlich anders: Doppelgänger, Monster, Schattenwesen im Kino* (Berlin, Germany: Bertz and Fischer, 2005), 53–68.

12. Wulff, "Die entmachtete Sexualität. Politik, Klonieren und Replikation im neueren Kino," 142.

13. Les Daniels, *Superman: The Complete History: The Life and Times of the Man of Steel* (San Francisco: Chronicle Books, 1998); Bradford W. Wright, *Comic Book Nation: The Transformation of Youth Culture in America* (Baltimore: Johns Hopkins University Press, 2003).

PART FOUR:
Reception

Finding Clark Kent

Sites of Nostalgia and Affect

GREGORY BRAY and
JOHN PATRICK BRAY

In *Adaptation and Appropriation,* Julie Sanders writes, "Adaptation and appropriation are dependent on the literary canon for the provision of a shared body of storylines, themes, characters, and ideas upon which their creative variations can be made. The spectator or reader must be able to participate in the play of similarity and difference perceived between the original, source, or inspiration to appreciate fully the reshaping or rewriting undertaken by the adaptive texts."[1] In other words, an audience already knows—to some extent—the story that is being retold. There are many reasons why an artist may wish to adapt a known work, and one of those reasons has to do with evoking a particular affect (and effect) within the audience, relying on an audience's nostalgia for the "source" material in order to shed some new light on beloved fictitious characters and stories. And as Sarah Warner and Erin Hurley suggest,

> The affective turn signals a renewed interest in embodiment and sensorial experience; [...] [t]his paradigm shift represents the desire to carve out some conceptual space for aspects of human motivation and behavior that are not tethered to consciousness, cognitive processes, and rationality, to validate physical and social dynamics that are inchoate and unpredictable, and to explore impulses and responses that social conventions shape but do not circumscribe.[2]

Most important for this essay, affect theory "elevates aesthetics of experience over those based in representation, freeing dramaturgy and spectacle from the Aristotelian requirements of wholeness and unity."[3]

Affect theory can be an effective tool in the field of adaptation studies, as our experiences with a given work are haunted by our previous experiences. As Marvin Carlson suggests, "Derrida and others have argued that all texts are in fact haunted by other texts and can be best understood as weavings together of preexisting textual material—indeed, that all reception is based upon this intertextual dynamic."[4] For Carlson, just as theatrical performances are haunted by other performances, so are characters haunted by actors, and actors by characters. Christopher Reeve, for example, will always be remembered as Superman. Furthermore, prior to the early twenty-first century, Basil Rathbone haunted the character Sherlock Holmes. There are times when these can overlap, and in other instances the actor is forever haunted (Rathbone, who played Holmes in fourteen films from 1939–1946, is a prime example), yet the character moves on and finds new life (for Holmes: Peter Cushing, Jeremy Brett, Benedict Cumberbatch, and Robert Downey, Jr., among others).

Superman is a haunted character. When considering the adaptations of Superman, there are various sites of nostalgia—Superman's hair, his cape, the various Superman themes that all are built on a triad, staring with the Max Fleischer cartoons—which become *canonical* for audiences. These canonical or iconic sites become so ingrained in a culture, it becomes difficult to separate what an audience remembers from one incarnation of a character, that a new incarnation/adaptation may have an assumed lack. In a work as popular as Superman, not only are the adapted texts influenced by the source material, but they also often redefine the source material and garner a new acceptance so that the adaptation then influences the source medium in a haze of mutually shared intertextuality. Despite this, there is a horizon of expectation that the central character in contemporary folklore will bear resemblances to his or her previous incarnations. More than simply a linear history of adaptation, Superman's earlier incarnations are in constant evocation as specters with each subsequent series or project. After decades of projects, this has created a cultural ideal of who and what the central character is. This simultaneously causes the story in *Smallville* to build to the familiar while it is also weighed down by it. The question, then, is "How is *Smallville*'s Clark Kent, and by extension, the world of story, impacted by previous incarnations?" This leads into a further consideration into affect theory and affective gesture and relies on (1) expectations for an adaptation, (2) sites of nostalgia which double as marks of legitimacy for spectators, and (3) the ways in which those creating an adaptation rely on sites of nostalgia to mark their adaptations as being as legitimate— if not more than—the predecessors.

We offer the term "sites of nostalgia" building on Pierre Nora's notion of "sites of memory." When writing about Nora's distinction between memory and history, Barbara A. Misztal suggests, "memory is no longer authentically lived and specific places of memory do not simply arise out of lived experience—instead they have to be created."[5] According to Nora, these creations (or sites of memory) include physical locations, such as libraries, or rituals, such as anniversaries, and weddings. For our purposes, a site of nostalgia has more to do with how a culture perceives an aspect of their own personal folklore, which can include songs, poems, books, films, and television series. While memory studies theorists tend to look at nostalgia as potentially violent (insofar as nostalgia creates imagined communities with dangerous borders), affect theorists (who have argued in various ways the positives of feeling) working in media and performance studies have given a closer look at nostalgia as something that can bring social awareness and effect positive change.[6] In the world of adaptation studies, sites of nostalgia are self-conscious moments used by artists who wish to let the audience know that they are aware of the audience's expectations.

Over the past few years, television producers and filmmakers have capitalized on audience nostalgia with some excellent results. For example, in Christopher Nolan's *Batman Begins* (2005), actor Christian Bale performs the "I'm Batman" line as a throwback to Michael Keaton's same line in Tim Burton's 1989 film. In *Skyfall* (2012), Daniel Craig's James Bond drives the Aston Martin made popular decades earlier by Sean Connery's Bond in *Goldfinger* (1964). These moments are supposed to simultaneously make us nostalgic for previous iterations of the character and convince us that Bale and Craig have rightfully inherited the onscreen mantle of Batman and Bond respectively. In other words, these moments make us nostalgic, and that nostalgia makes us accept "the new." However, Batman has a much different history than Superman concerning onscreen adaptations. The Caped Crusader has generally changed with the times, while Superman has remained more-or-less grounded in the same ideas that were originally presented not in Action Comics #1, but with the Fleischer Studios cartoons.

Creating the Site of Nostalgia and Affect

In 1941, Paramount commissioned Fleischer Studios (later reorganized into Famous Studios) to create a series of short Superman cartoons for theatrical release. Max and David Fleischer were at first reluctant to tackle the project, and asked for $100,000 per short (approximately four times the typical amount for a six-minute short at that time). Paramount negotiated and ended up paying $50,000 per short. Fleischer/Famous studios created sixteen shorts, which are all in public domain. In his review of the shorts, Martin R. Thomas writes:

> There are lots of firsts in these shorts, like making Superman fly (before that, in the comics, he only "leapt tall buildings in a single bound"), and the famous

opening line of the radio production and live-action TV series that came after the animated shorts ("Faster than a speeding bullet...") [...] There is a very art-deco look to them, which is natural given when they were made, but there's also this futuristic early science fiction look and feel to the shorts which anybody who appreciates early science fiction would love. The music, by Sammy Timberg (who also wrote the Popeye and Betty Boop music for Fleischer Studios) fits just right with the artistic style, especially the opening "Superman March" theme. It has this very retro and somewhat kitschy feel, but is still majestic in its way.[7]

In short, all Superman stories—including the comics—are haunted by the Fleischer cartoons: his powers and his quest for truth and justice (the "American way" would come later, first during World War II and again during the Cold War) would become commonplace in the comics and in other adaptations for the radio and screen. The art deco "look" of the cartoon would also later inspire the creators of *Batman: The Animated Series* (1992–1995) and *Superman: The Animated Series* (1996–2000), and the spin-offs *Justice League* (2001–2004) and *Justice League Unlimited* (2004–2006). "The Superman March" by Sammy Timberg, with its majestic brass, would influence both Leon Klatzkin's "Superman's March" for *The Adventures of Superman* (1952–1958) and John Williams's sweeping score for *Superman: The Movie* (1978). Already, we can see how much the Flesicher cartoons influenced many subsequent versions of Superman stories.

In 1948, Sam Katzman produced the first Superman serial for Columbia Pictures, aptly titled *Superman*. It starred an uncredited Kirk Alyn as Superman and Noel Neill as Lois Lane (who would reprise the role on the television series *The Adventures of Superman*). Thomas Carr, who would also direct a number of *The Adventures of Superman* episodes, helmed the serial. The *Superman* serial tells the entire backstory of the character in the first episode, from Krypton to Smallville to Metropolis, and the rest of the serial concentrates on his battle with a criminal mastermind known as the Spider Lady. The serial was so successful that a second serial, *Atom Man vs. Superman* (in which Superman faces Lex Luthor for the first time on screen) was released in 1950. Unlike the first project, which used animation for the flight sequences, director Spencer Gordon Bennet turned a camera on its side, and put Kirk Alyn in a wind cyclorama to create the sense that Superman was really up, up and away. Though the serials were cheaply made, and the special effects were lackluster even for their time, they were highly successful with audiences who were clamoring for more. *The Adventures of Superman*, starring George Reeves, was the next screen incarnation. Phyllis Coates played Lois Lane in the early episodes, and would later be replaced by Noel Neill. As mentioned, Leon Klatzkin's theme was known as "Superman's March," and as with the Fleischer Cartoons, was based on a triad, matching the three syllables in the name Superman, thereby cementing expectations for future Superman scores, including the one composed by John Williams for the 1978 film.

At this point, it would be take significantly less space to find places where Superman might not be haunted by prior incarnations. The 1978 film begins with a boy opening an issue of Action Comics. The notion is that we, the audience, are the child and we are supposed to be in the land of Superman. The affect/effect is supposed to be one of nostalgia. Additionally, Noel Neill would make an uncredited blink-and-you-miss-it appearance as Lois's mother, adding another ghost to this haunted Superman. The poster promised, "You will believe a man can fly," and audiences were not let down. This haunting only continued throughout *Smallville*'s ten year run on television in the twenty-first century.

Locating the Affect in Smallville

From the very beginning of *Smallville*, we are introduced to Clark Kent's specters as a way of resurrecting the audience's nostalgia and desire for "legitimacy" in the adaptation. There is the casting of Martha Kent. Though originally portrayed by Cynthia Ettinger in the pilot (2001), she was recast with Annette O'Toole, whom Superman fans would immediately recognize as Lana Lang opposite Christopher Reeve in *Superman III* (1983). In a sense, this gives the entire location its first site of nostalgia. *Superman III*, though a mixed effort at best, explores the theme of homecomings for Clark, and Lana is central to his thinly explored catharsis. Coming home does not mean returning to Ma Kent on the farm, it means whisking Lana away from her overbearing boyfriend. This theme continues in *Smallville,* as the first eight seasons feature Clark's failed courtship of Lana. The bond between the mother and Smallville as a home puts this casting in a particular light. O'Toole represents home and nostalgia for both Reeve's and Tom Welling's Clark. The location is also secure in its nostalgic familiarity, as the fields of corn and the white farmhouse evoke the nostalgia for an idealized America. Jeffrey K. Johnson asserts that Superman would not be the recognizable character he is today without the Smallville upbringing, and were Superman to be raised elsewhere, such as in Metropolis, we would have a far more cynical super-being.[8] In order to situate his magnificent powers with a conscience that prevents him from using them for ill gains, Superman/Clark must arrive to a small town in Kansas and be cared for by the Kents.

Smallville's portrayal of Clark's arrival on Earth is also familiar, while adding a new dimension. Though the pilot episode provides the familiar space shuttle crashing to Earth and the subsequent Kent discovery, it also depicts a meteor shower that shields Clark's arrival. This allows for the Kryptonite meteor rocks to affect a host of characters in and out of Smallville, who then mutate into superpowered antagonists for Clark to battle again and again (this is known as the series' "Freak of the Week" storytelling formula). We are then introduced to an ambitious freshman Clark stumbling in front of Kristin Kreuk's Lana, who is unknowingly wearing a Kryptonite necklace. When Lana assists Clark with his disheveled books, she sees that he is reading Frederich Nietzsche (a remarkable feat for a high school freshman). Undaunted, Lana asks Clark, "So what are you? Man or Superman?" To which a nervous Clark responds, "I haven't figured that out yet." The intentional play on words is done to give the audience the immediate sense of the familiar—remember, we are viewing no ordinary WB program about teenage angst—this is the man who will be Superman. There are moments where Welling even looks as though he is a young Christopher Reeve, giving the audience an even deeper sense that *Smallville* is the extended backstory present to fill in the gaps provided by the quick Smallville prologue in *Superman: The Movie*. The locations and casting of Martha are just the beginning. Indeed, there are plenty of affectionate nods woven into the series' narrative that acknowledge the passing of the torch.

The Smallville Torch

The school newspaper at Smallville High School is simply called the *Smallville Torch*. This evokes two immediate images. The first is the metaphorical torch, which is passed from Superman actor to Superman actor. As Jeffrey K. Johnson asserts that "No superhero, besides Superman and Batman can lay claim to having numerous appearances each month since the late 1930s."[9] Although he is speaking of the comics, this statement can be broadened out to engage the audience's nostalgia for previous screen adaptations. The second image is the Statue of Liberty, whose torch can represent the three ideals most identified with Superman: truth, justice, and the American Way.

In consideration of the first torch, there is a key moment in the second season that relies heavily on our nostalgia for previous incarnations of Superman—that is when we are introduced to the character Virgil Swann, an astronomer whose moniker is "the Man of Tomorrow." Most importantly, Swann is portrayed by Christopher Reeve, the most famous actor to take on the Superman role. In "Rosetta" (2003), Clark burns a Kryptonian symbol on the side of the Kent barn. The symbol catches Swann's watchful eye and he then invites Clark to visit him in his observatory. Portrayed as part Stephen Hawking and part Bill Gates, Swann tells Clark of his Kryptonian heritage—

literally telling Clark Kent that he is Kal-El of Krypton, and that he has a destiny on Earth. This destiny is one the audience is very aware of, while the inclusion of John Williams's "The Fortress of Solitude" and "Superman Theme" also lets the audience know that the torch is being passed from Superman to Superman in a style that meets the horizon of expectations, and situates Welling as the new and accepted Superman. This is a rather large responsibility. Though Reeve and the audience acknowledge Welling's Clark, the expectation is that Welling must fill Reeve's boots without tarnishing the audience's appreciation for the previous incarnations of the character. It is, as a paradox, a gesture of liberation and one that also provides this Clark (and Welling) with a larger responsibility to the audience than he previously had to endure.

Later, when Reeve's health worsened, we meet another character from Swann's institute, portrayed by Margot Kidder, otherwise known as Lois from the Reeve-era films. Kidder's Bridgette Crosby is introduced in "Crusade" (2004) where she visits an unnerved Martha. It is a reunion for O'Toole and Kidder, who have not shared the screen since they portrayed Lois and Lana respectively in *Superman III* as part of an underdeveloped love triangle during Reeve's time as Clark/Superman. During the conversation, it is revealed that Kidder had a relationship with Swann; she adds that it was "in a different lifetime." Again, this scene, designed on a plot-level as a *deus ex machina* to allow Clark to return to the Kent farm, features an imbued self-awareness powered by knowing casting and the echoes of previous performances.

As the series progresses, there are far too many moments like this to enumerate, including the casting of Dean Cain as a Vandal Savage-inspired Curtis Knox in "Cure" (2007), whose "CK" embroidering on his handkerchief is a reminder of his previous role on *Lois and Clark: The New Adventures of Superman* (1993–1997), and Marc McClure, who portrayed Jimmy Olsen opposite Reeve and Kidder, as Kryptonian Dax-Ur in "Persona" (2008). While there are many nods from season to season, the cumulative effect is one in which the audience is situated well within a nostalgic territory—a comfort until the new arrives, which then has the possibility to upset expectations. However, there are two key examples worth exploring in further detail. The first is the casting of Jor-El's disembodied voice (first heard in the spaceship and then later in the Fortress of Solitude), and the second is Lois's arrival in Smallville.

When we first encounter Jor-El in "Rosetta," it is through a written message in Clark's spaceship. The message tells Clark to rule over humanity, and Clark recoils as he realizes he has been sent as a possible conqueror. This is a departure from any previous Jor-El, where the character was presented as a brilliant scientist and one with a balanced sense of justice. Take for example, Marlon Brando's handling of the character in Richard Donner's *Superman: The Movie*. He offers a sage and calming presence, and tells his son that the human race "can be a great people, Kal-El." The initial shock of Jor-El as a potential antagonist is muddled, in part, due to the casting of Terence Stamp as Jor-El. Superman fans in the audience would recognize Stamp from his portrayal of General Zod in the Reeve-era films (and his "Kneel before Zod" chant). Stamp's previous Superman-related work gave his presence as Jor-El an additional layer of meaning, and perhaps some gravitas to the character's more villainous perspective. Thus, Stamp and Jor-El offers both nostalgia and something entirely new for the audience.

When Lois arrives in season four, *Smallville* faces a balancing act between narrative necessity (a conspicuous nod to the early *Superboy* comics that introduced a teenage Lois) and the disrupted expectations of viewers who expect Clark and Lois to meet well after the former leaves Smallville behind him. Almost immediately in her first appearance in "Crusade," *Smallville* presents a version of Lois who is fairly connected to previous iterations. She struggles with nicotine addiction, which evokes Kidder's characterization in the Superman films, and she is naturally investigative in looking into her cousin Chloe Sullivan's possible murder. This Lois is also tenacious, showcasing a strong wit and stubbornness that is common with every incarnation of the character, and she refers to Clark as "Smallville," a nickname given to him during *Superman: The Animated Series*. The nickname works in the animated program, as Lois and Clark are both in Metropolis at the *Daily Planet* when they meet. However, it is a bit conspicuous in *Smallville*, as Lois meets Clark in Smallville, and winds up taking a portion of her final year of high school in Smallville High. Why call him (and only him) as "Smallville" if she is present in the same space? Lois may refer to any character as such, but is compelled to do so by reasons that exist external to the text.

This Lois does not escape specters very easily either. Aside from the familiar adapted backstory (daughter of General Sam Lane, portrayed by standby military character actor Michael Ironside, and the presence of her sister Lucy Lane), the character in *Smallville* is never too far removed from previous performers. Like Clark, her immediate circle includes a cast recognizable to Superman fans, especially her mother, Ella Lane (previously named Ellen Lane in *Lois and Clark*) played by *Lois and Clark*'s Teri Hatcher. This is a particularly interesting passing of the torch, as it evokes two previous moments in Superman's history. The first is a re-inserted scene from *Superman: The Movie* where Noel Neill sits on a train with a young child, as the child witnesses Clark outrun the train. We learn that the child is Lois, and when she describes what she has just seen out the train's window, Noel Neill tells her "Lois Lane, you have a writer's gift for invention." Here, the torch has been passed from Noel Neill to the next Lois (though not Margot Kidder, certainly her character), in the presence of (presumably) her grandfather played by the first live action Superman Kirk Alyn. The second occurs in *Lois and Clark*'s "The House of Luthor" (1994) where Ellen (instead of Ella) Lane stands with Lois moments before Lois's ultimately failed marriage to Lex. In this scene, Ellen Lane is played by Phyllis Coates, the first live action Lois.

In *Smallville* Erica Durance's Lois does not have an onscreen interaction with her mother, as it is established that her mother died some years earlier. Instead, in "Abandoned" (2010) Lois views a video of her mom, played by Hatcher, who is wearing a wig that mirrors how *her* Lois wore her hair—pin straight and shoulder length. In a sense, this makes Durance's Lois the granddaughter of the Phyllis Coates (and due to the recasting in the George Reeves series) and Noel Neill as well. The lineage is all the more interesting due to Neill's presence in the 1978 *Superman* film, which of course also starred Margot Kidder, who *also* appeared on *Smallville* and shares so many familial connections to previous incarnations.

In the same episode, Clark sees a hologram of his parents in the Fortress of Solitude. He had previously encountered a clone version of his mother Lara during season seven, but this is the first encounter with his "real" mother during her final moments. The episode deals with ghosts that have surrounded Clark throughout *Smallville*, but then also reminds the audience that Welling's Clark is the son (in a way) of the Reeve-era Supergirl Helen Slater, who portrays Lara on the series. With both Clark's biological and adoptive mothers and Lois's biological mother coming from previous. Superman adaptations, *Smallville* evokes the familiar to produce emotionally satisfying storytelling. However, with that said, the familiar also weighs down Clark's narrative. Part of *Smallville*'s conceit is that it must showcase a Superman who does not fly, does not wear the tights and cape, and does not always strictly adhere to his previous incarnations as the writers attempt to find new dramas to create for networks (the WB and later the CW) that specialize in serialized teen dramas, and it does take ten full seasons for Clark to become Superman.

Truth, Justice, and the Other Torch

In addition to Clark's personality characterizations, the theme consistently present in all Superman adaptations is his never-ending battle for truth, justice, and the notion of American values. Clark, therefore, is imbued with much more than the text simply allows. He is haunted by the previous incarnations of himself, from the Donner-inspired Fortress of Solitude, to the cast around him, to his final costume being the one developed for and worn by Brandon Routh in Bryan Singer's *Superman Returns* (2006). Furthermore, *Smallville*'s Clark must continue to be representative of the American way.

Though the definition may change over time, there are core tenets that must be present to keep Superman as an obviously *American* hero. Depending upon the iteration, he stands for truth and justice (Fleischer cartoons), truth, justice, and tolerance (Kirk Alyn serials), truth, justice, and the American way (George Reeves's iteration—though the "American way" is never clearly defined), and "Truth, justice ... and that kind of stuff" (Welling and *Smallville*).[10] What is instructive is not only the scale and scope of destruction Clark must deal with from season to season, whether it be a tornado (season one), a full-on alien attack (season four, and to a lesser extent season five), or Darkseid's coming apocalypse (season ten), but how Clark/Superman has to handle the attack and devastation.

There is no doubt that *Smallville* is a post–9/11 Superman, which means that the notion of American way is a particular torch that Clark/Superman must carry. Modern popular cinema and television, as many theorists and critics have pointed out, can give us a clear sense of our collective social and political barometers. In looking at the trailers for upcoming films, there seems to be a consistent visual pattern—buildings tumbling down, bodies whizzing past the camera, and a post-apocalyptic nihilism. The blockbuster films those trailers preclude present similar darkened visual palettes, war aesthetic, and an urgent sense of us versus them, with "them" portrayed as a particularly cold or otherwise brainless swarm of villains. The ultimate evildoers have no conscience, no concern for humanity, and are thus the perfect enemy. A particularly worrisome trend is how images of actual war or catastrophes have become trivialized to, if one were to channel Slavoj Žižek, create a fantasy image for coping, or turning real tragedy to fantasy in order to process it.[11] Escapist films and television of yesteryear may release us from our worries, but contemporary escapist films are there to justify it, to fetishize it, and to confirm the Mean World Syndrome, the notion that the world is actually a darker place than it really is.[12] In *Smallville*'s case, some fans viewed a handful of actions as a step too far, and as a noticeable pushback against the traditional ideals of the American Way.

A few moments in *Smallville* seem to signal how the notion of the American way is to be processed. Much of it is handled with the usual pro-military imagery, but some of it settles into a pattern that unintentionally sets the stage for how the controversial film *Man of Steel* (2013) finds its ending. Although Superman has had a "no kill" rule in the comics for quite some time, Clark has been put in several situations where he has caused the death of a living being or sentience.[13] In "Prototype" (2007), Clark's actions cause the death of a character that is behaving like a villain due to an implant. It is also unclear if Clark delivers Darkseid a deathblow during the series finale. While much of this can be explained away in the story's exposition, the one plot point and image that created a notable ripple among fans was season nine's "Persuasion" (2010), which featured Clark burning down twin towers erected by Major Zod. The towers were part of a device intended to alter the sun's power, allowing Zod and his minions to possess superpowers, while reducing Clark to a mere mortal. As a means of wrapping up the towers storyline without much conflict, "Persuasion" shows Clark burning the towers to the ground with his heat vision. The towers tumble, reporters shriek and dash away, and we are left with an unsettling image. Superman has burned down twin towers.

The letdown expectation comes from what Peter Coogan describes as the "Superhero as Metaphor." He postulates:

> The metaphor the superhero most often embodies outside the superhero genre is the idea of effortless efficacy, the power to right wrongs without danger to oneself ... the superhero has a unique signifying function. It can be used to express ideas that other genres cannot portray as well. Superheroes embody a vision of the use of power unique to America. Superheroes enforce their own visions of right and wrong on others, and they possess overwhelming power, especially in relation to ordinary crooks.... This vision of power fits quite well with the position American finds itself in after the Cold War.[14]

The use of power, then, must signify the American way; somehow, the superhero must have a strong moral center and not betray basic views on right and wrong. This act, the burning of the towers, operates too much as a meta-critique of Superman, himself. He has this power that must be used responsibly, but at times this responsibility, at least according to *Smallville,* means destruction of the enemy—or in this case, the enemy's resources. This notion fails our understanding of Superman, as this view is in essence a justification for war, imperialism (Superman, himself, is a foreigner)—things that Superman operates against in other iterations. Though Zod's towers were unoccupied, the visual still evokes (almost) Superman engaging in a terrorist act similar to the 9/11 attacks. Presumably, any challenge to the quest for truth, justice, and the American way should still be done in the quest for moral good, not in an act of destruction—especially one that vividly mirrors powerful real world events.

Furthermore, as a cultural figure, Superman tends to hold rigid and binary views of right and wrong, heteronormative values, and sexuality, while maintaining vaguely defined Christian undertones. Clark betrays two of these ideas by engaging in sexual intercourse with Lana and Lois (and almost doing so with Alicia Baker), and through his use of force and destruction that creates imagery that is disturbing to the American psyche. These moments stand out, as they are not in keeping with the familiar, or the nostalgic, and at times seem to betray the basic tenets of the character. Nevertheless, despite a winding journey that sometimes undercuts familiar tenants of the character, *Smallville* ends with Clark as a generally familiar version of the character. In "Finale"

(2011), he rescues a seemingly doomed Air Force One flight (as he did in *Superman Returns*), while literally "inspiring" people away from Darkseid's omega beams. The familiarity is especially present in the finale's coda, a scene at the *Daily Planet* with Lois, Clark, Jimmy Olsen (the younger brother of the series' previous version of the character, played by the same actor, Aaron Ashmore), Perry (seen, but not heard, shouting "Great Caesar's Ghost," as was common in *The Adventures of Superman*), and the announcement that Lex running is for president (as was the case in the comics). This all builds to one last inclusion of the Williams theme and Welling enacting the classic shirt-rip exposing the "S" emblem as Superman flies off to save the day.

What Does an Adaptation Do?

In discussing *Smallville* and its connections to previous adaptations, the use of affect theory and affective gestures, and a nod toward memory studies, brings out new dimensions to consider iconic characters. Though these theories have gained traction in performance studies, their applicability becomes immediately apparent when discussing media-based adaptations and contemporary folklore. By bridging the frameworks together, we can see how in this version of the story, the characters are richer due to our cultural memories and expectations of them. The sites of nostalgia serve more than simple shocks to engage the audience, but rather an homage and love letter to the audience, recognizing their memories of the past as a key component of a successful adaptation.

If superheroes teach us how to behave, or perhaps how to live, what we learned from *Smallville* is that if a super villain comes to Earth (representing one-dimensional absolute darkness personified), that we must not give up hope, as there will be a savior (absolute light personified) who will guide us, never let us down. There will be perilous times, but absolute good will always triumph over absolute evil, and we must behave accordingly. As Robert Grant notes,

> these [Superhero] stories [...] explore our society and the advances in technology and science fiction that seem to be de-humanizing us to the extent that we have forgotten how to behave towards each other. While the big crime boss or supervillain is a key ingredient to a lot of superhero stories [....] in fighting or defeating them our superhero is showing us a better way to behave.[15]

Smallville ultimately teaches us that finding a moral center relies upon connections with the past—and literal past iterations of the protagonist's world—while also negotiating new territory. That it ends with the familiar Williams theme and shirt rip should satisfy most fans, despite an uneven journey. Superman's future may be another story, as the 2013 *Man of Steel* film emptied itself of any nostalgia for the previous in an attempt to create more of a new character from the ground up. What future adaptations should remember is that for many of us who wear our nostalgia a little too proudly, a character like Superman is not just a touch of light¬—he is light personified. If we cannot remember that, then Superman will become a casualty in our (post-post) modern cinema. *Smallville*, however jagged, ultimately provides the audience with the sense of nostalgia, the location of nostalgia, and affective gestures that provide a horizon of expectation consistent with audience desires.

NOTES

1. Julie Sanders, *Adaptation and Appropriation (The New Critical Idiom)* (London: Routledge, 2005), 45.

2. Erin Hurley and Sara Warner, "Special Section: Affect, Performance, Politics," *Journal of Dramatic Theory and Criticism* 46 (Spring 2012): 99–100.

3. Ibid., 100.

4. Marvin Carlson, *The Haunted Stage: The Theater as Memory Machine* (Ann Arbor: University of Michigan Press, 2003), 100.

5. Barbara A. Misztal, *Theories of Social Remembering* (Philadelphia: Open University Press, 2003), 105.

6. For a comprehensive discussion regarding affect theory, see *The Affect Theory Reader,* ed. Melissa Gregg and Gregory J. Seigworth (Durham: Duke University Press, 2010). See also Jill Dolan's *Utopia in Performance* (Ann Arbor: University of Michigan Press, 2005), which deals specifically with communal feelings at live performance.

7. Martin R. Thomas, "Related Genres: Animation- Max Fleischer Superman Animated Shorts," *Daddy Rolled a 1*, March 11, 2011, http://daddyrolleda1.blogspot.com/2011/03/related-genres-animation-max-fleischer.html.

8. J.K. Johnson, "The Countryside Triumphant: Jefferson's Ideal of Rural Superiority in Modern Superhero Mythology," *The Journal of Popular Culture* 43 (2010): 720–737.

9. Johnson, "The Countryside Triumphant," 723.

10. "Drone," *Smallville*, The WB (April 30, 2002).

11. Slavoj Žižek, "The Politics of Batman," *New Statesman*, August 23, 2012, http://www.newstatesman.com/culture/culture/2012/08/slavoj- percentC5 percentBEi percentC5 percentBEek-politics-batman.

12. George Gerbner, Larry Gross, Michael Morgan, Nancy Signorielli, and James Shanahan, "Growing up with Television: Cultivation Processes," in *Media Effects: Advances in Theory and Research,* 2d ed., ed. Jennings Bryant and Dolf Zillmann (Mahwah, NJ: Lawrence Erlbaum, 2002), 43–67.

13. Though there are notable exceptions, as in Alan Moore's *Whatever Happened to the Man of Tomorrow* (Little, Brown, DC Comics, 2010), and the post–John Byrne handling of Zod and his minions in issues.

14. Peter Coogan, *Superhero: The Secret Origin of a Genre* (Austin: MonkeyBrain, 2006), 231.

15. Robert Grant, *Writing the Science Fiction Film* (Saline, MI: Michael Wiese Productions, 2013), 21.

"Chlark" Versus "Clois"

Shippers, Anti-Fans, and Anti-Fan Fans in Smallville

CORY BARKER

For a series that aired for a full decade, *Smallville* is not foremost known for its rabid fans. It never reached mainstream popular culture consciousness like *Star Trek* (1966–1969), *The X-Files* (1993–2002), or even *Buffy the Vampire Slayer* (1997–2003), and as such, its fans were never really target for celebration or scorn. Similarly, only a few scholars have explored the series' fandom.[1] Although we might not first think of *Smallville* when considering impressive fan activity or intra-fan debates, perhaps we should. Any series that survives multiple timeslot changes, the death of one network and the unstable life of another, and the highly-competitive twenty-first century television landscape is bound to have a large amount of dedicated viewers. This essay attempts to rectify *Smallville*'s minimal presence in fan-related discussions and concentrates on a particularly compelling—and in some ways still ongoing—conversation among sub-sections of the series' fandom.

Despite *Smallville*'s lesser prominence, one of the primary tensions among its fans is a fairly typical one: who should end up with whom? The disputes over which romantic pairing makes the most sense, a process known as "shipping," dominate much of the contemporary fan discussion online in comment threads, message boards, and Tumblr pages; *Smallville* fans were, and continue to be, no different. What makes *Smallville* more compelling in the context of shipping is that its lead character Clark Kent had a presumed romantic destination given his decades-long relationship with Lois Lane in other Superman stories. Nevertheless, the series' narrative trajectory, beginning with Clark's high school days, introduced fans to non–Lois possibilities. The primary example is Lana Lang, another long-standing Superman universe character known for serving as Clark's early love. However, the more notable example for the purposes of this essay is Chloe Sullivan, Clark's best friend, sidekick, and super-sleuthing journalist (and later hacker). Chloe, a wholly original character to *Smallville*'s universe, quickly became a fan favorite in the series' early seasons. Among a vocal group of the online fandom, Chloe was and is the best romantic option for Clark—predetermined outcomes be damned.

Complicating matters further is a theory developed by fans early in the series' run that Chloe would somehow grow up to be the *Smallville* universe's version of Lois Lane. This speculation, known as the "Chlois theory" made some sense in *Smallville*'s initial seasons. Chloe embodied the honorable dogged pursuit of the truth through investigative journalism, quick wit, and crackling chemistry with Clark that all viewers hope the eventual Superman will have with Lois. *Smallville* deflated this theory by introducing Lois in the fourth season, but Chloe's most ardent supporters held out hope that the Chlois theory would come true. Consequently, among this portion of the fandom, Chloe became the measuring stick that Lana and eventually Lois had to measure up to, despite the fact that *Smallville* never truly paired Clark and Chloe together romantically.

I argue here that these particular *Smallville* fans represent and ultimately conflict Jonathan Gray's conceptualization of the "anti-fan," those media consumers who "strongly dislike a given text or genre, considering it inane or stupid, morally bankrupt, and/or aesthetic drivel."[2] However, in this case, one of the more intriguing consequences of the conflict among shippers is the balance between like and dislike, or between love and hate. Meaning, while these fans enjoy *Smallville* and their chosen relationship (or "ship"), they can often grow to "strongly dislike," and even hate, other possible pairings within the series' universe. Chloe-Clark (or "Chlark") supporters and Lois-Clark (or "Clois") supporters can simultaneously enjoy the series as a whole and particularly the portions that support their ship, but also despise or ignore the portions that directly conflict with their romantic hopes. The tension between these two groups (and others) manifests through fan productions, debates, and in certain instances boycotts, making for quite the complicated corner of *Smallville* fandom. Therefore, these shippers are not anti-fans as Gray defines them; instead they are what I refer to as "anti-fan fans."

In this chapter, I present examples of the various conflicts among *Smallville* shippers. The examples all come publicly available websites and platforms online. Although it is always useful to speak directly with fans, following the threads of conversation and argumentation across different online locations provides a quality substitute in the absence of interviews. I do not simply take fan statements at face value, but my analysis here assumes that fans advocating for particular positions or relationships online are doing so earnestly (and thus not "trolling" for trolling's sake). In my research, I primarily followed the notable and long-running *Smallville* message board, *Kryptonsite* and the *Smallville* forums at popular television website *Television Without Pity* (*TWoP*). However, it is worth noting here that as a longtime fan of the series myself, I spent many hours lurking on both forums and was thus very familiar with their rhythms and conventions. This acknowledgement does not mean my interpretations here are *more* valid, but I wish to put this information up-front to show that my choices were not entirely random, nor was my time spent online short-lived. My observations on *Kryptonsite* and *TWoP* sent me to other corners of the Internet, to smaller and perhaps more specific password-protected forums, Live Journal pages, and social media accounts.

Furthermore, it is also important to note that the majority of my research initially took place in the spring of 2010, in the middle of *Smallville*'s ninth season. Although much of my material has been subsequently updated (something the archiving of the Internet allows researchers to do), this is a very particular snapshot of a specific time in not only the series' run, but in the fan response to story developments. Two primary points of interest with this research are examining how these opposing shipper groups interact with one another and how their conflicts ultimately affected the enjoyment of *Smallville*. The concluding section of this chapter attempts to support this initial string of research by returning to these shipper debates in 2014, a few years after *Smallville* concluded its run on the CW. My hope is to offer a brief update of where fan discourse has traveled after the series ended, which in theory concluded any in-text debate about who "belongs" with Clark.[3] With this section, I try to parse out what—if any—lasting impacts the shipper conflicts had on fan enthusiasm and whether or not these conflicts are ongoing.

Fans, Shippers, and Haters

Scholarly interest in fandom has developed quite a bit since Henry Jenkins's seminal work on *Star Trek* fans in the early 1990s.[4] The last three decades of research have helped destigmatize long-standing stereotypes of fans as "pathological," "excessive," or passive consumers.[5] The key recent catalysts for the improved perception of fan activity are the Internet and related digital media technologies/applications. These tools expand the scope, speed, and visibility in which consumers can engage with media, and with one another, giving rise to what Jenkins refers to as "participatory culture." Fan groups were actively responding to their favorite texts and producing their own projects in response long before the Internet, YouTube, and Twitter, but those tools have certainly made it easier for active fans (and all active consumers) to engage.

Although the Internet and related digital media tools have aided in a certain mainstreaming of fandom in recent years, the tools that bring fans closer together also provide similar resources to anti-fans. In describing anti-fans, Gray notes that the assumption about these consumers is that they

> know little about [a specific text], do not watch it, and thus are poor informants. But, anti-fans must find cause for their dislike in *something* [original emphasis]. This something may vary from having previously watched the show and having found it intolerable; to having to dislike for its genre, director or stars; to having seen previews or ads, or seen or heard unfavourable reviews. ...In this or any other case, clearly anti-fans construct an image of the text—and what more, an image they feel is accurate—sufficiently enough that they can react to and against it.[6]

For Gray, anti-fans are not unknowing, blind haters but instead generally knowledgeable consumers who form their opinions through the circulation of "paratexts," the "semi-textual fragments" surrounding a primary work, to make a more educated opinion based in distaste.[7] In his theorization of the paratext, Gerard Genette points to books, offering cover art, prefaces, and reviews as key examples that fill in the textual blanks. Gray expands this conversation of paratexts to television, adding credit sequences, promotional material, spoilers, and more to the list.[8] The Internet and social media allow for many more paratexts to circulate and also allow for industry- and fan-made paratexts to blend and build from one another.[9] Thus, contemporary anti-fans can procure information about the things they dislike very easily online, whether they actively choose to find that information by reading a detailed *Wikipedia* page or passively stumble across it by browsing Twitter during primetime hours or reading the comments of an article about the results of the latest awards show. This increase in available information does not necessarily mean that 2014's anti-fans hold more educated opinions than 1999's anti-fans, but they certainly can "construct an image" of a text using paratexts in an unparalleled fashion.

Recent work from Catherine Strong and Sarah Harman and Bethan Jones and have explored how anti-fans infiltrate forums, YouTube comment sections, and social media to criticize popular fiction series *Twilight* and *Fifty Shades of Grey* and the fans who love them.[10] In these particular cases, anti-fans tout the much-maligned novels' perceived lack of quality as a way to construct taste hierarchies between those who dislike the work (those with "good" taste) and those who love it (those with "bad" taste). And again, the wide circulation of paratextual content about *Twilight* and *Fifty Shades of Grey*—both of which have scored popular culture ubiquity—makes it easy for disinterested anti-fans to decide, for whatever reason, to dislike the series and then find material on the Internet that supports their dislike.

However, not all anti-fans are outsider-esque antagonists using parody videos on YouTube to discredit the enjoyment of gushing supporters. There is a very fine line between fans and anti-fans; Gray argues that the activity of the two groups often resembles one another.[11] Furthermore, I would argue that many anti-fans actually actively consume the text they purport to be against—they watch every episode, read every book, and play every game in the series. This behavior manifests in a few ways. First, as Francesca Haig and Harman and Jones argue, many anti-fans fully engage with the text through "hate-reading" or "hate-watching" with the text's flaws in mind.[12] Haig posits *Twilight* anti-fans find a substantial amount of pleasure in approaching the series with "snark" in mind:

> This is what seems to me to be distinctive about *Twilight* snark: the criticisms aren't incidental to the pleasure taken in the texts; they appear, in large part, to constitute that pleasure. This form of critical fandom does not simply recognise *Twilight* as rubbish and enjoy it *in spite of* that recognition; the recognition *itself* and the analysis, discussion, and parody that it permits, provide much of the fans' pleasure [original emphasis].[13]

Harman and Jones augment Haig's arguments in their analysis of *Fifty Shades of Grey* anti-fans by suggesting that the series' anti-fans pleasure can also develop through "performing and sharing distinctions of taste." Thus, while most *Fifty Shades of Grey* anti-fans are of the opinion that the series is drivel, there many anti-fans who actually read the books first, *then* refer to it as drivel. This latter group is what Harman and Jones refer to as "close-reading anti-fans."[14]

Second, although Harman and Jones's close readers gain satisfaction out of sharing their anti-fandom with one another, certain anti-fans seriously enjoy portions of the text and despise others. There are those anti-fans who indeed actively consume the text with a close reading, but in doing so attempt to create more contentious debate among the larger fandom. Different subgroups within the fandom come into conflict with one another over which portions are better for any number of reasons, but never lose sight of a larger devotion to the text. A significant way that this tension manifests is through shipping, as fan investment in romantic pairings can be especially divisive.

Although scholars have long been interested in fan productions— fan/slash fiction, videos, etc.,—related to character romance, the tensions between different shipper groups are less prominent in fan studies research. Scholars have taken interest in the conflicts between shippers and non-shippers, however. Christine Scodari and Jenna L. Felder and Leora Hadas examine how these shipper/non-shipper clashes develop online between

X-Files and *Doctor Who* fans respectively.[15] One of the fascinating results of both projects is how often questions of genre percolate in these online discourses. Namely, in these cases, both *X-Files* and *Doctor Who* fans against shipping were found to be disinterested and dismissive of romance all together, because it disrupted the series' science fiction conventions and turned them toward soap opera tendencies. Therefore, ships served as "feminine" threats to *The X-Files*' and *Doctor Who*'s perceived primary narrative and generic concerns.

These are useful case studies for thinking about how different segments of a larger fan group interact online, but they ignore "shipper versus shipper" processes that, frankly, dominate much of fan discourse online (and it was happening long before the Internet as well). The conflicts between opposing shipper groups within a fandom have driven a number of franchises to worldwide success and forces within the culture industries now key in on these conflicting groups when developing promotional materials. The rise of #TeamJacob– and #TeamEdward–like discourse is one of the simplest ways to recognize how pervasive shipping is in contemporary media reception. What is most compelling about these conflicts is how love for one ship and hatred for another does not, ultimately, disrupt affection for the text as a whole. Thus, these fans are very strongly anti-*something* within the text, yet still fans. They are anti-fan fans. What I hope to provide with my *Smallville* case study are some notable examples of how these conflicts play out and how they impact anti-fan fan enjoyment of the series.

The *Smallville* Shipper Context

Before discussing particular *Smallville* fan behavior, it is useful to provide some of the broader context regarding the series' storylines, characters, and relationships. *Smallville* began as an exploration of the teenage years of Clark Kent, the boy who would become Superman. Over its ten seasons, the series presented numerous characters from the DC Comics universe and decades of Superman stories, starting with Clark's parents Jonathan and Martha, future nemesis Lex Luthor, buddy Pete Ross, and love interest Lana. As the series progressed, more and more characters from the DC/Superman universe arrived in Clark's hometown of Smallville, Kansas, or in the bustling big city of Metropolis, including Jimmy Olsen, Perry White, Oliver Queen (Green Arrow), Bart Allen (Flash), Zod, Doomsday, Darksied, and of course, Lois. However, *Smallville* also integrated its own original characters into storylines, most notably Chloe Sullivan, who spent the entire run of the series as Clark's best friend, confidant, and superhero sidekick. In fact, Clark and Chloe were the only characters to appear as series regulars in all ten seasons, and the only two to appear in at least 200 of *Smallville*'s 218 episodes. Chloe's consistent prominence in the series cannot be ignored.

Although the series is based on comic book stories full of superheroes, action, and regular excursions into science fiction territory, *Smallville*'s existence on the WB and later the CW, networks predominantly aimed at female viewers, often means that a substantial amount of the episodes deal with the characters' romantic issues. As such, there are *Smallville* shippers of all sorts, each with their amalgamated names: Clana (Clark-Lana), Clex (Clark-Lex), Chlark (Clark-Chloe), Clois (Clark-Lois), Chimmy (Jimmy-Chloe), and Chlollie (Oliver-Chloe), among others. In *Smallville*'s later years, the most vocal—and thus the most often opposition to one another—groups support Chlark and Clois. The tension between these two groups prevails throughout the forums of popular *Smallville* fan site, *Kryptonsite*, and in the comment sections of more general and popular press websites. However, the skirmishes also developed so much that each group created private communities that allow them to enjoy their favorite pairing without the debate or hostility of the other group.

Chloe and Lois: A Brief History

It is also useful to describe Lois's and Chloe's role in *Smallville* and how they interact with Clark, as those things shape shippers' feelings and reactions to the various partnerships, and the series as a whole. In the first three seasons, Chloe stars as Clark's sidekick, but also appears to be something of a Lois placeholder. Separate from the relationship with Clark, Chloe is the editor of the Smallville High newspaper, the *Smallville Torch*, and displays the tenacity to hunt down any story, sometimes to the detriment of her personal relationships. In the second and third seasons, Chloe becomes intertwined with the Luthors (both Lex and his overbearing, evil father Lionel), often serving as the foil to their various misdeeds. Chloe's conflict with Lionel goes so far that in the season three finale "Covenant" (2004), he tries to have her killed in a safe house explosion. As the series progresses, Chloe fosters a multitude of expert sources and eventually makes her way to the bullpen of the *Daily Planet*. Generally speaking, these traits are associated with the Lois character in Superman comics, animated series, and films. *Smallville* pushed the comparison further by having Chloe use "Lois Lane" (her cousin), as her pen name in season three's "Delete" (2004).

Moreover, when Lois is introduced into *Smallville*'s world in season four, she is not quite the character recognizable to beloved by Superman fans. Lois is a pushy fifth-year high school senior that struggles with nicotine addiction and has very little interest in a journalism career. In her first few years on the series, Lois lacks a clear direction as a character. She very briefly attends Metropolis University and then becomes Jonathan's campaign manager in his senate race against Lex. By the sixth season, her interest in the weird occurrences happening around her turns Lois onto reporting and a job at the *Metropolis Inquisitor* tabloid, and in the seventh season, Lois's reporting acumen score her a job at the *Planet*. Despite this career trajectory, Lois (and the actress playing her, Erica Durance) is often used for sex appeal when placed in skimpy outfits and costumes, or as the love interest of a cavalcade of would-be-superheroes (Arthur Curry and Oliver Queen).

During seasons four through seven, it often seems like the *Smallville* writers had no idea what to do with Lois. They clearly wanted the cachet of having the character in the series' universe, but were also unwilling (or not ready) to dedicate enough time to her to develop a full character arc. In short, Lois is often playing second, third, and fourth fiddle to other characters like Lana, Chloe, and even Kara, Clark's Kryptonian cousin. This changes starting with the eighth season when *Smallville*'s creators Alfred Gough and Miles Millar depart the series, along with lead cast members Kristin Kreuk (Lana) and Michael Rosenbaum (Lex). From that point onward, Lois is more of a central character in the series and begins to resemble the character as Superman fans know her. Meanwhile, as Lois progresses toward her presumed destiny, Chloe turns away from journalism, finds herself infected with remnants of Braniac DNA, and temporarily, love with Doomsday, and eventually grows into a more cerebral player in *Smallville*'s ever-expanding universe of superheroes and deadly villains.

Anti-Fan Fan Interactions

On the most basic level, *Smallville* shippers complicate Gray's definition of anti-fan by actively watching the series. In his construction of the fan and the anti-fan, Gray argues that fans are almost always "close readers," while anti-fans, though knowledgeable, gain awareness of texts from much more of a distance.[16] This demarcation is useful in thinking about the nuances of reception, but the actions of *Smallville* shippers provide yet another way to consider fandom. These fans are absolutely close readers, but what they do with that close reading, and the tension created by those actions, leads to something more than just positively-charged fandom.

Based on the forum postings after each episode found on *Kryptonsite*, Chlark and Chlois supporters watch most of the episodes, and use each episode as a way to further their side of the shipper debates. Each episode gets its own sub-section of the forum and many of the topics with the most activity in the ninth season focus on Chloe/Clark and/or Lois/Clois. For example, the most popular threads in the sub-section for "Escape" (2010), an episode primary about the series' various romantic entanglements, include "Clois Scenes," "Poll: Anyone think Clois kissing looks awkward?," "Who wants Clark more?," and "Chlark sex talk."[17] Although "Escape" tackles these kind of issues more heavily than the typical *Smallville* episode and thus could have prompted a more spirited output, other episode sub-forums are also filled with Chlark and Clois fans discussing the validity of their favorite relationship. Discussion topics for "Upgrade" (2010), an episode that was much more mythology-heavy, include "Dear Lois, Dump Your Boyfriend and Your Cousin: An Open Letter," "Clois scenes," and "Clark and Chloe."[18] This is a very brief survey of what *some* fans do in response to the series, and generally speaking these threads look like normal fan activity. It is participatory, interactive, and thoughtful.

However, when digging into many of the responses within these threads, we can begin to see how typical fan activity is actually more complicated. The original post in the "Dear Lois, Dump Your Boyfriend...." topic was actually a negative response from a Clois fan to "Upgrade," but in just a few responses, it turned into a Chlark-Clois conversation as one commenter said, "P.S. Encourage Chloe and Clark to get back together and live happily ever after. Whoops, did I just through in a Chlark reference in an entirely anti–Chloe and Clark thread? J."[19] Responses like this one are not reflective of an out-and-out hatred, but a frustration with a particular character or relationship creates tension between the different fan groups. Much of this tension dates back to a long-standing theory that is important to a certain segment of the *Smallville* fan base.

Smallville's portrayal of Chloe and Lois in the early seasons led to the development of an infamous theory that some fans still believe in (at least wishfully) today: The Chlois theory. Prominent Chlois fan website Carbon-Copy describes the Chlois theory as follows:

> What if Lois Lane, famous ace reporter for the *Daily Planet*, helpmate, co-worker and eventual spouse of Clark Kent/Superman, actually grew up with the name Chloe Sullivan? Well, then we have been unknowingly watching the story of young Lois Lane on *Smallville* since the Pilot. Fans who think so are Chloisers because they hope Chloe is the iconic Lois Lane. Currently, the most popular Chlois theory is that for some as yet unknown reason, the character played by Allison Mack, will adopt "Lois Lane" as a pen name for her work at the Daily Planet.[20]

The *Smallville* fan wiki refers to this part of the Chlois theory as the "pseudonym theory," and also provides two additional options for Chloe to be (or become) Lois: the "identity switch theory," wherein *Smallville*'s Lois would disappear or die, only for Chloe to take on the identity, and the "names don't matter theory," which suggests that Chloe could ultimately keep her name and still embody all the characteristics of the iconic Lois—including a romantic relationship with Clark.[21] The pseudonym theory took hold during *Smallville*'s first three seasons before Lois's introduction, and although one might think the series bringing in the "real" Lois would deter interest in the theory, Chloisers pushed onward, bringing in the other variations. The debate about Chloe and Lois persevered throughout *Smallville*'s run and was often one of the most-discussed topics among fans on the *Kryptonsite* and *Television Without Pity* forums. For example, the primary Chlois thread on *Television Without Pity* began on November 4, 2005, in the middle of the fourth season (Lois's first on the series) and continued until *Smallville*'s end in May 2011 with almost 18,000 posts. At one point in 2010, the *Kryptonsite* forums featured seven 4,000-plus-response threads specifically dedicated to Chlois (all have since been closed). The support for Chloe and the Chlois theory took on such a life of its own that Gough actually commented on it in an interview with Television Without Pity:

> No, it's funny, I've been hearing the rumors that Chloe is really Lois Lane. Then we put in that Lois was her cousin. When you actually put Lois on the show, you'd think that would quell that. I don't think Chloe goes into witness protection and comes out as Lois Lane.... When you actually introduce the character on the show, that to me would be the big hint. But people can dare to dream.[22]

Chlois fans often refer to Durance's Lois as "fake!Lois," "Nois," or "ED Lois" as a way to demarcate between the two characters. One of the primary issues Chloe and Chlois fans have with *Smallville*'s changes in the final seasons is how it maneuvers to put Lois on the path to her iconic status while placing Chloe on a different trajectory. Within the fandom, these maneuvers are known as "light switches," suggesting that the series' new showrunners from season eight onward *simply decided* to have Lois become *the* Lois (and to a lesser extent, Clark become *the* Clark), despite the fact that these changes do not track with previous storylines or characterizations. Television Without Pity poster Tobi summed up this line of thinking in an extended and insightful October 21, 2008 entry:

> ...this season feels like "Clark's at the *Planet* because." "Lois is in love with him because." They had seven years to set up Clark at Central Kansas or Met U studying journalism or working at The Ledger. They had four seasons of EDLois around to have her decide she liked Clark and didn't want to belittle him. In that vein, they had four seasons to start writing it so Chloe didn't want to be a journalist anymore. Almost being murdered by Lionel would be reason enough to back off. But they didn't so instead they create Chloiac and wave a magic wand and boom! Chloe's out and Nois and Clark at the DP as reporters and ICONIC!

> Iconic and mythos are derided because they seem like a cheap excuse for poor writing and a desperate rush to match with the comics when NOTHING matches. Lois loved the Green Arrow first and had sex with Lex's little clone brother. She was first published for a story she stole from Clark. Clark never finished college and he ended up not hired by Perry White but HR and working in the basement sans glasses. That doesn't really match with the comics as I understood them but that's okay because as long as Cnois are at the DP in some way it matches up and we're done. So forget the last seven years of *Smallville*.
>
> It's just insulting. And that's what Chloisers are frustrated with. The reporter of the story. The girl on teh [sic] trail of meteor freaks and Level Three (before there was ever 33.1) is shunted aside as a LITERAL Pod!Person so that her cousin who didn't even graduate from high school, worked for a tabloid, had an affair with her boss and has to rely on Clark, Chloe or JIMMY OLSEN to handhold her through her investigations can be the journalist at the DP.[23]

Although Chloe and Chlois supporters are generally more vocal within the thread, there are those that acknowledge that Lois's increased role is worthwhile, despite the noted light switches. As user Dragon Knight posits:

> I'm not sure. Lois played a very prominent role in the first 5 episodes of the [eighth] season, and this role had her interacting not only with Clark, but also with the other characters. The elements in which she hasn't had direct involvement were areas in which knowledge of Clark's secret would have been required. I already think there have been some lighswitches [sic] this season, I don't think the fact that Lois hasn't been given an even more prominent role either in Clark's life or in terms of plot development is somehow evidence that the character's not all that important.[24]

What is fascinating about these debates is that the fans clearly recognize what the "iconic" version of Lois is, yet have a differing opinion about which of *Smallville*'s leading ladies truthfully embodies those traits. Despite these differences, the intense discussion itself illustrates that these posters are well-informed consumers of Lois's character history across different stories. Although these posters could have, in theory, accumulated this knowledge through paratextual content alone, it is hard to believe they would debate the matter so heavily unless they were both intimately familiar with both *Smallville*'s universe and Lois as a character. The frustration from Chloe fans and Chlois believers is noticeable throughout the discussion threads, but they still want what is best for *Smallville*—or at least what they think is best for *Smallville*.

Furthermore, other Chloe and Chlois fans started to believe that the series' changes for Lois in season eight and beyond were part of some course correction that would have initially ended with the Chlois theory coming true. User Bkwurm reflects this perspective:

> While reading this forum does renew my hope, I am no longer certain that Chlois is the endgame for PS3 [showrunners Brian Peterson, Kelly Souders,

Todd Slavkin, and Darren Swimmer]. One thing this season has made me certain of is that Chlois was/is truely [sic] the only logical ending and the manner in which Lois has been refitted to now play the part of Chloe Sullivan only reinforces my surety [sic] that Chlois was intended all along."[25]

This type of response reflects a negotiation of *Smallville*'s dominant textual meanings.[26] Fans like Bkwurm are willing to acknowledge that the Chlois theory is unlikely within *Smallville*'s universe, but are not willing to admit that the theory never played a role in the series' possible endings. Instead, the changes in Lois's character are some kind of proof that the Chlois believers were correct all along. For Chloisers, this is the only way the story and character transformations make sense, and it is the only way to enjoy *Smallville*'s later seasons without letting disappointment or hatred of Lois get in the way.

Wins and Losses

These particular *Smallville* fans often turn the debates into "wins" and "losses," bending the narrative to fit their interpretations. On *Kryptonsite*'s forum, each episode sub-section has a "Best Actor/Actress" poll where the two groups compete, albeit on a minor level, over which one of the actresses/characters did the "best" in a given week. Furthermore, while Gray's anti-fans rely on the paratext to garner textual fragments to help build a case of distanced dislike, *Smallville* shippers use paratextual content as "data" or "proof" to back up their specific claims. This proof comes in the form of Nielsen ratings, critical reception, the number of comments on posts about *Smallville* on popular news websites, and more. Elliotxoxo's November 2009 blog post is a nice example of how *Smallville* fans use this paratextual proof to state their case: "If you're still watching *Smallville*, which most of you aren't (considering the ratings), then you've witnessed the fake!Lois Lane steal everything that once belonged to Chloe Sullivan. I believe the intuitive rejection of the shallowly written EDLois Lane drove SV [*Smallville*] to push Chloe into an obscure arch [sic] of her own in these later seasons."[27] This post points to the series' declining ratings in season nine as indication that the larger *Smallville* fandom is disappointed in how Chloe and Lois are presented. Similarly, when the ratings for each episode are released, the reactions can often focus on blaming lower ratings on one character or celebrating higher ratings for another. For example, the comments on an April 2010 *Hollywood Reporter* article about season nine's ratings quickly turned to the blame game. One anti–Chloe commenter said, "The ratings fell off a cliff in the second half of last season too. The common denominator? More Chloe-focused episodes," while an anti–Lois commenter replied with "Not surprised, nobody wants to see Cnois."[28] To be fair, *Smallville* moved from its plum Thursday timeslot to Friday nights, one of the least-watched nights of the week, in season nine, so a drop in ratings was almost guaranteed. Nevertheless, this is a fine example of the ways fans find paratextual content to discredit the characters and relationships they dislike.

The two groups are also active on more mainstream media websites operated by *Entertainment Weekly* and *TV Guide*. When popular "spoiler journalist" Michael Ausiello worked for *EW*, he posted "scoops" about *Smallville* more than any other series aside from the much more traditionally-popular *House* (2004–2011) and *Grey's Anatomy* (2004–), which is itself an acknowledgement that news about the series draws valuable web traffic. Perhaps unsurprisingly, many of Ausiello's updates about *Smallville* turned toward the pros and cons of Chloe and Lois in the comments. For example, a March 30, 2010 Ausiello entry about a *Smallville* series regular dying garnered more than 800 comments as of April 17, 2010. There one fan noted that "No Chloe, no *Smallville*," which caused a few Lois supporters to say, "You don't mean that." Then, one Chloe fan chimed in with an extended comment: "I KNOW a ton of people who already left (only watching the Chloe scenes online and some who refuse to even do that) I'm sure once Chloe is gone, several people will leave and never come back. Once Chloe is gone, I will feel no temptation to watch ANY of the scenes" [original emphasis].[29] Gray acknowledges that "dislike is potentially as powerful an emotion and a reaction is like."[30] These instances display the fans using the paratexts as a way to spread the word about the characters and pairings they support, but also using them to cut down the ones they do not like. And with the use of "I KNOW a ton of people who already left," we see fans positioning their statements as facts regarding the fan base as a whole.

The crusade for wins and losses reflects the fine line between love and hate for some *Smallville* fans, but also represent the distribution of Sarah Thornton's "subcultural capital." Thornton's conceptualization of subcultural capital modifies Pierre Bourdieu's cultural capital, wherein members of a subcultural group distinguish themselves through certain knowledges, skills, or tastes that make them look "hipper" or more "authentic" in comparison to other members. For Thornton, members of the subculture rely on the "mainstream" and media to create their oppositional identities and obtain subculture capital.[31] In the case of *Smallville*, fans oppose one another—and not some nebulous idea of the mainstream—but they certainly rely on the media, and paratextual content, to gain subcultural capital. When the series reciprocates the fans' feelings, they are further emboldened in the shipper discussions. Thus, when episodes predominantly highlight Clark and Lois or Clark and Chloe, the fans that support that relationship feel like they have gained an upper hand, and some distinction, because they are so emotionally invested in that relationship. A positive moment for the couple means a positive moment for their supporters.

Impact of the Tensions

In *Smallville*'s final few seasons, the tension between Chloe and Lois supporters led to the creation of separate spaces for two groups. Although both groups still actively participated in conversations and debates on *Kryptonsite* and *Television Without Pity*, or argued in the *TV Guide* comment sections, many fans moved to their own shipper-specific web communities where they knew they would not be bothered by the opposition and could freely celebrate their favorite characters/relationships. In spring of 2010, *CarbonCopy.org*, www.two-of-us.svtometropolis, and www.flybacktome.suddenlaunch3 were among the notable Chloe/Chlark spaces, while *DivineIntervention.com* served as the prominent Lois/Clois community. (Of course, this just a small sample.) Interestingly, each of these communities requires users to sign up for a username and password not just to post on forums or chat rooms, but to read the majority of the content as well. Perhaps the opposing factions wanted to create space between themselves and "other" fans, whether they supported a different relationship or not. This is an example of the fans creating additional levels of distinction between one another. It takes a more dedicated or "true" Chloe fan to make the effort, however small, to create a username and be an active member of a relationship-specific website instead of just lurking around on the general spaces. Moreover, it seems that the need to create distinctive, separated groups at least partially violates Jenkins's ideas of fan enjoyment through interactive, participatory cultures. Without the full group of *Smallville* fans together, the "collective intelligence" does not quite exist in the way that it could, or is at least skewed towards one ideology or another. The scope of response, something Jenkins celebrates about the Internet and fandom, is perhaps more limited than it could be.[32]

Moreover, as *Smallville*'s storylines shifted, there were episodes throughout the ninth season where Durance's Lois was more prominently featured than Allison Mack's Chloe. In a few of these instances, a small section of Chloe supporters attempted to organize boycotts on Twitter in hopes of dragging down *Smallville*'s ratings, and ultimately to teach the series' producers some kind of lesson.[33] These boycotts did not go especially far, but are notable nonetheless because they signal the most overt anti-fan behavior in Gray's sense of the word: these fans chose to avoid the series, even for a week, because of strong feelings of dislike. Yet, the fans turned to boycotts not out of real hatred, but out of love and what they view as in *Smallville*'s best interest. The hatred was thus directed a just a small section of the series.

Nevertheless, amid the visible tension between two segments of the *Smallville* fandom, it is important to acknowledge that said tension did not destroy all fan discourse and community online. For a series that ran for a decade, there is something to be said for such a dedicated fan base, whether they agree on much or not. Plus there is real-world evidence for the fervent support for *Smallville*, as its move to Friday did not substantially affect its ratings. Entertainment media consistently celebrated its performance throughout the 2009–2010 season and in the middle of my initial research, *Smallville* was renewed for a tenth and final season.[34] Although the series was not a massive hit in traditional television standards, a ten-year run, jam-packed Comic-Con panels, and expansive discussion online signals that *Smallville* had a real impact on many people, no matter what romantic pairing they supported. This suggests that Jenkins's positive outlook for participatory culture exists within *Smallville* fandom. The collective intelligence pool might not have been as large as could it have been at points, but under the circumstances, it still existed in a substantial way. Moreover, the creation of different, relationship-specific communities fits Jenkins's idea of the expansion of communities fairly well. Fans might have splintered away from one another and from a major hub like *Kryptonsite*, but the creation of new websites can be read as a positive growth for the fandom.

Returning to the Chloe and Lois Debates

When I completed my initial round of research, *Smallville* was about to finish its ninth season to establish storylines for the tenth and final year. In that final season, Lois and Chloe generally continued down the paths set forth in seasons eight and nine. Lois became the iconic version of the character: ensconced at the *Daily Planet*, engaged to Clark, aware of his superhuman abilities, and more prominently involved in the series' narrative. Meanwhile, Chloe married Oliver and grew further into her role as a superhero mentor, but also eventually took a "day job" working as a journalist at the *Star City Register*, returning to the vocation she seemed so dedicated to in the early seasons. Yet, the tenth season was also the first where Lois appeared in more episodes than Chloe, who became more of a supporting character as *Smallville* reached its conclusion. Ultimately then, Chlois supporters did not get what they wanted. Chloe did not turn into Lois, or take over the iconic Lois identity, or end up romantically involved with Clark. Yet, Chloe survived the series' full run, something many thought she would not do considering her previous nonexistence in the Superman mythology, and she returned to reporting, something her biggest fans longed for as the series moved toward the end.

Smallville ended nearly three years ago and though I am sure I could write another essay about how *Smallville* fans reacted to the final season and the series finale specifically, I have instead decided to jump to the present day.

Of course, this is a very brief check-in, but hopefully returning to the discussions between Chloe and Lois fans in 2014 will provide some additional insight into how fandom does or does not change over time.

Perhaps unsurprisingly, the discussion has slowed on *Kryptonsite*'s forums. The popular and seemingly never-ending threads on *Television Without Pity*'s forums are now closed. Other prominent communities like *CarbonCopy* and *Divine Intervention* are still up and running in some form, but the activity is less frequent than it was during *Smallville*'s run. However, though engagement may be down in previously notable locations, the rise of social platform Tumblr has helped keep all things Chlark, Clois, and Chlois alive. Tumblr's emphasis on photos, GIFs, and short videos allows still-dedicated fans to flex their fandom relatively quickly and easily. Tumblr's with titles such as *everythingchlark*, *fyeahchlark*, *chlarkcaps*, and simply *chlark* are keeping the Chloe and Clark romance alive, while *fyeahclois*, *cloisismyfairytale*, and *itscloisforever* are doing the same for Lois and Clark. The most interesting of this sub-section of Tumblrs are those that, through the magic of photo editing, use screencaps from the last few seasons to bring the Chlois theory to life. These photos, like those on *chloisverse*, feature strategically framed shots of Clark and Chloe at the *Daily Planet* (often from different seasons, considering Clark did not work there until season eight, after Chloe was fired), with her having darker hair and in certain cases, taking on the Lois Lane name. Similarly, the final few seasons' run of "adult" events—proposals, weddings, near weddings—make it easy for these intuitive Tumblr users to recontextualize these images to fit their relationship-related ends. Thus, though the arguments appear to be diminished (and again, this is a small sample), *Smallville* fans are still displaying their affection for romantic pairings and in certain cases, still holding onto a world where the series' final outcomes were different. It is unfair to say that the Internet and platforms like Tumblr mean that fans are holding onto their fandom longer than they were before these tools existed, but I would suggest that the tools at least make it easier to do so.

Conclusion

Gray's work on the fan and anti-fan (and non-fan) illustrates that fandom and reception are not one size fits all. With this project, I set out to further complicate those conceptualizations, particularly the lines between fandom and anti-fandom. Across two different periods of time, I found evidence that displays how fans on either side of the Chloe and Lois debates exist as anti-fan fans: people who enjoy *Smallville* as a series and certain characters in particular, but also strongly dislike other characters within the series. Anti-fan fans actively work against their opposition through message board postings, fan-made productions, and the presentation of "facts," ultimately creating an environment that is often driven by conflict and attempts to "prove" some form of "truth." But as the *Smallville* case study shows, the conflict is not always destructive; it emboldens fans, encourages discussion, and requires a certain dedication and impressive knowledge of the text.

The *Smallville* case is special because of the complicated history behind the Chlois theory, but the issues between segments of the fandom are not new; this kind of activity is almost certainly happening in every fandom online. The further segmentation of Internet and social media fandom, with fans often retreating to password protected forums or Tumblrs instead of congregating in one primary space might close off certain conversations, but it certainly has not limited the discourse. In fact, it is very likely that fans, anti-fans, and anti-fan fans split their time online between more "mainstream" spaces and more private communities, perhaps based on the complicated tastes they have about a given series. Ultimately then, we need to keep pushing the boundaries of categories like fan, anti-fan, and non-fan. Anti-fan fan is perhaps not the most eloquent term, but it makes room for the multitude of responses fans can have. Hopefully the more we think about the complications in media reception, the better we will understand individual fan identity, fan productions, and fan communities.

Notes

1. There are very few, but some of the notable works on *Smallville* fandom include Melanie E.S. Kohnen, "The Adventures of a Repressed Farm Boy and the Billionaire Who Loves Him: Queer Spectatorship in *Smallville* Fandom," in *Teen Television: Essays on Programming and Fandom*, ed. Sharon Marie Ross and Louisa Ellen Stein (Jefferson, NC: McFarland, 2008), 207–223; Juli Stone Pitzer, "Vids, Vlogs, and Blogs: The Participatory Culture of *Smallville*'s Digital Fan," in *The Smallville Chronicles: Critical Essays on the Television Series*, ed. Lincoln Geraghty (Lanham, MD: Scarecrow Press, 2011), 109–128; and Michaela Meyer, "Slashing *Smallville*: The Interplay of Text, Audience, and Production on Viewer Interpretations of Homoeroticism," *Sexuality & Culture* 17.3 (2013): 476–493.

2. Jonathan Gray, "New Audiences, New Textualities: Anti-Fans and Non-Fans," *International Journal of Cultural Studies* 6.1 (2003): 70.

3. It is worth noting that while *Smallville* completed its story on television in the tenth season, the story technically continued in comic form with the *Smallville Season 11* series, written by former series staff writer Bryan Q. Miller. The comic and its related spin-offs are still running as of early 2014.

4. Henry Jenkins, *Textual Poachers: Television Fans and Participatory Culture* (New York: Routledge, 1992).

5. Joli Jenson, "Fandom as Pathology: The Consequences of Characterization," in *The Adoring Audience: Fan Culture and Popular Media*, ed. Lisa A. Lewis (New York: Routledge, 1992), 9–29; Sara Gwenllian-Jones, "The Sex Lives of Cult Television Characters," *Screen* 43.1 (2002): 73–90.

6. Gray, "New Audiences, New Textualities," 71.
7. Ibid., 72.
8. Gerard Genette, *Paratexts: Thresholds of Interpretation*, trans. Jane E. Lewin (Cambridge: Cambridge University Press, 1997).
9. For a more detailed look at the relationship between industry- and fan-made paratexts see Jonathan Gray, *Show Sold Separately: Promos, Spoilers, and Other Media Paratexts* (New York: New York University Press, 2010).
10. Catherine Strong, "'... It Sucked Because It Was Written for Teenage Girls' – *Twilight*, Anti-Fans, and Symbolic Violence," presented at *The Future of Sociology: The Annual Conference of the Australian Sociological Association*, Australian National University, December 1–4, 2009; Sarah Harman and Bethan Jones, "Fifty Shades of Ghey: Snark Fandom and the Figure of the Anti-Fan," *Sexualities* 16.8 (2013): 951–968.
11. Jonathan Gray, "Antifandom and the Moral Text: Television Without Pity and Textual Dislike," *The American Behavioral Scientist* 48.7 (2005): 840–858.
12. Harman and Jones, "Fifty Shades of Ghey"; Francesca Haig, "Critical Pleasures: *Twilight*, Snark, and Critical Fandom," in *Screening Twilight: Critical Approaches to a Cinematic Phenomenon*, ed. Sarah Harman and Wickham Clayton (London: I.B. Tauris, 2013), n.p., cited in Harman and Jones, "Fifty Shades of Ghey." See also: Anonymous, "The Joys of Live-Reading the Hated Book," *In Media Res*, September 23, 2012, http://mediacommons.futureofthebook.org/imr/2012/09/23/joys-live-reading-hated-book.
13. Haig, "Critical Pleasures."
14. Harman and Jones, "Fifty Shades of Ghey," 956.
15. Christine Scodari and Jenna L. Felder, "Creating a Pocket Universe: 'Shippers,' Fan Fiction, and *The X-Files* Online," *Communication Studies* 51.3 (2000): 238–257; Leora Hadas, "Resisting the Romance: 'Shipping' and the Discourse of Genre Uniqueness in *Doctor Who* Fandom," *European Journal of Cultural Studies* 16.3 (2013): 329–343.
16. Gray, "New Audiences, New Textualities," 71.
17. "#9–16 Escape," *Kryptonsite* Forums, accessed January 31, 2014, http://www.ksitetv.com/forums/forumdisplay.php?618-9-16-Escape.
18. "#9–18 Upgrade," *Kryptonsite* Forums, accessed January 31, 2014, http://www.ksitetv.com/forums/forumdisplay.php?634-9-18-Upgrade.
19. Britas15, "Dear Lois, Dump Your Boyfriend and Your Cousin: An Open Letter," Kryptonsite Forums, April 16, 2010, http://www.kryptonsite.com/forums/showthread.php?t=141748.
20. Massena, "Some Achieve Greatness: Part I—An Overview of Evidence," *Carbon Copy.org*, January 6, 2006, http://www.carboncopy.chlois.org/essays/reasons/some-achieve-greatness-part-i-overview-evidence.
21. "Chlois Theory," *Smallville Wikia*, accessed May 21, 2013, http://smallville.wikia.com/wiki/Chlois_theory.
22. Omar G, "Al Be There for You," *Television Without Pity*, January 18, 2006, http://www.televisionwithoutpity.com/show/smallville/.
23. Tobi, "The Chlois Discussion Thread: Which Anvils Do You Believe?" post #14014, *Television Without Pity*, October 21, 2008, http://forums.televisionwithoutpity.com/topic/3132457-the-chlois-discussion-thread-which-anvils-do-you-believe/page-468.
24. Dragon Knight, "The Chlois Discussion Thread: Which Anvils Do You Believe?" post #14044, *Television Without Pity*, October 21, 2008, http://forums.televisionwithoutpity.com/topic/3132457-the-chlois-discussion-thread-which-anvils-do-you-believe/page-469.
25. Bkwurm, "The Chlois Discussion Thread: Which Anvils Do You Believe?" post #14016, *Television Without Pity*, October 21, 2008, http://forums.televisionwithoutpity.com/topic/3132457-the-chlois-discussion-thread-which-anvils-do-you-believe/page-468.
26. The dominant and negotiated reading positions come from Stuart Hall's seminal

essay, "Encoding and Decoding in the Television Discourse," *Centre for Critical Cultural Studies*, 507–517, Birmingham: University of Birmingham, 1973.

27. Elliottxoxo, "The 'What If' That Is '*Smallville*,'" *Spider Fan's Web*, November 14, 2009, http://spiderfansweb.wordpress.com/2009/11/14/the-what-if-that-is-smallville/.

28. Comments on James Hibberd, "'*Smallville*' Drops Again, Hits Season Low," *The Live Feed*, April 17, 2010, http://livefeed.hollywoodreporter.com/2010/04/smallville-ratings-low-.html#disqus_thread.

29. Comments on Michael Ausiello, "'*Smallville*' Exclusive: Someone Is Going to [Major Spoiler Alert]!" *The Ausiello Files at EW.com*, March 30, 2010, http://ausiellofiles.ew.com/2010/03/30/smallville-finale-death-spoiler/-comments.

30. Gray, "New Audiences, New Textualities," 73.

31. Sarah Thornton, *Club Cultures: Music, Media, and Subcultural Capital* (Cambridge: Polity Press, 1995), 9–14, 158–162.

32. Henry Jenkins, *Convergence Culture: Where Old and New Media Collide* (New York: New York University Press, 2006).

33. Derek Russell, "Starkville's House of El Episode 135 – 'Kandor,'" *Starkville's House of El Podcast*, November 11, 2009, www.smallvillepodcast.com.

34. James Hibberd, "CW Renews '*Smallville*' for 10th Season," *Hollywood Reporter*, March 4, 2010, www.heatvisionblog.com/2010/03/cw-renews-smallville-for-10th-season.html.

Selected Bibliography

Abbott, Stacey, and David Levery, ed. *TV Goes to Hell: An Unofficial Roadmap of Supernatural*. Toronto: ECW Press, 2011.
Abrams, Natalie. "*Smallville*'s Allison Mack Excited About Directing Again—and a New Coupling." *TV Guide*. February 11, 2010. http://www.tvguide.com/News/Smallville-Allison-Mack-1014927.aspx.
Andre, Judith. "Stereotypes: Conceptual and Normative Considerations." In *Racism and Sexism: An Integrated Study*, edited by Paula Rothenberg. New York: St. Martin's Press, 1988.
Ausiello, Michael. "'*Smallville*' Exclusive: Someone Is Going to [Major Spoiler Alert]!" *The Ausiello Files at EW.com*. March 30, 2010. http://ausiellofiles.ew.com/2010/03/30/smallville-finale-death-spoiler/-comments.
Badiou, Alain. *Saint Paul: The Foundation of Universalism*, translated by Ray Brassier. Stanford: Stanford University Press, 2003.
Badiou, Alain. "Thinking the Event." In *Philosophy in the Present*, edited by Peter Engelmann, translated Peter Thomas and Alberto Toscano, 1–47. Cambridge: Polity Press, 2009.
Banks, Miranda. "A Boy for All Planets: *Roswell*, *Smallville*, and the Teen Male Melodrama." In *Teen TV: Genre, Consumption, and Identity*, edited by Glyn Davis and Kay Dickinson, 17–28. London: BFI, 2004.
Battis, Jess. "The Kryptonite Closet: Silence and Queer Secrecy in *Smallville*." In *The Smallville Chronicles: Critical Essays on the Television Series*, edited by Lincoln Geraghty, 45–63. Lanham, MD: Scarecrow Press, 2011.
Beeler, Karin. "Televisual Transformations: Myth and Social Issues in *Smallville*." In *The Smallville Chronicles: Critical Essays on the Television Series*, edited by Lincoln Geraghty, 25–44. Lanham, MD: Scarecrow Press, 2011.
Beeler, Stan. "From Comic Book to *Bildungsroman*: *Smallville*, Narrative, and the Education of a Young Hero." In *The Smallville Chronicles: Critical Essays on the Television Series*, edited by Lincoln Geraghty, 3–24. Lanham, MD: Scarecrow Press, 2011.
"The Best TV Series of the 2000s." *The A.V. Club*. November 12, 2009. http://www.avclub.com/article/the-best-tv-series-of-the-00s-35256.
Billson, Anne. *Buffy the Vampire Slayer (BFI TV Classics)*. London: British Film Institute, 2006.
Blüher, Dominique. "Französische Ansätze zur Analyse der filmischen Figur." In

Der Körper im Bild: Schauspielen, Darstellen, Erscheinen, edited by Heinz-B. Heller, Karl Prümm, und Birgit Peulings, 61–70. Marburg, Germany: Schüren, 1999.

Booker, M. Keith, ed. "Feminism." *Encyclopedia of Comic Books and Graphic Novels, Volume 1*. Santa Barbara: Greenwood, 2010.

Britas15. "Dear Lois, Dump Your Boyfriend and Your Cousin: An Open Letter." *Kryptonsite* Forums. April 16, 2010. http://www.kryptonsite.com/forums/showthread.php?t=141748.

Byrne, Craig. *Smallville: The Official Companion Season 5*. London: Titan, 2007.

Campbell, Joseph. *The Hero with a Thousand Faces*. Princeton: Princeton University Press, 1968, 1973. [See also Campbell, Joseph. *The Hero with a Thousand Faces*. Novato, CA: New World Libraries, 2008.]

Campbell, Joseph. *Thou Art That: Transforming Religious Metaphor*. Novato, CA: New World Library, 2001.

Carlson, Marvin. *The Haunted Stage: The Theater as Memory Machine*. Ann Arbor: University of Michigan Press, 2003.

"The Chlois Discussion Thread: Which Anvils Do You Believe?" Pages 450–500. *Television Without Pity*. October 21, 2008. http://forums.televisionwithoutpity.com/topic/3132457-the-chlois-discussion-thread-which-anvils-do-you-believe/page-450.

"Chlois Theory." *Fanlore*. Accessed January 2, 2014. http://fanlore.org/wiki/Chlois_theory.

"Chlois Theory." *Smallville Wikia*. Accessed May 21, 2013. http://smallville.wikia.com/wiki/Chlois_theory.

Coffin, Tristram Potter. *The Female Hero in Folklore and Legend*. New York: The Seabury Press, 1975.

Coogan, Peter. *Superhero: The Secret Origin of a Genre*. Austin: MonkeyBrain, 2006.

Commentary on "Lazarus." *Smallville: The Complete Tenth Season*. Warner Home Video, 2011. DVD feature.

The CW Source. "Cassidy Freeman Introduces Tess Mercer to the CW Source." *YouTube*. August 14, 2008. http://www.youtube.com/watch?v=OLzMKsZelo0.

Daniels, Les *Superman. The Complete History, the Life and Times of the Man of Steel*. San Francisco: Chronicle Books, 1998.

Darwin, Charles. *The Descent of Man and Selection in Relation to Sex*. New York: Merrill and Baker, 1874.

Denison, Rayna. "It's a Bird! It's a Plane! No, It's DVD! *Superman*, *Smallville*, and the Production (of) Melodrama." In *Film and Comic Books*, edited by Ian Gordon, Mark Jancovich, and Matthew P. McAllister, 160–179. Jackson: University Press of Mississippi, 2007.

Denison, Rayna. "No Flights, No Tights: *Smallville* and the Roles of Special Effects in Television." In *The Smallville Chronicles: Critical Essays on the Television Series*, edited by Lincoln Geraghty, 65–86. Lanham, MD: Scarecrow Press, 2011.

DiBattista, Maria. *Fast-Talking Dames*. New Haven: Yale University Press, 2001.

Dolan, Jill. *Utopia in Performance: Finding Hope at the Theater*. Ann Arbor: University of Michigan Press, 2005.

Dooley, Dennis. "The Man of Tomorrow and the Boys of Yesterday." In *Superman at Fifty*, edited by Dennis Dooley and Gary Engel, 19–35. New York: Collier, 1987.

Duffy, Michael S. "Sacrifice or Salvation? *Smallville*'s Heroic Survival and Changing Television Trends." In *The Smallville Chronicles: Critical Essays on the Television Series*, edited by Lincoln Geraghty, 153–172. Lanham, MD: Scarecrow Press, 2011.

Eder, Jens. *Die Figur im Film: Grundlagen der Figurenanalyse*. Marburg, Germany: Schüren Verl, 2008.

Eder, Jens, Fotis, Jannidis, and Schneider, Ralf. "Characters in Fictional Worlds. An Introduction." In *Characters in Fictional Worlds: Understanding Imaginary Beings in Literature, Film, and Other Media*, edited by Fotis Jannidis, Ralf Schneider, and Jens Eder, 3–66. Berlin: Walter de Gruyter, 2008.

Elliottxoxo. "The "What If" That Is '*Smallville*.'" *Spider Fan's Web*. November 14, 2009. http://spiderfansweb.wordpress.com/2009/11/14/the-what-if-that-is-smallville/.

Engle, Gary. "What Makes Superman So Darned American?" In *Superman at Fifty*, edited by Dennis Dooley and Gary Engel, 79–87. New York: Collier, 1987.

"Episode List: *Smallville* Season 2." *TV Tango*. Accessed March 3, 2014. http://www.tvtango.com/series/smallville/episodes?filters%5Bday%5D=&filters%5Bseason%5D=2&filters%5Bbroadcast%5D=No&filters%5Bmedia%5D=&commit.x=13&commit.y=13.

Estés, Clarissa Pinkola. *Women Who Run with the Wolves*. New York: Ballantine Books, 1992.

"Fan Episode Reviews." *TV.com*. Last modified June 21, 2012. http://www.tv.com/shows/smallville/subterranean-864005/reviews.

"The 50 Best TV Dramas of All Time." *Complex*. March 20, 2013. http://www.complex.com/pop-culture/2013/03/best-tv-dramas-of-all-time.

Fludernik, Monika. "Histories of Narrative Theory (II): From Structuralism to the Present." In *A Companion to Narrative Theory*, edited by James Phelan and Peter J. Rabinowitz, 36–59. Malden, MA: Blackwell, 2005.

Frankel, Valerie Estelle. *Buffy and the Heroine's Journey*. Jefferson, NC: McFarland, 2012.

Frankel, Valerie Estelle. *From Girl to Goddess: The Heroine's Journey in Myth and Legend*. Jefferson, NC: McFarland, 2010.

Fried, Alexandra. "Transformation von Charakteren. Das Alter Ego als narratives Element im Animationsfilm." Thesis, University of Applied Sciences Upper Austria, Hagenberg, 2010.

Gardies, André. "L'acteur dans le système textuel du film." *Etudes Littéraires* 13.1 (1980): 71–108.

Genette, Gerard. *Paratexts: Thresholds of Interpretation*, translated by Jane E. Lewin. Cambridge: Cambridge University Press, 1997.

Geraghty, Lincoln. *American Science Fiction Film and Television*. New York: Berg, 2009.

Gerbner, George, Larry Gross, Michael Morgan, Nancy Signorielli, and James Shanahan. "Growing up with Television: Cultivation Processes." In *Media Effects: Advances in Theory and Research*, 2d ed., edited by Jennings Bryant and Dolf Zillmann, 43–67. Mahwah, NJ: Lawrence Erlbaum, 2002.

Girl Friday: A Chloe Sullivan/Allison Mack Worship Site. Accessed December 31, 2013. http://www.loony-archivist.com/girlfriday/.

Gordon, Andrew. "*Star Wars*: A Myth for Our Time." *Literature/Film Quarterly* 6.4 (1978): 314–326.

Gordon, Ian. "Nostalgia, Myth, and Ideology: Visions of Superman at the End of the 'American Century.'" In *Comics and Ideology*, edited by Matthew P. McAllister, Edward H. Sewell, and Ian Gordon, 177–194. New York: Peter Lang, 2001.

Goyer, David S. (w), Sepulveda, Miguel (p), and Paul Mounts (i). "The Incident." *Action Comics* #900, 75. Little, Brown/DC Comics, 2011.

Grant, Robert. *Writing the Science Fiction Film*. Saline, MI: Michael Wiese Productions, 2013.

Gray, Jonathan. "Antifandom and the Moral Text: Television Without Pity and Textual Dislike." *The American Behavioral Scientist* 48.7 (2005): 840–858.

Gray, Jonathan. "New Audiences, New Textualities: Anti-Fans and Non-Fans." *International Journal of Cultural Studies* 6.1 (2003): 64–81.

Gray, Jonathan. *Show Sold Separately: Promos, Spoilers, and Other Media Paratexts*. New York: New York University Press, 2010.

Gregg, Melissa, and Gregory J. Seigworth. *The Affect Theory Reader*. Durham: Duke University Press, 2010.

Greimas, Algirdas Julien. "Actants, Actors, and Figures." In *On Meaning. Selected Writings in Semiotic Theory*, 106–120. Minneapolis: University of Minnesota Press, 1987.

Gunderson, Seth. "Smallville, Kansas, The Biggest Little Town You've Ever Seen." *The Trades*. November 5, 2001. http://www.the-trades.com/article.php?id=908.

Gwenllian-Jones, Sara. "The Sex Lives of Cult Television Characters." *Screen* 43.1 (2002): 73–90.

Hadas, Leora. "Resisting the Romance: 'Shipping' and the Discourse of Genre Uniqueness in *Doctor Who* Fandom." *European Journal of Cultural Studies* 16.3 (2013): 329–343.

Haig, Francesca. "Critical Pleasures: *Twilight*, Snark, and Critical Fandom." In *Screening Twilight: Critical Approaches to a Cinematic Phenomenon*, edited by Sarah Harman and Wickham Clayton. London: I.B. Tauris, 2013.

Hall, Stuart. "Encoding and Decoding in the Television Discourse." *Centre for Critical Cultural Studies*, 507–517. Birmingham: University of Birmingham, 1973.

Harman, Sarah, and Bethan Jones. "Fifty Shades of Ghey: Snark Fandom and the Figure of the Anti-Fan." *Sexualities* 16.8 (2013): 951–968.

Hedegaard, Erik. "Tall Tales from *Smallville*." *Rolling Stone* #892. March 28, 2002.

Heidbrink, Henriette. "Fictional Characters in Literary and Media Studies: A Survey of the Research." In *Characters in Fictional Worlds: Understanding Imaginary Beings in Literature, Film, and Other Media*, edited by Fotis Jannidis, Ralf Schneider, and Jens Eder, 67–110. Berlin: Walter de Gruyter, 2010.

Hibberd, James. "CW Renews '*Smallville*' for 10th Season." *Hollywood Reporter*. March 4, 2010. www.heatvisionblog.com/2010/03/cw-renews-smallville-for-10th-season.html.

Hibberd, James. "'*Smallville*' Drops Again, Hits Season Low." *The Live Feed*. April 17, 2010. http://livefeed.hollywoodreporter.com/2010/04/smallville-ratings-low-.html#disqus_thread.

Highsmith, Doug. "The Long, Strange Trip of Barbara Gordon: Images of Librarians in Comic Books." In *The Image and Role of the Librarian*, edited by Wendi Arent and Candace R. Benefiel. Binghamton, NY: Haworth Press, 2002.

Hurley, Erin, and Sara Warner. "Special Section: 'Affect, Performance, Politics.'" *Journal of Dramatic Theory and Criticism* 46.2 (Spring 2012): 99–108.

Iaccino, James F. *Jungian Reflections Within the Cinema: A Psychological Analysis of Sci-Fi and Fantasy Archetypes*. Westport, CT: Praeger, 1998.

"In the Director's Chair: Behind the Scenes and Calling the Shots with Allison Mack." *Smallville: The Complete Eighth Season*. DVD Feature. Warner Home Video, 2009.

Inness, Sherrie A., ed. *Action Chicks: New Images of Tough Women in Popular Culture*. New York: Palgrave Macmillan, 2004.

Jagodzinski, Jan. *Television and Youth Culture: Televised Paranoia*. New York: Palgrave Macmillan, 2008.

Jannidis, Fotis. "Character." In *The Living Handbook of Narratology*, edited by Peter Hühn, John Pier, Wolf Schmid, and Jörg Schönert. Hamburg, Germany: Interdisciplinary Center for Narratology. http://hup.sub.uni-hamburg.de/lhn/index.php/Character.

Jenkins, Henry. *Convergence Culture: Where Old and New Media Collide*. New York: New York University Press, 2006.

Jenkins, Henry. *Textual Poachers: Television Fans and Participatory Culture*. New York: Routledge, 1992.

Jenson, Joli. "Fandom as Pathology: The Consequences of Characterization." In *The Adoring Audience: Fan Culture and Popular Media*, edited by Lisa A. Lewis, 9–29. New York: Routledge, 1992.

Johnson, J.K. "The Countryside Triumphant: Jefferson's Ideal of Rural Superiority in Modern Superhero Mythology." *The Journal of Popular Culture* 43.4 (2010): 720–737.

Jowett, Lorna. *Sex and the Slayer: A Gender Primer for the Buffy Fan*. Middletown, CT: Wesleyan University Press, 2005.

"The Joys of Live-Reading the Hated Book." *In Media Res*. September 23, 2012. http://mediacommons.futureofthebook.org/imr/2012/09/23/joys-live-reading-hated-book.

Jung, Carl. *The Collected Works, Volume 4: Freud and Psychoanalysis*, translated by R. F.C. Hull. Princeton: Princeton University Press, 1990.

Jung, Carl. *The Collected Works, Volume 9 Part I: The Archetypes and the Collective Unconscious*, translated by R. F.C. Hull. Princeton: Princeton University Press, 1990.

Jung, Carl G. *The Collected Works, Volume 9, Part II: Aion: Researches into the Phenomenology of the Self*, translated by R. F.C. Hull. Princeton: Princeton University Press, 1990.

Jung, Carl. *Collected Works, Volume 11: Psychology and Religion: West and East*, edited by Herbert Read and Gerhard Adler, translated by R. F.C. Hull. Princeton: Princeton University Press, 1968.

Keitz, Ursula von. "Orlacs Hände und die Körperfragment-Topik nach dem Ersten Weltkrieg." In *Unheimlich anders: Doppelgänger, Monster, Schattenwesen im Kino*, 53–68. Berlin: Bertz and Fischer, 2005.

Keppler, Angela. "Zur Wahrnehmung medialer Akteure im Fernsehen." In *Fernsehen als Beziehungskiste: Parasoziale Beziehungen und Interaktionen mit TV-Personen*, edited by Peter Vorderer, 11–24. Opladen, Germany: Westdeutscher Verlag, 1996.

Kohnen, Melanie E.S. "The Adventures of a Repressed Farm Boy and the Billionaire Who Loves Him: Queer Spectatorship in *Smallville* Fandom." In *Teen Television: Essays on Programming and Fandom*, edited by Sharon Marie Ross and Louisa Ellen Stein, 207–223. Jefferson, NC: McFarland, 2008.

Kozloff, Sarah R. "Superman as Saviour: Christian Allegory in the *Superman* Movies." *Journal of Popular Film and Television* 9.2 (1981): 78–82.

Kuhn, Markus. *Filmnarratologie: Ein erzähltheoretisches Analysemodell*. Berlin: Walter de Gruyter, 2011.

Lefebvre, Benjamin. "Adolescence through the Looking-Glass: Ideology and the Represented Child in *Degrassi: The Next Generation*." *Canadian Children's Literature* 33.1 (2007): 82–106.

Levine, Elana, and Lisa Parks, ed. *Undead TV: Essays on Buffy the Vampire Slayer*. Durham: Duke University Press, 2007.

Levy, Steven. *Hackers: Heroes of the Computer Revolution*. Garden City, NY: Anchor Press, 1984.

Lundegaard, Erik. "Trust, Justice and (Fill in the Blank)." *The Chicago Tribune*. June 30, 2006, A23(L).

"The Making of a Milestone: *Smallville*'s 100th Episode." *Smallville: The Complete Fifth Season*. DVD feature. Warner Home Video, 2006.

Margolin, Uri. "Character." *Routledge Encyclopedia of Narrative Theory*, edited by Manfred Jahn and Marie-Laure Ryan, 52–57. London: Routledge, 2005.

Massena. "Some Achieve Greatness: Part I—An Overview of Evidence." *Carbon Copy.org*. January 6, 2006. http://www.carboncopy.chlois.org/essays/reasons/some-achieve-greatness-part-i-overview-evidence.

McManus, Robert M., and Grace R. Waitman. "*Smallville* as a Rhetorical Means of Moral Value Education." In *The Amazing Transforming Superhero! Essays on the Revision of Characters in Comic Books, Film and Television*, edited by Terrence R. Wandtke, 174–191. Jefferson, NC: McFarland, 2007.

"Meteor Freak," *Smallville Wikia*. Accessed December 31, 2013. http://smallville.wikia.com/wiki/Meteor_freak.

Meuleners, Matthew. "Treat Students Right by Valuing Their Diversity." *Education Digest* 67.4 (2001): 46–51.

Meyer, Michaela. "Slashing *Smallville*: The Interplay of Text, Audience, and Production on Viewer Interpretations of Homoeroticism." *Sexuality & Culture* 17.3 (2013): 476–493

Misztal, Barbara A. *Theories of Social Remembering*. Philadelphia: Open University Press, 2003.

Mitovich, Matt. "*Smallville*'s Allison Mack, Part 2: Here Comes the Bride?" *TV Guide.com*. October 8, 2008. http://www.tvguide.com/News/Allison-Mack Smallville-20069.aspx.

Moore, Alan (w), Dave Gibbons (i). *Whatever Happened to the Man of Tomorrow?* Little, Brown/DC Comics, 2010.

Morrison, Grant. *Supergods*. New York: Spiegel and Grau, 2011.

Nama, Adilifu. *Black Space: Imagining Race in Science Fiction*. Austin: University of Texas Press, 2008.

Ngai, Mae. *Impossible Subjects: Illegal Aliens and the Making of Modern America*. Princeton: Princeton University Press, 2004.
"#9–16 Escape." *Kryptonsite* Forums. Accessed January 31, 2014. http://www.ksitetv.com/forums/forumdisplay.php?618-9-16-Escape.
"#9–18 Upgrade." *Kryptonsite* Forums. Accessed January 31, 2014. http://www.ksitetv.com/forums/forumdisplay.php?634-9-18-Upgrade.
Norris, Christopher. *Badiou's Being and Event: A Reader's Guide*. London: Continuum, 2009.
Omar G. "Al Be There For You." *Television Without Pity*. January 18, 2006. http://www.televisionwithoutpity.com/show/smallville/.
Omi, Michael, and Howard Winant. "Racial Formation." In *Racial Formation in the United States: From the 1960s to the 1990s*, 2d ed. New York: Routledge, 1994.
O'Shea, Tara. "The Allison Chronicles." *Allison-Mack.com*. July 29 2003. http://allison-mack.com/exclusive2.htm.
Pearson, Carol, and Katherine Pope. *The Female Hero in American and British Literature*. New York: Bowker, 1981.
Pitzer, Juli Stone. "Vids, Vlogs, and Blogs: The Participatory Culture of *Smallville*'s Digital Fan." In *The Smallville Chronicles: Critical Essays on the Television Series*, edited by Lincoln Geraghty, 109–128. Lanham, MD: Scarecrow Press, 2011.
Radish, Christina. "Erica Durance Interview: *Smallville*." *Collider.com*. January 30, 2011. http://collider.com/erica-durance-interview-smallville/73448.
Ramírez Berg, Charles. "Immigrant, Aliens, and Extraterrestrials: Science Fiction's Alien "Other" as (among Other Things) New Hispanic Imagery." In *Latino Images in Film: Stereotypes, Subversion, and Resistance*, 153–182. Austin: University of Texas Press, 2002.
Regalado, Aldo. "Modernity, Race, and the American Superhero." In *Comics as Philosophy*, edited by Jeff McLaughlin, 84–99. Jackson: University Press of Mississippi, 2005.
Ross, Andrew. "Hacking Away at the Counterculture." *Postmodern Culture* 1.1 (1990).
Rubin, Rachel, and Jeffrey Melnick. *Immigration and American Popular Culture*. New York: New York University Press, 2007.
Russell, Derek. "Starkville's House of El Episode 135 – 'Kandor.'" *Starkville's House of El Podcast*. November 11, 2009. www.smallvillepodcast.com.
Ryan, Christopher, and Cacila Jethá. *Sex at Dawn*. New York: HarperCollins, 2010.
Sanders, Julie. *Adaptation and Appropriation (The New Critical Idiom)*. London: Routledge, 2005.
Schweinitz, Jörg. "Stereotypes and the Narratological Analysis of Film Characters." In *Characters in Fictional Worlds: Understanding Imaginary Beings in Literature, Film, and Other Media*, edited by Fotis Jannidis, Ralf Schneider, und Jens Eder, 276–289. Berlin: Walter de Gruyter, 2010.
Scodari, Christine, and Jenna L. Felder. "Creating a Pocket Universe: 'Shippers,' Fan Fiction, and *The X-Files* Online." *Communication Studies* 51.3 (2000): 238–257.
Seidman, Robert. "Super Friday Night for the CW; Strategy of Pairing '*Smallville*'/ '*Supernatural*' Again on the Night Paid Off." *TV by the Numbers*. September 25, 2010. http://tvbythenumbers.zap2it.com/2010/09/25/super-friday-night-

for-the-cw-strategy-of-pairing-smallvillesupernatural-again-on-the-night-paid-off/65167/.
Simpson, Paul. *Smallville: The Official Companion Season 1*. London: Titan, 2004.
Simpson, Paul. *Smallville: The Official Companion Season 3*. London: Titan, 2005.
Smith, Murray. *Engaging Characters. Fiction, Emotion, and the Cinema*. Oxford: Clarendon Press/Oxford University Press, 1995.
"The Son Becomes the Father." *Smallville: The Complete Tenth Season*. DVD feature. Warner Home Video, 2011.
Steinhauer, Jennifer. "Pow! Slam! Thank You, Ma'am." *New York Times*. November 5, 2000. http://www.nytimes.com/2000/11/05/weekinreview/ideas-trends-pow-slam-thank-you-ma-am.html.
Strong, Catherine. "'...It Sucked Because It Was Written for Teenage Girls' – *Twilight*, Anti-Fans, and Symbolic Violence." Presented at *The Future of Sociology: The Annual Conference of the Australian Sociological Association*. Australian National University, December 1–4, 2009.
"Supergirl: The Last Daughter of Krypton." *Smallville: The Complete Seventh Season*. DVD Feature. Warner Home Video, 2008.
Taylor, Henry, and Tröhler, Margrit. "Zu ein paar Facetten der menschlichen Figur im Spielfilm." In *Der Körper im Bild: Schauspielen, Darstellen, Erscheinen*, edited by Heinz-B. Heller, Karl Prümm, and Birgit Peulings, 137–151. Marburg, Germany: Schüren, 1999.
Thomas, Martin R. "Related Genres: Animation—Max Fleischer Superman Animated Shorts, *Daddy Rolled a 1*. March 11, 2011. http://daddyrolleda1.blogspot.com/2011/03/related-genres-animation-max-fleischer.html.
Thornton, Sarah. *Club Cultures: Music, Media, and Subcultural Capital*. Cambridge: Polity Press, 1995.
"26 Best Cult TV Shows Ever." *Entertainment Weekly*. March 14, 2013. http://www.ew.com/ew/gallery/0,,20741515_20620965_21199219,00.html.
Van Eenwyk, John R. *Archetypes and Strange Attractors: The Chaotic World of Symbols*. Toronto: Inner City Books, 1997.
Vernet, Marc. "Le personnage de film." *Iris* 7 (1986): 81–110.
Vogler, Christopher. *The Writer's Journey: Mythic Structure for Writers*, 3d ed. Studio City, CA: Michael Wiese Productions, 2007.
Weber, Lynn. "A Conceptual Framework for Understanding Race, Class, Gender, and Sexuality." *Psychology of Women Quarterly* 22.1 (1998): 13–32.
Wee, Valerie. "Teen Television and the WB Television Network." In *Teen Television: Essays on Programming and Fandom*, edited by Sharon Marie Ross and Louisa Ellen Stein, 43–60. Jefferson, NC: McFarland, 2008.
Wilcox, Rhonda V., and Sue Turnbull, eds. *Investigating Veronica Mars: Essays on the Teen Detective Series*. Jefferson, NC: McFarland, 2011.
Williams, Raymond. *Culture and Society: 1780–1950*. New York: Columbia University Press, 1983.
Wright, Bradford W. *Comic Book Nation: The Transformation of Youth Culture in America*. Baltimore: Johns Hopkins University Press, 2003.
Wulff, Hans Jürgen. "Charaktersynthese und Paraperson: Das Rollenverhältnis der gespielten Fiktion." In *Fernsehen als Beziehungskiste: Parasoziale Beziehungen und Interaktionen mit TV-Personen*, edited by Peter Vorderer, 29–48. Opladen, Germany: Westdeutscher Verlag, 1996.

Wulff, Hans Jürgen. "Die entmachtete Sexualität: Politik, Klonieren und Replikation im neueren Kino." In *Unheimlich anders: Doppelgänger, Monster, Schattenwesen im Kino*, edited by Christine Rüffert, 141–152. Berlin: Bertz Plus Fischer, 2005.

Žižek, Slavoj. "Badiou: Notes from an Ongoing Debate." *International Journal of Žižek Studies* 1.2 (2007): 28–43.

Žižek, Slavoj. *In Defense of Lost Causes*. London: Verso, 2008.

Žižek, Slavoj. "Introduction: Between the Two Revolutions." In *Revolution at the Gates: Žižek on Lenin: The 1917 Writings*, 1–14. London: Verso, 2004.

Žižek, Slavoj. "Neighbors and Other Monsters: A Plea for Ethical Violence." In *The Neighbor: Three Inquiries in Political Theology*, 134–190. Chicago: University of Chicago Press, 2005.

Žižek, Slavoj. "The Politics of Batman." *New Statesman*. August 23, 2012. http://www.newstatesman.com/culture/culture/2012/08/slavoj-%C5%BEi%C5%BEek-politics-batman.

Žižek, Slavoj. *The Puppet and the Dwarf: The Perverse Core of Christianity*. Cambridge: Massachusetts Institute of Technology, 2003.

Zubernis, Lynn, and Katherine Larsen, eds. *Fan Phenomena: Supernatural*. Chicago: Intellect Books and the University of Chicago Press, 2014.

Media Referenced—*Smallville*

Smallville. Creat. Alfred Gough and Miles Millar. Perf. Tom Welling, Kristin Kreuk, Michael Rosenbaum, Allison Mack. The WB, 2001–2006. The CW, 2006–2011.
Specific episodes:
"Abandoned." *Smallville*. The CW. November 12, 2010.
"Absolute Justice." *Smallville*. The CW. February 5, 2010.
"Abyss." *Smallville*. The CW. November 13, 2008.
"Accelerate." *Smallville*. The WB. May 6, 2003.
"Action." *Smallville*. The CW. October 25, 2007.
"Ageless." *Smallville*. The WB. May 4, 2005.
"Arctic." *Smallville*. The CW. May 15, 2008.
"Arrival." *Smallville*. The WB. September 29, 2005.
"Arrow." *Smallville*. The CW. October 19, 2006.
"Asylum." *Smallville*. The WB. January 14, 2004.
"Beacon." *Smallville*. The CW. February 11, 2011.
"Beast." *Smallville*. The CW. April 30, 2009.
"Bizarro." *Smallville*. The CW. September 27, 2007.
"Blank." *Smallville*. The WB. April 27, 2005.
"Bloodline." *Smallville*. The CW. November 6, 2008.
"Blue." *Smallville*. The CW. November, 15 2007.
"Booster." *Smallville*. The CW. April 22, 2011.
"Bound." *Smallville*. The WB. November 17, 2004.
"Bride." *Smallville*. The CW. November 20, 2008.
"Bulletproof." *Smallville*. The CW. January 22, 2009.
"Calling." *Smallville*. The WB. May 13, 2002.
"Charade." *Smallville*. The CW. April 23, 2010.
"Checkmate." *Smallville*. The CW. April 9, 2010.

"Collateral." *Smallville*. The CW. February 4, 2011.
"Combat." *Smallville*. The CW. March 22, 2007.
"Commencement." *Smallville*. The WB. May 18, 2005.
"Covenant." *Smallville*. The WB. May 19, 2004.
"Craving." *Smallville*. The WB. November 27, 2001.
"Crimson." *Smallville*. The CW. February 1, 2007.
"Crisis." *Smallville*. The WB. March 3, 2004.
"Crusade." *Smallville*. The WB. September 22, 2004.
"Crush." *Smallville*. The WB. May 7, 2002.
"Cure." *Smallville*. The CW. October 18, 2007.
"Delete." *Smallville*. The WB. January 28, 2004.
"Devoted." *Smallville*. The WB. October 13, 2004.
"Dichotic." *Smallville*. The WB. November 19, 2002.
"Doomsday." *Smallville*. The CW. May 14, 2009.
"Drone." *Smallville*. The WB. April 30, 2002.
"Duplicity." *Smallville*. The WB. October 8, 2002.
"Escape." *Smallville*. The CW. April 2, 2011.
"Eternal." *Smallville*. The CW. April 2, 2009.
"Exile." *Smallville*. The WB. October 1, 2003.
"Exodus." *Smallville*. The WB. May 20, 2003.
"Extinction." *Smallville*. The WB. October 15, 2003.
"Façade." *Smallville*. The WB. October 6, 2004.
"Fallout." *Smallville*. The CW. November 6, 2006.
"Fever." *Smallville*. The WB. February 18, 2003.
"Fierce." *Smallville*. The CW. October 11, 2007.
"Finale." *Smallville*. The CW. May 13, 2011.
"Forever." *Smallville*. The WB. May 11, 2005.
"Forsaken." *Smallville*. The WB. May 12, 2004.
"Fortune." *Smallville*. The CW. February 25, 2011.
"Fracture." *Smallville*. The CW. February 14, 2008.
"Gone." *Smallville*. The WB. September 29, 2004.
"Harvest." *Smallville*. The CW. October 29, 2010.
"Heat." *Smallville*. The WB. October 1, 2002.
"Hex." *Smallville*. The CW. March 26, 2009.
"Hidden." *Smallville*. The WB. October 13, 2005.
"Homecoming." *Smallville*. The CW. October 15, 2010.
"Hostage." *Smallville*. The CW. May 7, 2010.
"Hothead." *Smallville*. The WB. October 30, 2001.
"Hourglass." *Smallville*. The WB. November 21, 2001.
"Hug." *Smallville*. The WB. February 5, 2002.
"Hydro." *Smallville*. The CW. January 11, 2007.
"Hypnotic." *Smallville*. The WB. March 30, 2006.
"Icarus." *Smallville*. The CW. December 10, 2010.
"Identity." *Smallville*. The CW. October 30, 2008.
"Idol." *Smallville*. The CW. November 13, 2009.
"Infamous." *Smallville*. The CW. March 12, 2009.
"Injustice." *Smallville*. The CW. May 7, 2009.
"Instinct." *Smallville*. The CW. October 9, 2008.

"Isis." *Smallville*. The CW. October 22, 2010.
"Jinx." *Smallville*. The WB. November 3, 2004.
"Jitters." *Smallville*. The WB. December 11, 2001.
"Justice." *Smallville*. The CW. January 18, 2007.
"Kandor." *Smallville*. The CW. November 6, 2009.
"Kent." *Smallville*. The CW. April 15, 2011.
"Kinetic." *Smallville*. The WB. February 26, 2002.
"Labyrinth." *Smallville*. The CW. January 25, 2007.
"Lazarus." *Smallville*. The CW. September 24, 2010.
"Leech." *Smallville*. The WB. February 12, 2002.
"Legacy." *Smallville*. The WB. April 14, 2004.
"Legion." *Smallville*. The CW. January 15, 2009.
"Lineage." *Smallville*. The WB. November 5, 2002.
"Luthor." *Smallville*. The CW. December 3, 2010.
"Magnetic." *Smallville*. The WB. November 12, 2003.
"Masquerade." *Smallville*. The CW. February 18, 2011.
"Metallo." *Smallville*. The CW. October 2, 2009.
"Metamorphosis." *Smallville*. The WB. October 23, 2001.
"Mortal." *Smallville*. The WB. October 6, 2005.
"Nemesis." *Smallville*. The CW. April 26, 2007.
"Nicodemus." *Smallville*. The WB. March 19, 2002.
"Nocturne." *Smallville*. The WB. October 22, 2002.
"Obsession." *Smallville*. The WB. February 18, 2004.
"Onyx." *Smallville*. The WB. April 13, 2005.
"Pariah." *Smallville*. The WB. February 2, 2005.
"Perry." *Smallville*. The WB. October 29, 2003.
"Persona." *Smallville*. The CW. January 31, 2008.
"Persuasion." *Smallville*. The CW. February 19, 2010.
"Phantom." *Smallville*. The CW. May 17, 2007.
"Phoenix." *Smallville*. The WB. October 8, 2003.
"Pilot." *Smallville*. The WB. October 16, 2001.
"Power." *Smallville*. The CW. January 29, 2009.
"Precipice." *Smallville*. The WB. April 22, 2003.
"Progeny." *Smallville*. The CW. April 19, 2007.
"Prophecy." *Smallville*. The CW. May 6, 2011.
"Prototype." *Smallville*. The CW. May 10, 2007.
"Quest." *Smallville*. The CW. May 8, 2008.
"Rabid." *Smallville*. The CW. October 9, 2009.
"Reckoning." *Smallville*. The WB. January 26, 2006.
"Recruit." *Smallville*. The WB. February 9, 2005.
"Red." *Smallville*. The WB. October 15, 2002.
"Redux." *Smallville*. The WB. October 29, 2002.
"Relic." *Smallville*. The WB. November 6, 2003.
"Requiem." *Smallville*. The CW. February 5, 2009.
"Resurrection." *Smallville*. The WB. February 25, 2003.
"Rogue." *Smallville*. The WB. January 15, 2002.
"Rosetta." *Smallville*. The WB. February 25, 2003.
"Run." *Smallville*. The WB. October 27, 2004.

"Rush." *Smallville*. The WB. February 4, 2003.
"Sacred." *Smallville*. The WB. February 23, 2005.
"Sacrifice." *Smallville*. The CW. April 30, 2010.
"Salvation." *Smallville*. The CW. May 14, 2010.
"Savior." *Smallville*. The CW. September 25, 2009.
"Scare." *Smallville*. The WB. December 1, 2004.
"Scion." *Smallville*. The CW. March 4, 2011.
"Skinwalker." *Smallville*. The WB. November 26, 2002.
"Sleeper." *Smallville*. The CW. May 1, 2008.
"Sneeze." *Smallville*. The CW. October 5, 2006.
"Spell." *Smallville*. The WB. November 11, 2004.
"Splinter." *Smallville*. The WB. November 10, 2004.
"Stray." *Smallville*. The WB. April 16, 2002.
"Subterranean." *Smallville*. The CW. December 7, 2006.
"Supergirl." *Smallville*. The CW. October 8, 2010.
"Talisman." *Smallville*. The WB. May 5, 2004.
"Tempest." *Smallville*. The WB. May 21, 2002.
"Tomb." *Smallville*. The WB. February 9, 2006.
"Toxic." *Smallville*. The CW. October 9, 2008.
"Transference." *Smallville*. The WB. October 27, 2004.
"Truth." *Smallville*. The WB. April 21, 2004.
"Turbulence." *Smallville*. The CW. March 19, 2009.
"Unsafe." *Smallville*. The WB. January 26, 2005.
"Velocity." *Smallville*. The WB. February 11, 2004.
"Vessel." *Smallville*. The WB. May 11, 2006.
"Visage." *Smallville*. The WB. January 14, 2003.
"Void." *Smallville*. The WB. April 6, 2006.
"Vortex." *Smallville*. The WB. September 24, 2002.
"Warrior." *Smallville*. The CW. February 12, 2010.
"Wither." *Smallville*. The CW. October 12, 2006.
"Witness." *Smallville*. The WB. April 29, 2003.
"Wrath." *Smallville*. The CW. November 8, 2007.
"X-Ray." *Smallville*. The WB. November 7, 2001.

Media Referenced—Non-*Smallville*

The Adventures of Superman. Perf. George Reeves, Noel Neill. American Broadcasting Company, 1952–1958.
    Specific episodes:
        "Superman on Earth." *The Adventures of Superman*. American Broadcasting Company. September 19, 1952.
Angel. Creat. Joss Whedon and David Greenwalt. Perf. David Boreanaz, Charisma Carpenter, Alexis Densiof. The WB, 1999–2004.
Batman. Dir. Tim Burton. Perf. Michael Keaton, Jack Nicholson, Kim Basiger. Warner Bros., 1989.
Batman Begins. Dir. Christopher Nolan. Perf. Christian Bale, Katie Holmes, Morgan Freeman. Warner Bros., 2005.

Batman: The Animated Series. Creat. Bruce Timm. Perf. Kevin Conroy, Efrem Zimbalist, Jr. Fox, 1992–1995.
Being John Malkovich. Dir. Spike Jonze. Perf. John Cusack, Cameron Diaz, Catherine Keener. Propaganda Films, 1999.
Breaking Bad. Creat. Vince Gilligan. Perf. Bryan Cranston, Aaron Paul, Anna Gunn. AMC, 2008–2013.
Buffy the Vampire Slayer. Creat. Joss Whedon. Perf. Sarah Michelle Gellar, Alyson Hannigan, Nicholas Brendon. The WB, 1997–2001, UPN, 2001–2003.
    Specific episodes:
    "Chosen." *Buffy the Vampire Slayer.* UPN. May 20, 2003.
    "Fear, Itself." *Buffy the Vampire Slayer.* The WB. October 26, 1999.
    "Two to Go." *Buffy the Vampire Slayer.* UPN. May 21, 2002.
Charmed. Creat. Constance M. Burge. Perf. Holly Marie Combs, Alyssa Milano, Rose McGowan, Shannen Doherty. The WB, 1998–2006.
Dawson's Creek. Creat. Kevin Williamson. Perf. James Van Der Beek, Katie Holmes, Joshua Jackson, Michelle Williams. The WB, 1997–2003.
The Exorcist. Dir. William Friedkin. Perf. Linda Blair, Ellen Burstyn, Max von Sydow. Warner Bros., 1973.
Fight Club. Dir. David Fincher. Perf. Brad Pitt, Edward Norton, Helena Bonham Carter. 20th Century Fox, 1999.
Firefly. Creat. Joss Whedon. Perf. Nathan Fillion, Gina Torres, Morena Baccarin, Alan Tudyk. Fox, 2002–2003.
The Fly. Dir. Kurt Neumann. Perf. David Hedison, Patricia Owens, Vincent Price. 20th Century Fox, 1958.
Goldfinger. Dir. Guy Hamilton. Perf. Sean Connery, Honor Blackman. Eon, 1964.
Hackers. Dir. Ian Softley. Perf. Jonny Lee Miller, Angelina Jolie, Jesse Bradford, Matthew Lillard. United Artists, 1995.
His Girl Friday. Dir. Howard Hawks. Perf. Rosalind Russell and Cary Grant. Warner Bros., 1940.
Justice League. Creat. Bruce Timm. Perf. Kevin Conroy, George Newbern, Carl Lumby. Cartoon Network, 2001–2004.
    Specific episodes:
    "Hereafter." *Justice Lague.* Cartoon Network. November 29, 2003.
Justice League Unlimited. Creat. Bruce Timm. Perf. Kevin Conroy, Carl Lumby, Michael Rosenbaum. Cartoon Network, 2004–2006.
Kill Bill: Vol. 2. Dir. Quentin Tarantino. Perf. Uma Thurman. Miramax, 2004.
Lois and Clark: The New Adventures of Superman. Perf. Dean Cain, Teri Hatcher. American Broadcasting Company, 1993–1997.
    Specific episodes:
    "The House of Luthor." *Lois and Clark: The New Adventures of Superman.* American Broadcasting Company. May 8, 1994.
The Maltese Falcon. Dir. John Huston. Perf. Humphrey Bogart, Mary Astor, and Lee Patrick. Warner Bros., 1941.
Man of Steel. Dir. Zack Synder. Perf. Henry Cavill, Amy Adams, Michael Shannon. Warner Bros., 2013.
The Matrix. Dir. The Wachowski siblings. Perf. Keanu Reeves, Laurence Fishburne, Carrie-Anne Moss, Hugo Weaving. Warner Bros., 1999.

Remy Zero (band members: Cinjin Tate, Shelby Tate, Cedric LeMoyne, Jeffrey Cain, and Gregory Slay). "Save Me." *Golden Hum*. Elektra Records, 2001.

Roswell. Creat. Jason Katims. Perf. Jason Behr, Shiri Appleby, Brandon Fehr. The WB, 1999–2001, UPN, 2001–2002.

Skyfall. Dir. Sam Mendes. Perf. Daniel Craig, Javier Bardem, Judi Dench. Eon, 2012.

Star Trek. Creat. Gene Roddenberry. Perf. William Shatner, Leonard Nimoy, DeForest Kelley. National Broadcasting Company, 1966–1969.

Star Trek: Deep Space Nine. Creat. Rick Berman. Perf. Avery Brooks, René Auberjonois, Terry Farrell. Syndicated, 1993–1999.

"Superman Comes to Earth as Clark Kent." *The Adventures of Superman*. The Mutual Broadcasting Company. August 31, 1942.

Superman Returns. Dir. Bryan Singer. Perf. Brandon Routh, Kate Bosworth, Kevin Spacey. Warner Bros., 2006.

Superman: The Animated Series. Creat. Bruce Timm. Perf. Tim Daly, Dana Delany. The WB, 1996–2000.

Superman: The Movie. Dir. Richard Donner. Perf. Christopher Reeve, Marlon Brando, Margot Kidder, and Gene Hackman. Warner Bros., 1978.

Superman III. Dir. Richard Lester. Perf. Christopher Reeve, Richard Pryor. Warner Bros., 1983.

Supernatural. Creat. Eric Kripke. Perf. Jensen Ackles, Jared Padalecki. The WB, 2005–2006, the CW, 2006-Present.

Terminator 2: Judgment Day. Dir. James Cameron. Perf. Arnold Schwarzenegger, Linda Hamilton, Robert Patrick, Edward Furlong. TriStar Pictures, 1991.

Veronica Mars. Creat. Rob Thomas. Perf. Kristen Bell, Percy Daggs III, Jason Dohring, Tina Majorino. UPN, 2004–2006, the CW, 2006–2007.

The Wire. Creat. David Simon. Perf. Dominic West, John Doman, Wendell Pierce, Clarke Peters. HBO, 2002–2008.

The X-Files. Creat. Chris Carter. Perf. David Duchovny, Gillian Anderson. Fox, 1993–2002.

About the Contributors

Roger **Almendarez**, a PhD candidate at Northwestern, is a media studies scholar specializing in Latina/o cultural productions. He is particularly interested in exploring how media convergence facilitates the formation of personal and communal identities.

Jonathan A. **Austad** is an associate professor of humanities at Eastern Kentucky University. His research interests include interdisciplinary aspects of cultural theory, art, pop culture, film, and literature, and his recent inquiries focus on the artistic influence on Hemingway's aesthetic and Marxism's influence on Richard Wright's *Native Son*.

Cory **Barker** is a PhD student at Indiana University. His research focuses on how television networks establish multi-platform brand identities and the intersections between television and social media. He also works as a staff writer and television critic for TV.com.

Gregory **Bray** is a filmmaker, writer, and an assistant professor of media at SUNY New Paltz. His media works have been broadcast nationally through Current TV and regionally in the northeast through WMHT/PBS and WAMC Northeast Public Radio. Research interests include popular culture, identity in cyberspace, and new media pedagogy.

John Patrick **Bray** is a playwright and lecturer at the University of Georgia. His research interests include geek theatre, new play development, and adaptation studies; he has published in *Theatre Topics, New England Theatre Journal, Platform, Texas Theatre Journal,* and *Theatre Symposium*.

Daniel P. **Compora** is an associate professor at the University of Toledo. He teaches a number of literature courses, including folklore, science fiction and fantasy literature, and the detective story. He has published in the areas of folklore, popular culture, and distance learning.

Valerie Estelle **Frankel** has won a Dream Realm Award, an Indie Excellence Award, and a *USA Book News* National Best Book Award for her Henry Potty parodies. She is the author of many books on pop culture, including *From Girl to Goddess: The Heroine's Journey through Myth and Legend* (McFarland, 2010), *Buffy and the Heroine's*

Journey (McFarland, 2012), *Teaching with Harry Potter* (McFarland, 2013), and *Women in* Game of Thrones (McFarland, 2014).

James F. **Iaccino** is an associate professor in the forensic psychology department at the Chicago School of Professional Psychology. His research interests include Jungian archetypal analyses of movie genres and television series. He has authored several seminal texts on the topic, including *Jungian Reflections Within the Cinema* (Praeger, 1998).

Bridget **Kies** is a PhD student at the University of Wisconsin–Milwaukee. Her research looks at masculinity on television and in fan practices. She has previously published on *Star Trek: Voyager* in the journal *Transformative Works and Cultures* and has two forthcoming essays on the television series *Supernatural*.

Daniel **Kulle**, an independent scholar and filmmaker in Hamburg, Germany, wrote his dissertation on Ed Wood and the concept of irony in trash cinema. He has also published on DIY cinema, dance and action cinema, and phenomenological film theory.

Peter **Melville** is an associate professor of English at the University of Winnipeg. He is author of *Romantic Hospitality and the Resistance to Accommodation* (Wilfred Laurier University Press, 2007), *Writing About Literature: An Introductory Guide* (Nelson Education, 2011), and articles published in *The Eighteenth Century: Theory and Interpretation*, *European Romantic Review*, *Mosaic*, and *The Dalhousie Review*.

Tara K. **Parmiter** is a senior language lecturer in the expository writing program at New York University. Her areas of interest include children's literature, literature and the environment, travel and captivity narratives, and popular culture.

Chris **Ryan** is a social media researcher in Vancouver, British Coluimbia. His research interests include contemporary horror films, tabletop role-playing books, and Internet folklore.

Myc **Wiatrowski** is an associate instructor in the department of folklore and ethnomusicology at Indiana University. His areas of research interest include folklore and the Internet, narratology, popular culture and politics, and critical ethnography. His publications include articles on the rhetoric of masculinity in television and co-edited collections on the study of popular culture.

Index

Acid Burn (character) 100
Action Comics 134, 163, 165
Adkins, Desirée 120, 153
The Adventures of Superman 25, 134–35, 143, 164, 172
affect theory 9, 161–73
Allen, Bart 129, 140, 155, 179; the Flash 91, 140, 156, 179; Impulse 91
Alyn, Kirk 164, 169–70
American 48, 118, 132–36, 138, 140, 142–43, 159; accent 138; African American 118; Americanness 134, 136–37; Anglo American 136; culture 4, 14, 132–33, 135–40, 142; family 145; history 16, 120, 138; idealism 55; landscape 49; myth 14, 21; popular culture 133, 143; psyche 56–57, 171; values 20, 169
anti-fan 175, 178; fan 10, 175, 181
Aquaman *see* Curry, Arthur
Archer, Iva 102
Arkin, Greg 119, 125
Arnold, Walt 119, 152
Ashmore, Aaron 172
Atom Man vs. Superman (serial) 164

Baker, Alicia 55, 68, 108, 120, 125, 129, 171
Bale, Christian 163
Batman 163, 166
Batman Begins 1, 163
Batman: The Animated Series 164
Belle Reve 153
Bible 84; *see also* Christianity; Jesus Christ
Bizarro (character) 22, 36, 151
Black Canary 91
Bloome, Davis 22, 67, 71–73, 76, 84, 88–99; Doomsday 4, 22, 59, 71, 84, 90–3, 95–6, 179, 181
Blue Beetle *see* Reyes, Jaime
The Blur *see* Kent, Clark
Bond, James 163

Booster Gold (character) 155
Brainiac 22, 66, 70–71, 73–74, 79–80, 85–87, 103, 110, 151; Milton Fine 22
Brando, Marlon 35, 167
Brice, Helen 123
Buffy the Vampire Slayer (television series) 1–2, 4–5, 10, 49, 101, 106, 156, 174

Cain, Dean 167
Campbell, Joseph 5, 14–5, 17–19, 26–27, 29, 40–41, 45–8, 53, 55–56, 61
Carter, Michael John *see* Booster Gold
Carver, Cassandra 119, 122
Charmed (television series) 49; *see also* the Halliwell Sisters
Checkmate (organization) 73, 111
Chlois 181–5, 188–9
The Chloe Chronicles 108–9
The Chlois Theory 104, 175, 182–5, 189–90
Christianity 84, 89, 98, 171
citizenship 4, 8, 90, 111, 120–21, 133–34, 137, 140, 143; non-citizenship 133
Clark-El *see* Kent, Clark
Clois 9, 175, 180, 182, 187, 189
clone 33, 37, 52, 61, 76, 85, 96, 149, 151, 169, 184
Coates, Phyllis 164, 169
Connery, Sean 163
Corben, John 2, 152; Metallo 21, 152
Craig, Daniel 163
Creek, Jeremy 118–19, 152
Crosby, Bridgette 167
Curry, Arthur 140, 181; Aquaman 140, 156
The CW (television network) 1–2, 10, 49, 57, 83, 142, 169, 176, 180
Cyborg *see* Stone, Victor

The Daily Planet 14, 41, 67, 71, 84–6, 90, 93, 101, 111, 168, 172, 180–83, 188–89

209

Damascus 89, 98
Darkseid (character) 18, 39–41, 154, 170, 172
Dax-Ur 167
DC Comics 4, 55, 132, 155, 179
Department of Domestic Security 158
Desaad 74
Dinsmore, Emily 61, 120, 151
Doctor Fate 74
Doctor Who 179
Donner, Richard 167, 169
Doomsday (character) *see* Bloome, Davis
Dorothy (character) 45–47, 56
Durance, Erica 4, 78, 169, 181, 183, 187

Edge, Morgan 123
Everdeen, Katniss 80

fans 2–3, 5, 9–10, 43, 55, 57–58, 65, 75, 97, 104, 114, 141, 165, 168, 170–72, 174–90
Faora 76, 80
"faster than a speeding bullet" 86, 164
feminism 7, 66–67, 79, 110, 179; power 73, 79; symbol 80
Fifty Shades of Grey (book series) 177–78
Fine, Abigail 128, 152
Fine, Elise 128, 152
Fine, Milton *see* Brainiac
The Flash *see* Allen, Bart
Fleischer, Max 162–63
Fleischer Studios 134, 163–64; cartoons 134, 162–64, 170
Fordman, Whitney 51–52, 59–61, 64, 119
Fortress of Solitude 17, 33–36, 38–40, 43, 52–53, 71, 136, 138, 167, 169
Freak of the Week 4, 152, 166
Freeman, Cassidy 5, 83

Gaines, Justin 152
Girl Friday 7, 101–7, 109, 111–14
Glover, John 4, 35
God 89; hand of 29
Goldfinger (film) 163
Gough, Alfred 1, 44, 79, 83, 108, 141, 181, 183
Grady, Kevin 152
The Green Arrow *see* Queen, Oliver
Greer, Eva 94, 96
Greer, Tina 61, 119, 125, 151
Grey's Anatomy 186
Griggs, Molly 153

Hackers (film) 100
Hall, Carter 41; Hawkman 41
The Halliwell sisters 49; *see also Charmed* (series)
Hamilton, Emil 72

Hamilton, Steven 121
Hatcher, Teri 168–69
Hawkman *see* Hall, Carter
heat vision 64, 79, 157, 171
The Helmet of Nabu 74
His Girl Friday 102
Holdsclaw, Jeremiah 126
Holmes, Sherlock 162
The Hunger Games (book series) 80

immigration 8, 16, 132–33, 135–36, 138–40, 142–44, 158–59
Impulse *see* Allen, Bart
Isis (character) 76, 154
Isis Foundation 71, 111

Jenkins, Earl 119
Jesus Christ 18, 89, 98; Son of God 107; *see also* Christianity
Johns, Geoff (character) 120, 152
Jor-El 6, 17, 23, 25–27, 30–43, 52–53, 55, 124, 128, 130, 136, 167–68
Judaism 84, 138
Judas Iscariot 84, 88, 89
Jung, Carl 5–6, 19, 26, 29, 42–43, 62–63, 73
Justice League (comic series) 132–33, 164
Justice League (group) 60, 70, 73, 101, 110–11, 132, 140–41
Justice League Unlimited (comic series) 164
Justice Society of America (group) 41

Kal-El *see* Kent, Clark
Kandor 80
Katzman, Sam 164
Kawatche Caves 17, 23, 33–34, 37, 98, 127
Keaton, Michael 163
Kent, Conner 54, 57
Kent, Clark 3–9, 13–36, 38–39, 41, 43–46, 48–57, 59–99, 101, 103–30, 132–45, 151–59, 161–62, 165–172, 174–176, 179–180, 182–84, 186, 188–89; the Blur 8, 50, 56, 67–68, 78, 111, 135–36, 141, 143; Clark-El 39, 43–44; DC Comics Character 1; Kal-El 26–28, 33–39, 43, 48, 92, 124, 127, 132–33, 136–37, 140–43, 167; the Red-Blue Blur 50, 107, 141; secret (Clark's) 32, 37, 60, 64, 67–69, 76–78, 86–87, 107, 111, 114, 123–25, 129–30, 140–43, 158, 184; Smallville (nickname) 49–50, 168; spaceship (Clark's) 26, 33, 52, 60, 124, 167; superpowers/abilities (Clark's) 3, 7, 16, 20, 28, 30–32, 35–36, 39, 41, 49, 53, 57, 62–63, 76, 115–16, 123, 126, 129–30, 133, 135, 141, 145, 153, 156–58, 188
Kent, Jonathan 4, 6, 16–17, 20–21, 25–42, 51–53, 107, 116–17, 121–24, 126–27, 129–30, 135–37, 179, 181

Index

Kent, Kara 5–7, 23, 31, 35, 37, 39, 60, 78–81, 110, 127, 155, 181; Supergirl 110, 169
Kent, Martha 4, 20–21, 26–27, 29, 31–32, 34, 39–40, 51–54, 57, 76, 78, 81, 88, 91, 107, 116–17, 121, 124, 127, 139, 165–67, 179; the Red Queen 53
Kent farm 6, 13, 16, 27, 33, 37, 51–52, 54, 92, 121, 123, 130, 165, 167
Kidder, Margot 167–69
Klatzkin, Leon 164
Knox, Curtis 167
Kreuk, Kristin 1, 166, 181
Krinn, Rokk 85
Krypton 15–17, 26, 37, 45, 130, 132, 136–37, 140, 142–43, 164, 167
Kryptonian (race) 8, 16, 22–23, 34, 37–38, 43, 48, 54, 67, 71, 76, 80, 94, 98, 113, 125, 127–128, 132, 136–38, 140, 167; cousin 23, 31, 60, 78, 127, 181 (*see also* Kent, Kara); father 17, 23, 25, 29, 35, 124 (*see also* Jor-El); heritage 4, 33–34, 43, 123, 130, 136, 140–41, 143, 166; powers 17, 19, 138–39; symbol(s) 28, 33, 40, 51, 166
Kryptonite 4, 8, 18, 27–28, 31, 34, 50–51, 57, 60–61, 66, 73, 77, 79, 94–95, 98–99, 104, 106, 115, 126–127, 129, 137, 145, 153, 157–58, 166; black 31, 34, 94–95, 127, 129, 153; blue 18, 153; gold 153; green 137, 153; red 28, 50, 57, 61, 104, 126, 137, 145, 153, 158; silver 153; *see also* meteor rock
Kryptonsite 176, 180–81, 183, 185, 187, 189

Lake, Linda 141, 151
Lance, Dinah *see* Black Canary
Lane, Ella 168–69
Lane, Ellen 168–69
Lane, Lois 4–7, 19, 23, 36, 38, 41, 48–50, 52, 55, 60, 67–68, 70, 74–78, 80–81, 86, 91, 100, 104, 107–8, 110–12, 117, 127–29, 141, 151, 154, 164–65, 167–69, 171–72, 174–75, 179–89
Lane, Lucy 128, 168
Lane, Sam (General) 168
Lang, Lana 5–6, 22, 31, 37, 48, 51, 54–55, 59–66, 71–72, 75–77, 79–81, 87, 103–4, 107, 110–11, 116, 119, 121–22, 124–26, 129–30, 136, 152–53, 165–67, 171, 175, 179–81
Lara-El 35, 38, 53, 169
The Legion of Super-Heroes 80, 85–86, 91, 144
The Legion Ring 80, 141, 144
Level 33.1 140, 184
Lois and Clark: The New Adventures of Superman (television series) 25, 55, 167–69
Luthor (family) 4, 38, 65, 69, 80, 90–91, 98, 122, 180

Luthor, Alexander 151
Luthor, Clark 22; Ultraman 22
Luthor, Julian 76, 151
Luthor, Lex 4, 6, 21–23, 31, 33, 51–52, 54–55, 57, 59–62, 64–67, 69, 71, 75, 78–80, 83, 87–88, 90, 94–96, 104, 107–8, 121, 126–27, 129–30, 140, 151, 158, 164, 169, 172, 179–81, 184
Luthor, Lionel 4, 21–23, 27, 31–32, 35, 37–40, 43, 51–53, 62–65, 68, 76, 88–90, 103, 107, 122–23, 126–28, 130, 151, 154, 180, 183
Luthor Manor 51, 88–89
LuthorCorp 22, 83, 86, 95, 98, 105, 120–22

Mack, Allison 5, 66, 71–74, 109, 113–14, 182, 187
Mackenzie, Cindy "Mac" (character) 101
The Maltese Falcon (film) 102
The Man of Steel (character) *see* Superman (character)
Man of Steel (film) 170, 173
The Man of Tomorrow *see* Superman (character)
Marsh, Eric 120–21, 152
Martian Manhunter 21, 132, 138, 144
masculine 49, 101; masculinity 48–49, 56, 208
The Matrix (film) 100, 111, 113
Maxima 153
McClure, Marc 167
McNulty, Van 125
Melville, Jodi 120–21
Mercer, Tess 5–7, 73–74, 77, 81–86, 88–99, 107–8
Metallo (character) *see* Corben, John
meteor freak 4, 8, 35, 64, 106–108, 115–18, 122, 125–26, 128–29, 140, 144, 152–55, 157–58, 184
meteor infectee 8, 104, 111, 113, 116, 118–22, 124–26, 152, 157; *see also* meteor freak
meteor powers 67, 106–7, 118
meteor rock 7–8, 51, 55, 115–30, 145, 152–53, 166; shower 4, 16, 22, 26, 45, 60, 83, 88, 90, 107, 109, 116–19, 122–23, 125, 130, 140, 156, 166; *see also* Kryptonite
Metropolis 4, 13, 27–28, 30, 40–41, 50–52, 56, 61, 64, 75, 86, 89, 93, 107, 111–12, 124, 126, 132, 164–65, 168, 179
Metropolis General Hospital 90
The Metropolis Inquisitor 31, 181
The Metropolis Marvel *see* Superman (character)
Metropolis University 75
Millar, Miles 1, 44, 83, 141, 181
Moore, Byron 120, 151
morality 7, 9, 13, 18, 46, 84, 86–88, 91–94,

96, 117, 119, 124, 129, 137, 139, 152–58, 171–72, 175
myth 13–14, 19, 22–23, 45–46, 49, 53, 57, 86, 90, 104, 110, 133, 145, 151, 188; archetypes 5, 19, 22, 37, 48; hero 14, 20, 42, 47, 56; journey 5; monomyth 5, 14–15, 25, 45–47, 51, 56, 61; pattern/structure 5, 13–15, 19, 23, 61

Naman 89–90, 98
Neill, Noel 164–65, 168–69
Nicodemus flower 61, 121, 153
Nietzsche, Frederick 43, 110, 166
9/11 4, 25, 56, 116, 170–71
Nixon, Roger 31

Olsen, Jimmy 14–15, 43, 46, 59, 67–68, 70–72, 76, 86, 90–91, 95–97, 99, 103–4, 107, 110, 141, 167, 172, 179–80, 184
O'Shaughnessy, Brigid 102
O'Toole, Annette 4, 54, 165

Parker, Chrissy 122
Perrine, Effie 102
Peterson, Brian 30, 184
The Phantom Zone 17, 22, 35–36, 51, 80, 93–95, 154; crystal 85; portal 94
Phelan, Sam 30, 158
power transfer 19, 23, 127–28, 151

Queen, Oliver 21, 52, 54, 56–57, 59, 67–68, 71, 73–75, 77, 81, 86–89, 91, 93, 96–98, 103, 112–13, 140–41, 153–54, 179–81, 188; Green Arrow 21, 56, 59, 68, 86, 111–12, 140–41, 156, 179, 184
Queen Industries 88

Ramirez, Javier 138–39
Randall, Ian 120
Ranzz, Garth 91
Rathbone, Basil 162
The Red-Blue Blur see Kent, Clark
The Red Queen see Kent, Martha
Reeve, Christopher 2, 9, 55, 98, 136, 162, 165–67, 169
Reeves, George 135, 164, 169–70
Reyes, Jaime 155; Blue Beetle 155
Rickman, Bob 119, 122, 153
Robbins, Brian 1
Rosenbaum, Michael 1–2, 4, 181
Rosenberg, Willow (character) 101, 106
Ross, Pete 122, 125, 127, 129, 145, 179
Roswell (television series) 3, 49, 57, 156
Routh, Brandon 169

Sageeth 89–90, 98
Salander, Lisbeth 101
Sands, Julian 37
Savage, Vandal 167
scarecrow 50, 52, 118
Schneider, John 30, 32–33
Schott, Winslow 21, 88; Toymaker 21
September 11, 2001 *see* 9/11
sex and sexuality 7, 46–48, 50, 52–57, 62–64, 75–76, 79, 100, 102, 115–18, 121, 131, 145, 152, 157, 171, 181–82, 184
shipper 9, 174–76, 178–81, 185–87
Shuster, Joe 25, 138
Siegel, Jerry 25, 138
Silver Banshee 76, 104
Singer, Bryan (director) 169
Skyfall (film) 163
Skywalker, Luke 45, 47, 56
Slade (General) 41
Slater, Helen 169
Slavkin, Todd 66, 185
Smallville (nickname) see Kent, Clark
Smallville, Kansas 6, 17, 26–28, 31, 35–37, 40, 42–43, 45–46, 48–52, 56, 61, 68, 83, 106, 116–17, 121–22, 124–25, 127–30, 137–38, 143, 164–67, 179
Smallville High School 50, 54, 116, 128, 158, 166, 168, 180
The Smallville Torch 101, 166, 180
Son of God *see* Jesus Christ
Souders, Kelly 184
Spade, Sam 102, 106
Stamp, Terence 33, 168
Star Trek (television series) 174, 176
Star Trek: Deep Space Nine (television series) 149
Star Trek: Voyager (television series) 208
Stone, Victor 140, 144, 152, ; Cyborg 140, 144, 152, 156
Sullivan, Chloe 5–7, 9, 15, 21, 34, 51, 54, 56–57, 59, 61, 65–78, 80–81, 85–89, 91, 93–96, 98–101, 103–114, 117, 124, 126–29, 141, 144, 151, 153, 168, 175, 179–89; Watchtower (character) 56, 59, 67, 69–70, 73, 75, 110–12
Sullivan, Moira 69
The Summerholt Institute 153
Summers, Buffy 49, 79, 100, 106, 113; as parody (Buffy Saunders) 64
Summers, Eric 19, 126, 151
super speed 102, 108
Supergirl *see* Kent, Kara
superhero 2–4, 6–7, 14, 17, 23, 25, 30, 38, 41–42, 44–45, 54, 56, 60, 65, 67–69, 72–73, 75, 77–78, 86, 107, 109, 111–13, 132–35, 140–41, 149, 155–59, 166, 171–72, 179–81, 188
superheroine 106–7, 110
Superman (cartoon) *see* Fleischer Studios

Superman (character) 2–10, 13–14, 18, 20, 22–23, 25–27, 29–30, 32, 34, 40–42, 44, 46, 49–50, 52, 55–57, 68, 77–78, 81, 83–84, 90, 92, 101, 104, 107, 110, 132–35, 138, 142–45, 153, 155–57, 162–75, 179–82, 188; Man of Steel 25, 36, 107, 132–34, 138, 142–43; Man of Tomorrow 68, 133, 135, 138, 143, 166; Metropolis Marvel 132–34, 143; *see also* Kent, Clark
Superman (film series) 55
Superman (serial) 164
Superman Returns (film) 169, 172
Superman: The Animated Series (television series) 83, 164, 168
Superman: The Movie (film) 35, 83, 136, 164, 166–69
Superman: III (film) 165
Supernatural (television series) 2–3, 5, 10, 49–50, 208; *see also* Winchester brothers
Swann, Virgil 98, 136, 166–67
Swimmer, Darren 185

The Talon 30, 121
Teague, Genevieve 63, 130
Teague, Jason 59–60, 62–64, 126, 129–130
Television Without Pity 176, 183, 187, 189
Terminator 2: Judgment Day 149
Theroux, Margaret Isobel (Countess) 60, 62–63, 65, 153
Tippet, Kyle 120, 122
Tollin, Mike 1
The Toymaker *see* Schott, Winslow
The Traveler 83, 88–89, 90, 98; *see also* Kent, Clark
Trinity (character) 101, 113
"truth, justice, and the American way" 105, 133–34, 166, 169–71
Twilight (book series) 177–78

Ultraman *see* Luthor, Clark

United States 8, 18, 51, 120, 133–34, 137–39, 142, 165, 171; Middle America 4, 116

Veritas (group) 98
The Veritas Journals 83, 88, 90
Veritas prophecy 89–91, 95–97
Veronica Mars (television series) 2–4, 11, 101
Vigilante Registration Act 54, 158
violence 65, 84, 87, 92, 118, 134, 163
Vogler, Christopher 5, 15, 17–19, 21–22

The Wall of Weird 21, 60, 68–69, 104, 117, 122
Waller, Amanda 73–74, 111; White Queen 111
Watchtower (character) *see* Sullivan, Chloe
Watchtower (location) 21, 73, 74, 111–12
The WB (television network) 1–2, 4, 49, 57, 83, 142, 166, 169, 180
weather girls 152
Welling, Tom 1, 3, 43, 135, 156–57, 165–67, 169–70, 172
White, Perry 77, 127, 172, 179, 184
The White Queen *see* Waller, Amanda
Williams, John 9, 164–65, 167, 172
Willowbrook, Joseph (professor) 126
Willowbrook, Kyla 122
The Winchester brothers 49–50; *see also Supernatural* (television series)
Woodman, Sasha 120
World War II 25, 134, 164

The X-Files (television series) 178–79
X-ray vision 101, 157
Xena (character) 79, 100, 113

Zatara, Zatanna 76
Zeus (Greek god) 149
Žižek, Slavoj 7, 84–85, 87, 92–95, 97, 99, 170
Zod (Major/General) 4, 22, 85, 96–98, 168, 171, 173, 179

www.ingramcontent.com/pod-product-compliance
Ingram Content Group UK Ltd.
Pitfield, Milton Keynes, MK11 3LW, UK
UKHW041957140426
5217IPUK00015B/838